ZAGATSURVEY

LOS ANGELES
MARKETPLACE
SURVEY

**Edited by Merrill Shindler
and Karen Berk**

with Linda Burum

**Published and distributed by
ZAGATSURVEY
4 Columbus Circle
New York, New York 10019
212 977 6000**

Acknowledgments

Because of the ethnic diversity and the unwieldy geography of Los Angeles, the task of compiling the data for this *Survey* was daunting. Thanks to Renee Shapiro for her fine attention to details and to Kathy Aaronson, Larry Ahlquist, Jeff Berk, Michael Berk, Mitzie Cutler, Gwen Lewis, Ann Martin, Andrea Michaels, Jan Weimer, Sherry Zelickson, and the Los Angeles Conservancy for the parts they played in making this book happen.

Contents

Introduction

Here are the results of our first *Survey* of the Los Angeles Food and Entertaining Marketplace. Over 2,200 people participated in this *Survey*, covering over 1,830 purveyors of baked goods, candy, caviar, cheese, coffee and tea, cookware, ethnic sources, fish, flowers, food specialty items, health food, herbs and spices, ice cream and yogurt, meat and poultry, prepared foods, produce and wine, plus top caterers, restaurant delivery services and cooking schools. The *Survey* has been designed to facilitate all aspects of dining at home or in the office and entertaining on a grand or small scale.

Knowing that the quality of this *Survey* is the result of their thoughtful voting and commentary, we sincerely thank each participant. We are especially grateful to our editors, Merrill Shindler, a distinguished restaurant commentator and Karen Berk, owner of The Seasonal Table cooking school and food consultant. Because Karen is the co-owner of The Seasonal Table cooking school, the treatment of that source was left solely to Merrill Shindler. We also wish to thank Linda Burum, a respected writer specializing in ethnic foods, who edited the Ethnic Food Sources section. They devoted much of the past year to organizing the present *Survey* and reporting its results.

While we have made every effort to be as accurate as possible, the Los Angeles marketplace scene is one of the most dynamic in the world, with ventures constantly opening and closing, or changing hours or formats as demand dictates. If you will be traveling out of your way to visit any of the stores listed in this book, it's always a good idea to phone ahead first.

Further, though we have included those shops that we believe to be among Los Angeles' best and most noteworthy, we simply did not have room to cover all of the city's countless food and entertaining sources. If you feel that we've missed something important, write to us and we'll consider adding your suggestion to our next *Los Angeles Marketplace Survey*.

New York, New York   Nina and Tim Zagat
November 27, 1995

Foreword

At first glance, LA is not a landscape awash with unique and wondrous markets. In the land of the car, the supermarket – with its convenient parking and helpful, smiling staff – is king. It's where most Southern Californians take care of their shopping; there are even markets with valet parking and eager helpers who load the goods in the car for you.

But while there's no denying the dominance of the supermarket, seeking out the more specialized food shops can be fun, a world of adventures open to anyone willing to drive. For those in the know, this is a land of cheese shops that may not make their Parisian counterparts tremble with concern, but which bring all the rich flavors of aged cow, sheep and goat milk to our tables. We are surrounded by some of the finest wine-making regions in the world, and the juices of those vines can be found all over town. And it goes without saying that fresh produce is one of our sun-blessed strengths.

Though myth has it that you can't get a good bagel outside of NYC, the many well-fed Californians who luxuriate in a weekend bagel and a schmear here on the Left Coast indicate that that fiction is a creation of the NY Chamber of Commerce. For those willing to look, this is a land filled with markets bursting with foods from around the world. From Europe across the Middle East and Russia to the Far East, from South America across the ocean to Africa, every cuisine is found in this melting pot that's about to boil over. And since we dance a fine fandango along the cutting edge of technology, we even have suppliers that exist only on the Internet – shopping along the Information Superhighway.

It's been great fun for us to put together the very first *Zagat Los Angeles Marketplace Survey*. And it's been a great adventure too, for this is a city that isn't so much an orange as an onion – no matter how much you think you know about the shopping scene here, peel away another layer and there's more waiting to be discovered.

Los Angeles, CA
November 27, 1995

Merrill Shindler
Karen Berk

Los Angeles

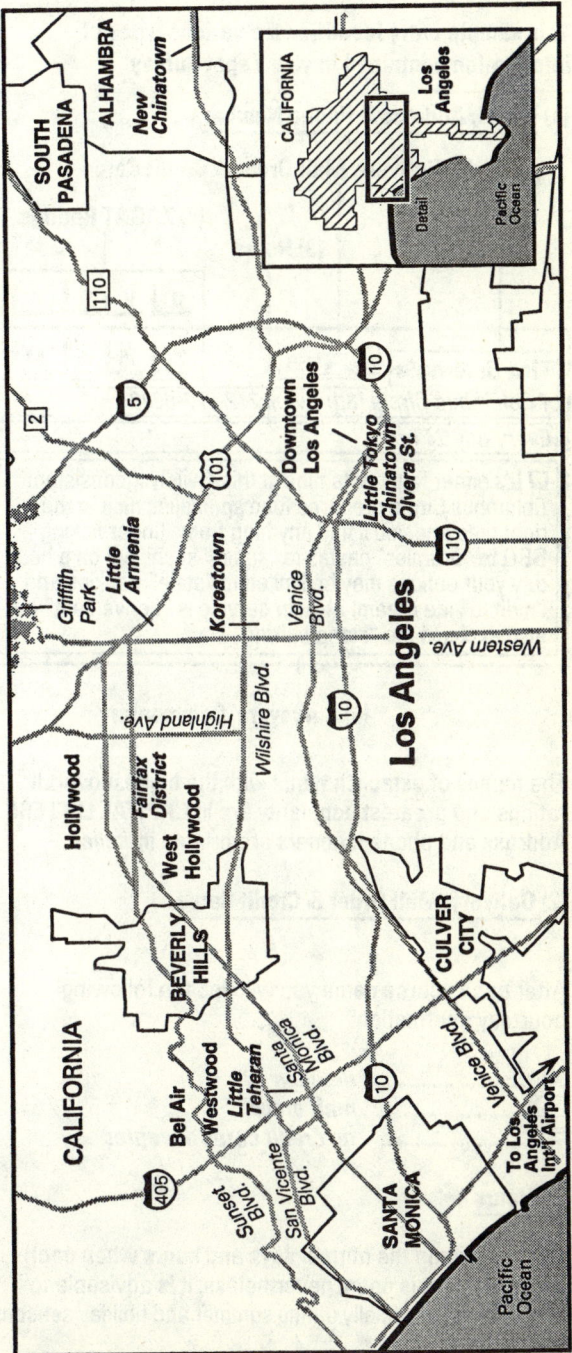

Key to Ratings/Symbols

This sample entry identifies the various types of information contained in your Zagat Survey.

(1) Name, Address & Phone Number

(2) Delivery, Mail Order & Credit Cards

(4) ZAGAT Ratings

(3) Hours

Ǫ	V	S	C
23	15	16	M

Tim & Nina's 🚲 ✉ ⊘
4 Columbus Circle (8th Ave.) 212-977-6000

Every day 24 hrs

◪ It's either feast or famine at this "wildly inconsistent" Columbus Circle prepared food specialist; hit it at the right time and you'll find anything from "finger-licking'" BBQ to "premier" pastas to "super" sushi, but on a bad day your options may be limited to "stale" cookies and "melted" ice cream; 24-hour service is "convenient" but also explains the "sleepwalking" staff.

(5) Surveyors' Commentary

The names of establishments with the highest overall ratings and greatest popularity are in **CAPITAL LETTERS**. Address and phone numbers are printed in *italics*.

(2) Delivery, Mail Order & Credit Cards

After each source name you will find the following courtesy information:

🚲 .... *delivers*
✉ .... *mail order*
⊘ .... *no credit cards accepted*

(3) Hours

We have listed the normal **days and hours** when each establishment is open; nevertheless, it is advisable to check them, especially during summer and holiday seasons.

(4) ZAGAT Ratings

Quality, **Variety** and **Service** are each rated on a scale of 0 to 30:

Q	V	S	C

Q .... *Quality*
V .... *Variety*
S .... *Service*
C .... *Cost*

23	15	16	M

0 - 9	.... *poor to fair*
10 - 19	.... *good to very good*
20 - 25	.... *very good to excellent*
26 - 30	.... *extraordinary to perfection*

▽ 23	15	16	M

▽ .... *Low number of votes/less reliable*

The **Cost (C)** column reflects estimated price range:

–	–	–	I

I .... *inexpensive*
M .... *moderate*
E .... *expensive*
VE .... *very expensive*

An establishment listed without ratings is either an important **newcomer** or a popular **write-in**.

(5) Surveyors' Commentary

Surveyors' comments are summarized, with literal comments shown in quotation marks. The following symbols indicate whether responses were mixed or uniform.

◩ .... *mixed*
◼ .... *uniform*

Top Ratings

Top 50 Overall*

28	Cheese Store	Cheese
27	Superior Meat	Meat & Poultry
	Bristol Farms	Meat & Poultry
	Bristol Farms	Produce
	Gelson's	Supermarkets
	Wally's	Wines & Liquors
	Gai Klass	Caterers
	Bristol Farms	Supermarkets
	Fish King	Fish
	Santa Monica Seafood	Fish
	Jacob Maarse	Flowers
	Bel-Air Prime Meats	Meat & Poultry
	Atlas Sausage	Meat & Poultry
	Owen's Market	Meat & Poultry
	Northridge Hills Liquors	Wines & Liquors
	Gelson's	Produce
	Marconda's	Meat & Poultry
26	Secret Garden	Flowers
	Mark's Garden	Flowers
	Edelweiss	Candy & Nuts
	European Deluxe Sausage	Meat & Poultry
	Wine House	Wines & Liquors
	Teuscher Chocolates	Candy & Nuts
	Campo dei Fiori	Flowers
	Jean Brady School	Cooking Schools
	Ten Ren Tea Co.	Coffee & Tea
	Aristoff Caviar	Caviar & Smoked Fish
	Kitchen for Exploring Foods	Caterers
	Standard Cutlery	Cookware & Supplies
	Gelson's	Meat & Poultry
	Schreiner's	Meat & Poultry
	Davy's Fish Market	Fish
	Chado Tea Room	Coffee & Tea
	Rosebud Cakes	Baked Goods
	Bristol Farms	Cheese
	Friedman Microwave	Cookware & Supplies
	Al Gelato	Ice Cream/Frozen Yogurt
	La Brea Bakery	Baked Goods
	Duke of Bourbon	Wines & Liquors
	Bristol Farms	Fish
	Williams-Sonoma	Cookware & Supplies
	Bristol Farms	Prepared Foods
	Wine Merchant/Bev. Hills	Wines & Liquors
	Lee Gelfond	Candy & Nuts
	Julienne	Prepared Foods
	Say Cheese	Cheese
25	David Jones	Flowers
	Gordon's Fish Market	Fish
	Silver Birches	Flowers
	Domingo's	Ethnic Food Sources

* Combines quality, variety and service ratings, and excluding
  sources with low voting and in outlying areas.

Top Overall by Category*

Bagels
24 Goldstein's

Breads
26 La Brea Bakery

Cakes
26 Rosebud Cakes

Candy & Nuts
26 Edelweiss

Caterers
27 Gai Klass

Caviar & Smoked Fish
26 Aristoff Caviar

Cheese
28 Cheese Store

Coffee
25 Graffeo

Cooking Schools
26 Jean Brady School

Cookware & Supplies
26 Friedman Microwave

Delis
25 Brent's Deli

Ethnic Food Sources
25 Domingo's (Italian)

Fish
27 Fish King

Flowers
27 Jacob Maarse

Health/Natural Foods
25 Mrs. Gooch's

Herbs & Spices
26 Co-Opportunity

Ice Cream
26 Al Gelato

Meat & Poultry
27 Superior Meat

Pastries
25 Sweet Lady Jane

Prepared Foods
26 Bristol Farms

Produce
27 Bristol Farms

Restaurant Delivery Services
23 LA to Go

Sausage
27 Atlas Sausage Kitchen

Supermarkets
27 Gelson's

Tea
26 Ten Ren Tea Co.

Wines & Liquors
27 Wally's

---

* Combines quality, variety and service ratings, and excluding
sources with low voting and in outlying areas.

Top 50 Best Buys*

1.	Southland Certified	Produce
2.	Atlas Sausage Kitchen	Meat & Poultry
3.	Topline Wine & Spirits	Wines & Liquors
4.	Monte Carlo	Ethnic Food Sources
5.	Wine House	Wines & Liquors
6.	Fish King	Fish
7.	Friedman Microwave	Cookware & Supplies
8.	Santa Monica Seafood	Fish
9.	Bharat Bazaar	Herbs & Spices
10.	Co-Opportunity	Herbs & Spices
11.	Davy's Fish Market	Fish
12.	Los Angeles Wine Co.	Wines & Liquors
13.	Bezjian's Grocery	Herbs & Spices
14.	Western Bagel	Bagels & Bialys
15.	Goldstein's	Bagels & Bialys
16.	Domingo's	Ethnic Food Sources
17.	Schreiner's	Meat & Poultry
18.	European Deluxe Sausage	Meat & Poultry
19.	Ten Ren Tea Co.	Coffee & Tea
20.	See's Candy	Candy & Nuts
21.	Brent's Deli	Delis
22.	Northridge Hills Liquors	Wines & Liquors
23.	Golden West Meats	Meat & Poultry
24.	Mark's Garden	Flowers
25.	Gloria's	Cookware & Supplies
26.	Superior Meat	Meat & Poultry
27.	Fosselman's Ice Cream	Ice Cream/Frozen Yogurt
28.	Larry's Shaver Shop	Cookware & Supplies
29.	99 Ranch	Fish
30.	Bagel Broker	Bagels & Bialys
31.	Wally's	Wines & Liquors
32.	C & K	Ethnic Food Sources
33.	Gordon's Fish Market	Fish
34.	Brooklyn Bagel Co.	Bagels & Bialys
35.	Jean Brady School	Cooking Schools
36.	Trader Joe's	Cheese
37.	Chado Tea Room	Coffee & Tea
38.	Cheese Store	Cheese
39.	I & Joy	Bagels & Bialys
40.	Kitchen for Exploring Foods	Caterers
41.	Marconda's	Meat & Poultry
42.	Bristol Farms	Meat & Poultry
43.	Bristol Farms	Cooking Schools
44.	Belwood Bakery	Baked Goods
45.	Red Carpet	Wines & Liquors
46.	Standard Cutlery	Cookware & Supplies
47.	Carrillo's Tortilleria	Ethnic Food Sources
48.	20/20 Wine Co.	Wines & Liquors
49.	Bristol Farms	Produce
50.	Bigg Chill, The	Ice Cream/Frozen Yogurt

---

* Derived by dividing overall ratings by surveyor cost estimates, and excluding sources with low voting and in outlying areas.

Top Overall Ranking By Cuisine Type*

Top American
27 Superior Meat (meat)
   Bristol Farms (meat)
   Gelson's (supermarket)
   Fish King (fish)
   Santa Monica (fish)

Top California
27 Gai Klass (caterer)
26 Kitchen for Expl. (caterer)
   La Brea Bakery (bakery)
   Bristol Farms (prep food)
   Julienne (prep food)

Top Chinese
26 Ten Ren (coffee/tea)
22 99 Ranch (fish/supermarket)†
21 Hong Kong (supermarket)†
20 L.A. Man (supermarket)†
— Kuo's Bakery (bakery)†

Top French
28 Cheese Store (cheese)
25 Belwood (bakery)
24 Q Bakery (bakery)
   Michel Richard
   (bakery/prep food)

Top German/Central European
27 Atlas Sausage (meat)
26 European Deluxe (meat)
   Schreiner's (meat)

Top Indian
24 Bharat Bazaar
   (herbs/spices)
22 Bombay Spiceland
   (groceries)†
20 India Sweets (groceries)†

Top Italian
27 Al Dente (prep food)†
26 Al Gelato (ice cream/yogurt)
25 Domingo's (groceries)†
   Monte Carlo (groceries)†
24 Divine Pasta (prep food)

Top Japanese
24 Yaohan (groceries)†
23 Safe & Save (groceries)†
22 Aloha (tofu)†
21 Nijiya (prep food)†

Top Jewish Deli
25 Brent's
24 Nate 'n Al's
   Langer's
— Art's
— Barney Greengrass

Top Kosher
25 Doheny Kosher (meat)
   G&K Kosher (meat)
22 Elite Cuisine (caterer)
— Ventura Kosher (meat)

Top Latin
23 El Cholo (caterer)
22 Carrillo's (prep food)†
21 Gallegos (prep food)†
   Empanada's (prep food)†
20 Grand Central (groceries)†
— Valley Food (supermarket)†

Top Mideast/Greek/Armenian
24 C&K (groceries)†
23 Tarzana Armenian
   (groceries)†
   Panos Pastry (bakery)†
   Bezjian's (groceries)†
— Food Bag (supermarket)†

---

* Combines quality, variety and service ratings, and excluding
  sources with low voting and in outlying areas.
† Listed in Ethnic Food Sources section.

Top Overall Ranking By Location*

Top Beverly Hills
28 Cheese Store (cheese)
26 Edelweiss (candy)
European Deluxe (meat)
Teuscher (candy)
Standard (cookware)

Top Chinatown
26 Ten Ren (coffee/tea)
24 Yaohan (ethnic)
22 99 Ranch (ethnic)
20 L.A. Man Wah (ethnic)
Enbun (ethnic)

Top Glendale/Burbank
27 Fish King (fish)
Atlas Sausage (meat)
26 Schreiner's (meat)
25 Red Carpet (wine)
Southland Farm. (produce)

Top Los Angeles
27 Superior Meat (meat)
Gai Klass (caterer)
Marconda's (meat)
26 Secret Garden (florist)

Top Monterey Park/ San Gabriel Valley
26 Ten Ren (coffee/tea)
23 Claro's (ethnic)
22 99 Ranch (ethnic)
21 Hong Kong (ethnic)

Top Outlying Areas
28 Wine Cask (wines),
Santa Barbara
26 Chino Ranch (produce),
Rancho Santa Fe
25 Zov's Bakery (bakery),
Tustin
R. Mondavi (cook. sch.),
Costa Mesa

Top Pasadena/San Marino/So. Pasadena
27 Bristol Farms (meat)
Bristol Farms (produce)
Bristol Farms (supermarket)
Jacob Maarse (florist)
26 Kitchen for Expl. (caterer)

Top San Fernando Valley
27 Gelson's (supermarket)
Fish King (fish)
Northridge Hills (wines)
Gelson's (produce)
26 Mark's Garden (florist)

Top Santa Monica
27 Santa Monica Seafood (fish)
26 Jean Brady (cook. sch.)
Co-Opportunity (herbs)
Willams-Sonoma (cookware)
25 Southland Farm. (produce)

Top South Bay
27 Al Dente (ethnic)
Bristol Farms (meat)
Bristol Farms (produce)
Bristol Farms (supermarket)
24 Yaohan (ethnic)

Top Westside
27 Gelson's (supermarket)
Wally's (wine)
Bel Air Prime Meats (meat)
Owen's Market (meat)
26 Wine House (wines)

---

* Combines quality, variety and service ratings, and excluding
sources with low voting.

Directory

Bagels & Bialys

New Yorkers, always trying to find reasons to dismiss Los Angeles as something less than a serious city, frequently refer to our lack of severe winters, the annoying affability of those in the service sector here, and – last but hardly least – our lack of a "real bagel" as proof that bulldozing LA would be a good idea.

What they forget is that this is not Manhattan, and the bagels found here aren't New York bagels because, of course, they're California bagels. Which means some of them taste like they were made in a basement in the Bronx or Brooklyn (out here, you always have a choice of boroughs), and others are languidly exotic, flavored with jalapeños, blueberries, chocolate chips and the like. They're also different because these aren't bagels eaten while huddling against the cold waiting for a bus that never comes. They're bagels made to be eaten in the convertible with the top down as you head up the coast to Malibu. With low-fat cream cheese, they're just fine.

Top Quality
25 Goldstein's
24 Bagel Broker
     Brooklyn Bagel Co.
     Western Bagel
23 NY Bagel Co.

Top Variety
26 Western Bagel
25 Goldstein's
     Brooklyn Bagel Co.
     I & Joy
24 Bagel Broker

Top Service
22 Western Bagel
     Goldstein's
21 Bagel Broker
     Hot Bagels
     I & Joy

Best Buys
     Western Bagel
     Goldstein's
     Bagel Broker
     Brooklyn Bagel Co.
     I & Joy

Q	V	S	C
24	24	21	I

Bagel Broker, The ⊕
- *7825 Beverly Blvd. (Fairfax Ave.), LA, 213-931-1258*
  M-F 6am-6pm/Sat 6am-5pm/Sun 6am-3pm

■ The "softest, freshest bagels" that "satisfy even a NYer" and "wonderful" bialys are the draw at this "independent" shop on Beverly Boulevard; along with "high-quality" baked goods it has the "best" schmears in town, including "yummy" lox spread and shallot butter.

22	23	19	I

Bagel Factory ⊕
- *8984 Cadillac Ave. (Robertson Blvd.), LA, 310-837-6046*
  Every day 6am-7pm
- *3004 Sepulveda Blvd. (National Blvd.), West LA,*
  310-477-8460
  M-Sat 6am-9pm/Sun 6am-6pm

Bagel Factory (Cont.)
- *21011 Hawthorne Blvd. (Torrance Blvd.), Torrance, 310-540-2077*
  Every day 7am-8pm

◪ "A decent variety" of "good, not great" fresh bagels ranging from the classics to jalapeño-cheese and pizza varieties are offered at this "convenient location" with "excellent early hours"; the downside, say critics, is that "factory is the operative word", meaning "mass-produced excuses" for the real thing.

Bagel Nosh   🚲   19 21 17 I
- *1629 Wilshire Blvd. (17th St.), Santa Monica, 310-451-8771*
  M-F 7am-4pm/Sat & Sun 8am-4pm
- *17201 Ventura Blvd. (bet. Balboa Blvd. & Louise Ave.), Encino, 818-995-4545*
  Every day 6:30am-8pm

◪ These "always-crowded" nosheries sell "well-made" but "heavy" bagels that "look pretty" but which some find "too big, too doughy" and "dry" tasting; in fact, critics claim that the only thing that's authentic about these "ersatz delis" is the "rude" service.

B&B Bagels ⊭   ▽ 18 19 17 I
- *7113 Beverly Blvd. (Detroit St.), LA, 213-933-8844*
  M-F & Sun 7am-3pm

◪ There are 20 varieties of bagels at this store in LA's orthodox Jewish district, but they're "not memorable" enough for any to be praised beyond "good"; those who find them "disappointing" and "too much like Wonderbread" say "you're better off buying at Ralphs."

Bronx Bagels ⊭   - - - I
- *5291 E. Second St. (bet. Glendora & La Verne), Long Beach, 310-438-2886*
  Sun-W 6am-9pm/Th-Sat 24 hrs.

In case the name didn't clue you in, NY-style bagels are the self-proclaimed specialty of this busy Long Beach bakery popular for its sizable selection of reasonably good bagels, bialys and well-whipped, flavored cream cheeses; if Queens and Staten Island had bagel styles, there'd probably be shops named for them as well.

Brooklyn Bagel Co. ⊭   24 25 20 I
- *2217 W. Beverly Blvd. (1½ blocks west of Alvarado Ave.), LA, 213-413-4114*
  Sun-Th 7am-11pm/F & Sat 7am-3am

■ Continuing the battle of the NY boroughs, this "great bagel shop" may be in a "funky", "industrial zone" (near the fabled Tommy's burger joint), but it attracts mavens from all over f H&H", it's "open all hours" and busy most of them – "now that's a bagel..."

⌐Q⌐ ⌐V⌐ ⌐S⌐ ⌐C⌐

GOLDSTEIN'S BAGEL BAKERY ⌐25⌐ ⌐25⌐ ⌐22⌐ ⌐I⌐

- *86 West Colorado Blvd. (1 block west of Fair Oaks Ave.), Pasadena, 818-792-2435*
  Sun-Th 7am-9pm/F & Sat 7am-10:30pm
- *412 N. Santa Anita Ave., Arcadia, 818-447-2457*
  Every day 6am-9pm

◪ The highest-rated of the Southland's bagelries is in the largely non-Jewish San Gabriel Valley, where locals line up for the likes of "chocolate chocolate-chip", "peanut butter chocolate-chip" and "banana nut" bagels spread with "peaches and cream", as well as "cheddar cheese bagel dogs"; a few troubled purists decry "froufrou bagels" that "aren't real", but masses of Goldstein's- goers insist these "specialty bagels" are "the best."

I & Joy Manhattan Bagel 🏍️🖨️ ⌐23⌐ ⌐25⌐ ⌐21⌐ ⌐I⌐

- *246 N. Beverly Dr. (north of Wilshire Blvd.), Beverly Hills, 310-274-5522*
- *1636 Westwood Blvd. (bet. Santa Monica & Wilshire Blvds.), Westwood, 310-441-1735*
- *9227 W. Pico Blvd. (bet. Doheny & Beverly Drs.), West LA, 310-858-9094*
- *4070 Lincoln Blvd. (south of Washington Blvd.), Marina Del Rey, 310-305-1939*
- *109 North Fairfax Ave. (south of Beverly Blvd.), LA, 213-932-9905*
- *713 W. Seventh St. (Flower St.), Downtown LA, 213-622-5216*
- *2216 Wilshire Blvd. (22nd St.), Santa Monica, 310-828-3228*
- *14423 ½ Ventura Blvd. (Van Nuys Blvd.), Sherman Oaks, 818-905-1315*
- *11974 Ventura Blvd. (Laurel Canyon Blvd.), Studio City, 818-760-9068*
- *7361 Sunset Blvd. (bet. La Brea & Fairfax Aves.), Hollywood, 213-850-9044*
- *16060 Ventura Blvd. (Woodley Ave.), Encino, 818-501-9267*
- *18539 Devonshire Blvd. (Reseda Blvd.), Northridge, 818-363-9879*
- *7535 Fallbrook Ave. (Saticoy St.), Canoga Park, 818-992-9792*
  Every day 6am-2pm
- *715 Pico Blvd. (Lincoln Blvd.), Santa Monica, 310-399-9631*
- *20048 Ventura Blvd. (Winnetka Ave.), Woodland Hills, 818-883-0166*
- *901 E. Del Mar (Lake Ave.), Pasadena, 818-356-0256*
- *16673 Roscoe Blvd. (east of Balboa Blvd.), Van Nuys, 818-830-3300*
  Every day 24 hrs.

I & Joy Manhattan Bagel (Cont.)
Hours for all locations are every day 6am-6pm, unless otherwise noted

■ "An institution", this well-loved chain is acclaimed for bagels and bialys that are "always fresh" and "as good as they get"; this is food that "brings joy to the palate": "crusty outside, soft and wonderful inside", but you "better nosh fast" or they make good "hockey pucks"; service "varies by outlet", from "efficient" to "surly."

New York Bagel Co. ⊄   23 | 23 | 18 | M
- *11640 San Vicente Blvd. (Darlington Ave.), Brentwood, 310-820-1050*
  Every day 7am-5pm

■ "Heavy-duty, chewy bagels" draw affluent Brentwoodians to this mini-mall shop that helps set the local trend for "big and fat", "fluffy and beautiful" specimens; apart from some "bad attitude", it's not quite as NY as the name implies, offering such only-in-LA versions as El Greco (sundried tomato, basil and rosemary).

Noah's New York Bagels ▣⊄   – | – | – | M
- *11911 San Vicente Blvd. (Montana Ave.), Brentwood, 310-472-5651*
  M-F 6:30am-7pm/Sat 7am-7pm/Sun 7am-6pm
- *2710 Main St. (Hill St.), Santa Monica, 310-396-4339*
  M-F 6:30am-7pm/Sat 7am-7pm/Sun 7am-6pm
- *320 Santa Monica Blvd. (bet. 3rd & 4th Sts.), Santa Monica, 310-394-3557*
  M-F 6am-7pm/Sat 7am-7pm/Sun 7am-5pm
- *1426 Montana Ave. (bet. 14th & 15th Sts.), Santa Monica, 310-587-9103*
  M-F 6:30am-7pm/Sat 7am-7pm/Sun 7am-5pm

Big, big bagels that stay fresh for days are sold at these SoCal branches of a hugely successful Bay Area bagel chain; halfway between bagel bakeries and delis, these retro shops also offer smoked fish and schmears to keep their yuppie/Gen-X clientele well-fed.

Sam's Bagels ⊄   – | – | – | I
- *1511 Montana Ave. (bet. 15th & 16th Sts.), Santa Monica, 310-260-0098*
  M-Sat 7am-5pm/Sun 7am-3pm
- *150 N. Larchmont Blvd. (½ block south of Beverly Blvd.), LA, 213-469-1249*
  M-Sat 6am-6pm/Sun 7am-5pm
- *544 S. Lake Ave. (California Blvd.), Pasadena, 818-564-9018*
  Every day 7am-4pm

A notable member of Santa Monica's 'Montana Avenue Bagel Explosion' that has bagelries competing with cappuccino houses for domination of the street; chewy, tasty, relatively authentic and, yes, very good are the early reports; how can you go wrong with a bagel made by a guy named Sam?

Q | V | S | C

St. Urbain Bagels ⊖   – | – | – | M
- *8593 Santa Monica Blvd. (bet. Robertson & La Cienega Blvd.), W. Hollywood, 310-657-6281*
  M-Sat 7am-7pm/Sun 8am-5pm
- *1232 Third St. Promenade (bet. Wilshire & Arizona), Santa Monica, 310-260-1511*
  M-Th 7am-7pm/F 7am-9pm/Sat 7am-11:30pm/Sun 8am-9pm
- *449 N. Beverly (Little Santa Monica Blvd.), Beverly Hills, 310-288-0219*
  M-F 6am-6:30pm/Sat 7am-6:30pm/Sun 7am-5pm

Named for the main street in Montreal's Jewish ghetto, this rapidly expanding, high-tech, in-and-out bagel chain serves very tasty, mostly traditional bagels; despite its Canadian roots, don't expect to find a bagel with back bacon and beer.

Union Bagel   – | – | – | I
- *Union Station, 800 N. Alameda St. (Cesar Chavez Blvd.), Downtown LA, 213-625-3734*
  Every day 6am-9:30pm

The place to go in Union Station for commuters in need of a bagel and a schmear on their way to Downtown LA, the Business District or the Courthouse; it offers close to 20 varieties, ranging from the basics to chocolate-chip.

Western Bagel ⊖   24 | 26 | 22 | I
- *7814 Sepulveda Blvd. (1 block north of Saticoy St.), Van Nuys, 818-786-5847*
  Every day 24 hrs.
- *21833 Ventura Blvd. (Topanga Canyon Blvd.), Woodland Hills, 818-887-5451*
  M-Th, Sun 5am-7pm/F & Sat 5am-9pm
- *12930 Ventura Blvd. (bet. Coldwater Canyon Ave. & Ventura Blvd.), Studio City, 818-906-7121*
  Every day 5:30am-7pm
- *11628 Santa Monica Blvd. (Barry), West LA, 310-826-0570*
  M-F 6am-7pm/Sat & Sun 6am-6pm
- *Redondo Shores Ctr., 403 N. PCH, Redondo Beach, 310-318-9686*
  M-Sat 6am-7pm/Sun 6am-5pm
- *North Ranch Mall, 3825 Thousand Oaks Blvd. (Westlake Blvd.), Westlake Village, 818-707-1469*
  M-Sat 6am-7pm/Sun 6am-5pm
- *23170 W. Valencia Blvd., Valencia, 818-778-6353*
  M-F 5am-6pm/Sat & Sun 6am-6pm
- *Larwin Sq., 506 E. First St., Tustin, 714-730-0611*
  M-Sat 6am-7pm/Sun 6am-5pm

■ This "old standby" is a leading candidate in the eyes of fans for SoCal's 'Big Boy of Bagels' title; the faithful say its outlets have the "best bagels both sides of the Mississippi", and though it does offer oddities like cranberry bagels and green bagels for St. Paddy's, it's basically a "unchanged classic"; the Van Nuys branch is a "24-hour heaven."

Baked Goods*

There was a time (admittedly, not so long ago) when our breads and pastries were kind of, to put it bluntly, dull. That was before the Modern Era in Los Angeles baking, when a new generation of dough devotees discovered the joys of making things in the oven that actually taste good and have great texture to boot. In the past decade and more, we've become a major haven for those looking to recreate the concept of bread in much the same way that many who live out here attempt to recreate their own lives. And treats like alligators, poppy seed strudel, rugalach, fruit cobbler, tarts and chocolate cakes keep personal trainers busy and Californians' sweet-tooth satisfied. Rather immodestly, we think we have some of the best baked goods in the world, created by highly innovative cooks willing to push the borders of what a baker can do. We're a city with crust.

BREADS & MUFFINS

Top Quality
29 La Brea Bakery
26 Röckenwagner
  Belwood Bakery
  Q Baker
25 Diamond Bakery

Top Service
24 Bristol Farms
  Belwood Bakery
  Misto Caffe & Bakery
23 Q Baker
  Pier Ave. Bakery

Top Variety
26 La Brea Bakery
25 Belwood Bakery
  Bristol Farms
  Q Baker
24 Beverlywood Bakery

Best Buys
  Belwood Bakery
  Fred's Bakery/Deli
  Diamond Baker
  Trader Joe's
  Pier Ave. Bakery

PASTRIES

Top Quality
27 Sweet Lady Jane
  Patticakes
  LA Desserts
  Cakeworks
  Michel Richard

Top Service
25 Rosebud Cakes
24 Cake & Art
  Cakeworks
  Cakeplace
  Patticakes

Top Variety
26 Rosebud Cakes
25 Cheesecake Factory
  Sweet Lady Jane
24 Bea's Bakery
  La Mousse

Best Buys
  Cobbler Factory
  Bea's Bakery
  Patticakes
  Beverlywood Bakery
  Sweet Lady Jane

---

* Top ratings lists exclude sources in outlying areas.

Babalu   <u>23</u> | <u>20</u> | <u>19</u> | <u>M</u>
● *1002 Montana Ave. (10th St.), Santa Monica, 310-395-2500*
Sun & T-Th 8am-10pm/F & Sat 8am-11pm

◪ Though there are grumbles about "dingbat" service, there's also plenty of praise for the "amazing" "crumbles and fruit pies" with "Caribbean flavors" at this "funky" Santa Monica "hole-in-the-wall" where the "desserts are impossible to refuse" even if the "coffee is served cold."

B & L Gourmet Pastries   <u>25</u> | <u>23</u> | <u>21</u> | <u>M</u>
● *8556 W. Third St. (1 block west of San Vicente Blvd.), LA, 310-271-8333*
M-F 7am-6pm/Sat 7am-5pm

■ The "alligators are great" at this Westside "pastry shop" that fans liken to a reasonably priced "Viktor Benes in mufti"; it's a bakery full of "family" feel and "old-time Vienna pastries" that invoke "memories of things past."

Bea's Bakery 🚴✉   <u>24</u> | <u>24</u> | <u>21</u> | <u>M</u>
● *18450 Clark St. (½ block north of Ventura Blvd.), Tarzana, 818-344-0100*
M-Sat 7am-9pm/Sun 7am-7pm

■ They're "always willing to give you a sample" at what some call the "best all-around bakery in the Valley"; it's a "homey" "Jewish pastry" shop that's "worth the wait" for the "strudel to die for" and "scrumptious rugalach", as well as "excellent" all-American "upside-down chocolate chocolate-chip muffins" and "great holiday stuff."

Belwood Bakery ✉   <u>26</u> | <u>25</u> | <u>24</u> | <u>M</u>
● *11625 Barrington Ct. (bet. Sunset Blvd. & Barrington Ave.), Brentwood, 310-471-6855*
M-Sat 6am-7pm/Sun 6am-6pm

■ "Man does not live by bread alone" and no wonder, given the "sublime apple tarts", "delicious Danish" and heavenly coffee cake at this slightly concealed Brentwood bakery that also has, yes, many "wonderful", "unusual breads and rolls"; "don't go...it's busy enough!"

Beverlywood Bakery ✉   <u>23</u> | <u>24</u> | <u>20</u> | <u>M</u>
● *9128 Pico Blvd. (Oakhurst), LA, 310-550-9842*
M-Sat 6am-6:30pm/Sun 6am-5:30pm

■ This "Jewish institution" is "a step back to childhood" for those who dream of "the best alligators", rugalach and "real Russian-quality" babkas and strudels offered in an "old-fashioned setting" where "they still give children free cookies"; the challah, raisin pumpernickel and corn rye breads are also "to die for", but the place can be so "crowded" some feel the need for "blinkers."

Baked Goods

Breadworks 🚴🚭
23 | 22 | 22 | M
- *7961 W. Third St. (entrance on Edinburgh St.), LA, 213-930-0047*
  M-Sat 8am-6pm

Breadworks Cafe
- *1301 Montana Ave. (13th St.), Santa Monica, 310-260-1931*
  M-Sat 7am-8pm/Sun 8am-6pm
- *131 Larchmont Blvd. (bet. 1st St. & Beverly Blvd.), LA, 213-464-8774*
  M-Sat 7am-8pm/Sun 8am-6pm

◪ A "divine" multibranch Californian-style bakery that has plenty of fans for its "terrific rosemary bread" and "great biscotti"; there are also "lots of no-fat and low-fat goodies" as well as an array of Mediterranean sandwiches and mini-pizzas; dissenters say the wares "look great, taste ordinary."

Bristol Farms
25 | 25 | 24 | E
- *See listing in Supermarkets section.*

◼ As you'd expect from a top-rated supermarket group, their well-respected bakery sections offer "high-quality" bagels and "sweet stuff" like "gooey cakes"; the "almost-overwhelming" variety is "a feast for the eyes and stomach" and besides, "doing your grocery shopping while eating a brownie is heaven"; just back your "Brinks truck" up to the register to pay for it.

Broadway Deli 🚴
20 | 20 | 17 | E
- *1457 Third St. Promenade (Broadway), Santa Monica, 310-451-0616*
  M-Th 7am-midnight/F 7am-1am/Sat 8am-1am/ Sun 8am-midnight

◪ "Too chichi", "crowded" and "uneven" for critics, this Santa Monica "deli with an attitude" nevertheless provides a "good variety" of baked goods, especially pastries "for the yuppie in you"; many go for "great people-watching" in a "predictably trendy" setting, but also leave grumbling that service is "terrible" and prices "high."

Brown's Victory Bake Shop 🚴🚭
– | – | – | M
- *12805 Victory Blvd. (1 block east of Coldwater Canyon Ave.), N. Hollywood, 818-766-3258*
  T-Sat 7am-7pm/Sun & M 7am-5pm

You'll find some of the best New York–style cookies and cakes, including a remarkable selection of pastries for Passover, at this San Fernando Valley bakery that supplies corn rye to many of the best delis in town; the young owners decided to revive the baking of their ancestors, and they've done a very good job of it.

Buona Forchetta ⌷

– | – | – | E

• 2229 S. Barry Ave. (Olympic Blvd.), West LA, 310-477-2229
M-Sat 8am-2pm

A hot contender for the title of 'best bread in town', this
well-hidden warehouse in West LA turns out a small
selection of exceptionally fine loaves under the skilled
hand of baker Suzanne Dunaway; most notable is the
extraordinary olive bread, which is about half olives and
impossible to resist during the drive home.

Cake and Art

24 | 24 | 24 | E

• 8709 Santa Monica Blvd. (Westbourne), W. Hollywood,
310-657-8694
M-Sat 10am-6pm

☑ "Beautiful and clever", this favorite of the entertainment
industry is known for its "outrageous", "amazing icings"
atop "fun, inventive cakes"; but despite "exotic" looks,
some say the "tastes are not all as good as the art"; don't
be "too chicken to see the X-rated" design book.

Cakeplace, The 🚲 🖃

25 | 24 | 24 | E

• 2221 S. Barry Ave. (½ block south of Olympic Blvd.),
West LA, 310-479-7783
M-F 9am-5pm/Sat 9am-4pm

■ Superlatives abound for the "best" carrot, lemon and
chocolate fudge cakes, as well as this bakery's ability to
"copy any photo" in icing on their cakes; it's a bit "pricey",
but the "special cakes for special occasions" are worth it.

Cakeworks 🚲

27 | 24 | 24 | E

• 117 N. La Brea Ave. (bet. Beverly Blvd. & 1st St.), LA,
213-934-6515
W-Sat 11am-6pm

■ "Unique cake designs" that are "masterpieces of
frosting" are the main attractions at this La Brea pastry
house, where the "rich and delicious" works include "great
chocolate and lemon cakes" and the "best birthday cake
ever"; it's "on the expensive side" but its creations inspire
"wows"; P.S. make an appointment for custom orders.

Cheesecake Factory, The 🖃

24 | 25 | 21 | M

• 364 N. Beverly Dr. (1 block south of Little Santa Monica
Blvd.), Beverly Hills, 310-278-7270
M-Th 11am-11:30pm/F-Sun 11am-12:30am
• 4142 Via Marina (Admiralty Way), Marina Del Rey,
310-306-3344
M-Th 11am-11:30pm/F & Sat 11:30am-12:30am/
Sun 10am-11:30pm
• 605 N. Harbor Dr. (Beryl St.), Redondo Beach,
310-376-0466
M-Th 11:30am-11pm/F & Sat 11:30am-12:30am/
Sun 10am-11pm
• 6324 Canoga Ave. (Erwin St.), Woodland Hills, 818-883-9900
M-Th 11am-11pm/F & Sat 11am-12:30am/Sun 10am-11pm

Cheesecake Factory, The (Cont.)
- *11647 San Vicente Blvd. (Barrington Ave.), Brentwood, 310-826-7111*
  M-Th 11:30am-11:30pm/F & Sat 11:30am-12:30am/ Sun 10am-11:30pm
- *26570 Agoura Rd. (¼ mile south of Malibu Canyon), Calabasas, 818-880-6015*
  M-Th 11:30am-9pm/F & Sat 11:30am-10pm
- *1141 Newport Ctr. Dr. (Jamboree Rd.), Newport Beach, 714-720-8333*
  M-F 11am-11pm/Sat 11am-11:30pm/Sun 10am-11pm
- *Mail order: 800-726-4225*

☒ Cynics grumble that "factory says it all", dismissing this chain's wares as "boring, fattening and bland", but the masses are in "cheesecake heaven" over "a-million-and-one" "awesome", "divine", "gooey indulgences" that are "fluffy rather than dense and creamy" in the NYC tradition; fans on a sugar-and-cholesterol high declare "cheesecake purists may blanch – screw 'em!"

Chez Nous　　　　　　　23 21 19 E
- *10550 Riverside Dr. (½ block east of Cahuenga Blvd.), Toluca Lake, 818-760-0288*
  M-F 7am-10:30pm/Sat 8am-11pm/Sun 8am-3:30pm

■ "Excellent pâtisserie and croissants" "that melt in your mouth" plus "the best French bread this side of France" draw patrons to this bakery/restaurant that also earns praise for "the best breakfast in the Valley", served in a setting only "slightly nicer than a diner"; the baking here is so authentic that the "ovens are French too", but it's not cheap and some say the staff has "an attitude."

Cobbler Factory　　　　　　25 19 23 I
- *33 N. Catalina Ave. (½ block north of Colorado Blvd.), Pasadena, 818-449-2152*
  T-Sat 10am-7pm

■ What some call the "finest cobblers in SoCal" are served "hot from the oven" at this "down-home" Pasadena shop that's "one of LA's culinary monuments"; despite charges that this baker "uses canned fruit", the consensus is that these "yum", "strictly upper-crust" cobblers "can't get better" – they'll "make you want to give up all other feeds."

Danish Pastry, The &ofb;　　　　21 18 21 M
- *11726 W. Pico Blvd. (Barrington), West LA, 310-473-8626*
  M-F 7am-6pm/Sat 7am-5pm/Sun 7am-3pm

☒ There are "very good pastries" with "butter and eggs galore" at this "little bit of Denmark" on West Pico; also "tempting" are raisin custard and chocolate pudding that are "better than mom's"; despite a few sour notes about "limited variety" and quality that "used to be better", it's nice for "a cup of coffee and quiet time with a friend."

Diamond Bakery ⊟ | 25 | 23 | 20 | M |
- *335 N. Fairfax Ave. (½ block north of Beverly Blvd.), LA,*
  213-655-0534
  M-Sat 5:30am-6:30pm/Sun 5:30am-5pm

◼ A major contender for the title of "top Jewish bakery in town", this "step back in time" is staffed by "lovely Russian ladies" who deal smartly with Fairfax Avenue hordes hungry for the "best challah by far – even by NY standards" and other gems such as raisin pumpernickel or corn rye bread, chocolate-brownie cake and cheesecake; it's a pleasing hotbed of "good old rude sarcasm and efficient service."

Emil's Swiss Pastry ⊟ | 25 | 22 | 22 | M |
- *1567 Barry Ave. (Barrington Ave.), West LA, 310-820-2666*
- *1751 Ensley Ave. (Santa Monica Blvd.), Century City,*
  310-277-1114
  M 7am-4pm/T-Sat 7am-5:30pm

◼ These West LA and Century City "favorites" draw crowds for "classic, classy" pastries, including "famous fruit tarts", a "coffee cake called Copenhagen" and "flaky apple strudel"; they're "a tradition" for "frothy, sugar-laden desserts" – "beats all the trendy bakeries" say loyalists.

Europane ⊟ | – | – | – | M |
- *950 E. Colorado Blvd. (Mentor St.), Pasadena, 818-577-1828*
  M-F 8am-5:30pm/Sat & Sun 8am-5pm

Sumi Chang, former breakfast chef at Campanile, opened this small Old Town Pasadena bake shop that offers a wide selection of exceptional pastries, especially strudels and tarts, along with muffins, scones, croissants and focaccia.

Fantasy Frosting ⊷⊟   ▽ | 29 | 23 | 22 | E |
- *10050 S. Mills Ave. (Mulberry St.), Whittier, 310-941-6266*
  By appointment only

◼ An "out-of-the-way place with ornate ideas", this Whittier shop near the Nixon Library satisfies fantasies for "tasty and beautiful" cakes with "died-and-gone-to-heaven flavors"; "I got my wedding cake here five years ago, and people are still talking about it."

Fred's Bakery ⊟ | 24 | 23 | 22 | M |
- *2831 S. Robertson Blvd. (north of National Blvd.), LA,*
  310-838-1204
  M-Sat 6am-5:30pm/Sun 6am-1pm

◼ Even the "nonfat cookies are too good to believe" at this Beverlywood landmark where locals crowd in for "excellent challah, bagels", rye and other "great breads", not to mention the "exceptional black-and-white cookies", all served by the "nicest people"; a few dissenters find it "uneven", but they're solidly outvoted.

Baked Goods

Q | V | S | C

Great Harvest Bread Co. ♥

– | – | – | M

- 11640 San Vicente Blvd. (Barrington St.), Brentwood,
  310-826-9400
  M-Sat 7am-7pm/Sun 7am-5pm

This friendly Brentwood shop offers customers large slices
of old-fashioned, preservative-free bread, made with organic
whole wheat flour that's milled at the store; 15 bread
varieties, available in one-kilo sizes, rotate throughout the
week, and there are also chewy chocolate-chip oatmeal
cookies to sample and buy.

Hansen Cakes 🚲

23 | 23 | 23 | E

- 1072 S. Fairfax Ave. (bet. Pico & Olympic Blvds.), LA,
  213-936-4332
  T-Sat 9am-5pm/Sun 8am-noon
- 193 S. Beverly Dr. (1 block south of Wilshire Blvd.),
  Beverly Hills, 213-272-0474
  T-Sat 10am-6pm
- 18432 Ventura Blvd. (Reseda Blvd.), Tarzana, 818-708-1209
  T-F 10am-6pm/Sat 10am-5pm/Sun 10am-11am

◼ A "treasury of beautifully decorated cakes" with "a
hundred fillings to choose from", this Beverly Hills "tradition"
(with LA and Valley branches) sets a sweet "standard";
dissenters claim the cakes "look better than they taste",
but the fact that this shop's "been around forever" says a
lot, and for many it remains "the only place I think of."

Hughes Markets

16 | 18 | 17 | I

- See listing in Supermarkets section.

◼ Some shoppers say the pastries and breads at this
ubiquitous chain are "decent", but for most the rule is "don't
get baked goods in a supermarket"; "cheap and not worth
the price", "dull but predictable", "just ok but convenient" –
talk about damning with faint praise!

Il Fornaio

25 | 22 | 20 | M

- 301 N. Beverly Dr. (Dayton), Beverly Hills, 310-550-8330
  M-Th 6:30am-11pm/F 6:30am-midnight/
  Sat 7:30am-midnight/Sun 7:30am-11pm
- 24 W. Union St. (bet. Fair Oaks & DeLacey Sts.),
  Pasadena, 818-683-8585
  M-Th 7am-9pm/Sat 8am-midnight/Sun 8am-9pm
- 1627 Montana Ave. (17th St.), Santa Monica,
  310-458-1562
  M-F 6:30am-6:30pm/Sat 7am-6:30pm/Sun 7am-5pm
- 3110 Main St. (Navy St.), Santa Monica, 310-450-2030
  M-F 6am-7pm/Sat & Sun 7am-7pm
- First Interstate Bank Bldg., 633 W. Fifth St., 2nd landing,
  Downtown LA, 213-623-8400
  M-F 6:30am-5pm

Il Fornaio (Cont.)
- *One Bunker Hill, 601 W. Fifth St. (Grand Ave.),*
  Downtown LA, 213-622-4122
  M-F 6:30am-6pm/Sat 8am-4pm/Sun 10am-4pm
- *650 Anton Blvd. (Bristol Ave.), Costa Mesa, 714-668-0880*
  M-F 7am-10:30pm
- *18051 Von Karman Ave. (Michelson Dr.), Irvine,*
  714-261-2202
  M-F 6:30am-6:30pm/Sat & Sun 8am-6pm

■ Though many think of this as an Italian restaurant chain first and foremost, its name refers to the wonderful baked goods sold at each branch (some carry nothing but baked goods); "close your eyes and you're in Europe" as you bite into its "authentic" ciabatta, olive bread and pastries; some find the goods so addictive they're left wondering "how do you stop eating focaccia?"

J & T Bread Bin ⮽   23 | 23 | 20 | M
- *Farmer's Market, Stall 330 (bet. Fairfax Ave. & 3rd St.),*
  LA, 213-936-0785
  M-Sat 9am-6:30pm/Sun 10am-5pm

■ "Very good variety" and "always consistent" quality make this Farmer's Market baker a popular "old standby"; favorites range from "wonderful" "double-baked sourdoughs" and "great English walnut bread" to "big chewy cookies"; shop here, "then eat at the Kokomo."

Konditori   24 | 21 | 20 | M
- *230 S. Lake St. (bet. Del Mar Ave. & Cordova St.),*
  Pasadena, 818-792-8044
  M-Sat 7:30am-5pm/Sun 8am-4pm

☑ This "nostalgic", "European" bakery in Pasadena does "wonderful things with marzipan" and provides warm service from a "longtime staff"; "the Budapest meringue" is singled out by some sweet tooths as a "favorite" among the Scandinavian and Continental specialties; critics say it's "not as good as it was" but still, "don't go hungry or you'll buy the store."

LA BREA BAKERY ⮽   29 | 26 | 23 | E
- *624 S. La Brea Ave. (bet. Wilshire Blvd. & Sixth St.), LA,*
  213-939-6813
  M-Sat 8am-6pm/Sun 8am-4pm

■ LA's highest-profile bakery is also the *Survey's* No. 1, and for good reason – baker Nancy Silverton "revolutionized the bread scene" in SoCal from this small shop adjacent to Campanile; a "paradise" for bread lovers, it sets the "gold standard" for baked goods on the West Coast, and though priced like gold, these "first-class" loaves are "worth every penny"; also available in markets all over town.

La Conversation   25 21 22 M

- *2118 N. Hillhurst Ave. (bet. Los Feliz Blvd. & Franklin Ave.), LA, 213-666-9000*
  M-F 7am-7pm/Sat 8am-6pm/Sun 8am-2:30pm
- *638 N. Doheny Dr. (1 block north of Santa Monica Blvd.), W. Hollywood, 310-858-0950*
  M 8am-7pm/Sat 8am-6pm/Sun 8am-4pm

■ Worth talking about, this minichain of boutique bakeries is popular for its "delicate" pastries, "great croissants and coffee", "wonderful" tarts and "sublime" cakes; they're "great neighborhood places" where the "stuffed croissants" also make a fine breakfast or lunch.

La Creme de la Creme ⊄   ▽ 23 22 23 M

- *3562 N. Sepulveda Blvd. (Rosecrans Ave.), Manhattan Beach, 310-416-9199*
  M-Sat 6:30am-6pm/Sun 8am-4pm

■ Confection-loving regulars make this Manhattan Beach bakery "the first stop Saturday mornings for great cinnamon rolls" and "the best Napoleons – strawberry or chocolate – around"; the "excellent fruit tarts" and "great cakes" are also worthy of the shop's name.

L.A. Desserts &   27 22 21 E

- *113 N. Robertson Blvd. (bet. 3rd St. & Beverly Blvd.), LA, 310-273-5537*
  M-Sat 10am-5pm

■ "A little on the rich side" is a wild understatement for "desserts you could die for" at this bakery inside the film-industry-favorite Ivy restaurant; "throw calorie counting to the wind" and dive into the "wonderful" tarte Tatin, "great" dark chocolate cake, "outstanding" raisin tart and "amazing" white-chocolate lemon cake; some call it "expensive sin", others call it "a knockout", while the succinct say "wow."

La Mousse   27 24 23 E

- *11162 La Grange Ave. (bet. Sepulveda Blvd. & Frwy. #405), West LA, 310-478-6051*
  M-F 8:30am-5pm

■ "Every chocolate freak likes" the "mouth-watering" mousse and blackout cakes at this West LA "chocoholic heaven" that's "still wonderful after all these years"; these "yummy creations for a crowd" are "expensive but unique" and "rich, rich, rich – but oh my!"

Mani's Bakery & Espresso Bar & ☰   22 22 21 M

- *519 S. Fairfax Ave. (bet. 5th & 6th Sts.), LA, 213-938-8800*
  M-Th 6am-midnight/F 6:30am-1am/Sat 7:30am-1am/ Sun 7:30am-midnight

Mani's Bakery & Espresso Bar (Cont.)

- *2507 Main St. (north of Ocean Park Blvd.), Santa Monica,
  310-396-7700*
  *M-Th 6am-11pm/F 6am-midnight/Sat 7:30am-midnight/
  Sun 7:30am-11pm*
- *Studio City Plaza Shopping Ctr., 3960 Laurel Canyon Blvd.
  (Ventura Blvd.), Studio City, 818-762-7200*
  *M-Th 6am-11pm/F 6am-midnight/Sat 7:30am-midnight/
  Sun 7:30am-11pm*
- *8801 Santa Monica Blvd. (east of San Vicente Blvd.), W.
  Hollywood, 310-659-5955*
  *M-Th 6am-2am/F 6am-3am/Sat 7:30am-3am/
  Sun 7:30am-2am*

■ LA's best-known "sugarless bakery" (fruit juices are the
main sweetener) is "crowded" with famous faces hungry
for "sugar-free muffins", "baked doughnuts called faux
nuts", cakes that are "great for the buns" and "healthy linzer
cookies"; but nonconverts say it all "tastes too healthy."

Michel Richard   27 23 21 E

- *310 S. Robertson Blvd. (Burton Way), LA, 310-275-5707*
  M-Sat 8am-10pm/Sun 9am-4pm

■ Though Michel Richard is now only connected by name,
this French pâtisserie still reflects the chef-entrepreneur's
first love: the sweetest, butteriest pastries that admirers rate
"simply the best" and the "closest we come to France"; it's a
"museum of desserts" that "look elegant" and "taste great."

Miss Grace Lemon Cake   25 20 23 E
Company &🖃

- *16571 Ventura Blvd. (1 block west of Hayvenhurst Ave.),
  Encino, 818-995-1987*
  M-Sat 8:30am-5:30pm
- *422 N. Cañon Dr. (north of Brighton Way), Beverly Hills,
  310-281-8096*
  M-Sat 10am-5:30pm
- *Mail order: 800-367-2253*

■ This venerable bakery has been sold and Miss Grace
has been gone for years, but the namesake lemon cakes
continue to earn praise as the "best ever" because they're
"consistently delicious without being icky sweet"; also
hailed is the "courteous service" and "ease of ordering"
from the catalog – is this the L.L. Bean of lemon cakes?

Misto Caffe & Bakery   24 21 24 M

- *24558 Hawthorne Blvd. (Via del Monte), Torrance,
  310-375-3608*
  M-Th 9am-9:30pm/F & Sat 9am-10pm/Sun 9am-9pm

■ One of several bakeries operated by the boys from Chez
Melange (they also run Pier Avenue Bakery), this is "a great
place to take the kids" for "the best pizza breads" and "fab
sandwiches" made with the "dense, flavorful" house loaves;
there's also a "limited selection but unusual choices" of
"yummy", "unique desserts."

Mrs. Beasley's 🚲 ✉️ | 23 | 22 | 22 | M |
- *255½ S. Beverly Dr. (bet. Wilshire & Olympic Blvds.),*
  Beverly Hills, 310-276-6404
  M-Sat 8am-4pm
- *Capri Plaza, 19572 Ventura Blvd. (bet. Tampa & Corbin*
  Aves.), Tarzana, 818-344-7845
  M-Sat 8:30am-5:30pm
- *Mail order: 800-683-3461*

☑ Best known for "excellent" gift baskets that are "always pretty, tasty and appropriate", these bake shops offer "fresh, rich" pastry for "the incurable sweet tooth"; many are also pleased by the "great variety of minimuffins" and the "best scones"; dissenters say "cute" but "often cloyingly sweet."

Mrs. Field's Cookies ✉️ | 21 | 18 | 18 | M |
- *West Covina Fashion Plaza, 603 Fashion Plaza (Vincent),*
  W. Covina, 818-960-7011
- *8910 W. Santa Monica Blvd. (San Vicente), W. Hollywood,*
  310-659-9330
- *Whittwood Mall, 15618 Whittwood Ln. (Whittier Blvd.),*
  Whittier, 310-947-1437
- *395 Santa Monica Blvd. (bet. 4th St. & Broadway),*
  Santa Monica, 310-395-3575
- *13350 E. Telegraph (Carmenita), Santa Fe Springs,*
  310-946-1035
- *15301 Ventura Blvd. (Sepulveda Blvd.), Sherman Oaks,*
  818-990-0932
- *1728 Montebello Town Ctr. (San Gabriel), Montebello,*
  213-720-1400
- *208 Plaza Pasadena (Marengo), Pasadena, 818-577-2124*
- *Heron Building, 516 W. Sixth St. (Grand St.), Downtown LA,*
  213-489-7740
- *Citicorp, 735 S. Figueroa St. (7th St.), Downtown LA,*
  213-683-0706
- *Crocker Court, 330 S. Hope St. (4th St.), Downtown LA,*
  213-617-2821
- *Eagle Rock Plaza, 2700 Colorado Blvd. (Sierra Villa),*
  Eagle Rock, 213-258-9992
- *Beverly Ctr., 8500 Beverly Blvd., 8th fl. (San Vicente), LA,*
  310-659-4221
- *2205 S. Sepulveda Blvd. (W. Olympic Blvd.), West LA,*
  310-479-0785
- *California Mart, 110 E. Ninth St. (Main St.), Downtown LA,*
  213-622-5561
- *907 Westwood Blvd. (Le Conte), Westwood, 310-208-0096*
- *4712 Admiralty Way (Mindanao Ave.), Marina del Rey,*
  310-827-8652
- *2235 Glendale Galleria (bet. Central & Brand Sts.),*
  Glendale, 818-502-0545
- *442 Puente Hills Mall (Azuza Ave.), City of Industry,*
  818-965-3367
- *Arco Plaza, 505 S. Flower St. (Fifth St.), Downtown LA,*
  213-622-8111

Mrs. Field's Cookies (Cont.)
- *Westside Pavilion, 1st fl., 10800 W. Pico Blvd. (Westwood Blvd.), West LA, 213-470-7100*
- *11740 San Vicente Blvd. (Gorham Ave.), Brentwood, 310-207-1604*
- *173 Fox Hills Mall (Stanson Ave.), Culver City, 213-398-2001*
- *Topanga Plaza, 6600 Topanga Canyon Blvd. (Van Owen), Canoga Park, 818-884-1626*
- *20700 S. Avalon Blvd. (Delamo Blvd.), Carson, 310-324-4682*
- *329 Los Cerritos (South St.), Cerritos, 310-402-1788 Hours vary according to location; please call to check.*
- *Mail order: 800-344-2447*

◪ This ubiquitous cookie chain that's in just about every mall in town offers "addictive" treats that hook many who find them "better than grandma's"; but foes lament that it's "too expensive at a dollar a cookie" and "too sweet" – the "sugar KOs the flavor of nuts and chocolate" and "more than one cookie is an overdose."

Mrs. Gooch's Whole   23 | 21 | 23 | E
Foods Market
- *See listing in Health/Natural Food section.*

◪ SoCal's best-known natural food markets offer "all manner of natural-grain" breads and muffins as well as "no-fat", "no-sugar", "no-wheat" pastries that satisfy the Birkenstock crowd; but burger eaters howl that "carob is no substitute for chocolate" and this stuff is "good only if you like things sweetened with honey and fruit juice"; still, it's *the* place to go for "hard-to-find vegan baked goods."

Nancy's Healthy Kitchen 🖃   – | – | – | M
- *17620 Ventura Blvd. (1 block east of White Oak Ave.), Encino, 818-380-6877 Every day 8am-8:30pm*

Yes, low-fat, low-calorie baked goods can be delicious, as attested to by this friendly Valley bakery/cafe's wide selection of cookies and cakes, all reduced in bad stuff but not in taste; for a clever gift, try one of their wooden boxes filled with innumerable packages of baked goods.

Nicolosi Pastries 🚲   24 | 22 | 21 | M
- *17540 Ventura Blvd. (2 blocks east of White Oak Ave.), Encino, 818-789-0922 T-Sat 9am-6pm/Sun 9am-4pm*

■ "The best cannoli west of the Hudson" and "irresistible biscotti" capture hearts at this Valley Italian bakery that also assembles the "best croquembouche ever" and leaves loaf lovers sighing "oh, that olive bread!"; in summer, "try the secret lemon and chocolate ices"; it's all a "good reason to go off your diet."

Odeon ⊅ | 21 | 20 | 19 | M |
• 625A Montana Ave. (7th St.), Santa Monica, 310-451-9096
  M-Sat 6:30am-9:30pm/Sun 6:30am-6:30pm

☑ "Terrific cinnamon rolls", "excellent cookies" and "yes –
sour-cream coffee cake" add to the "good vibes" at this
"neighborhood cafe" on Montana Avenue's Bakery Row; but
some critics find the baking "inconsistent", and others say
watch out for "pathetic", "snooty" service with "attitude."

Old Town Bakery & Deli | 24 | 24 | 18 | M |
• Tanner Market, 166 W. Colorado Blvd. (bet. Pasadena Ave.
  & DeLacey), Pasadena, 818-792-7943
  M-F 7:30am-10pm/Sat & Sun 7:30am-11pm

☑ Baker Amy Pressman is known for her "gorgeous", even
"obscene" desserts at this "drive-out-of-your-way" pastry
shop/restaurant on the western edge of Old Town Pasadena;
along with breads, "fabulous fruit pies" and "tempting
cookies" there's also the "best chicken pot pie"; the
downside is "compulsively poor service" – "for what they
charge, the customer deserves better."

Old Vienna Strudel Co. ♿⊅ | 24 | 15 | 22 | M |
• 10836 ½ Washington Blvd. (1½ blocks west of Overland
  Ave.), Culver City, 310-280-0282
  T-F noon-6pm/Sat 11am-6pm

■ A diminutive, "authentic" Viennese shop in an unexpected
Culver City locale offering "great, flaky, tasty" strudels ("the
apple is the best") that are still "warm from the oven",
including a "good low-fat, low-cal" model; but some are
stymied by the "odd hours" (i.e. no early AMs or late PMs).

Paris Pastry ♿ | 24 | 22 | 21 | E |
• 1448 Westwood Blvd. (Ohio Ave.), Westwood, 310-474-8888
  M-Sat 7am-6pm

☑ Westwood may be "a long way from Paris", but this
"most-authentic" baker remains a favorite for "beautiful",
"old-school" French pastries, including "excellent Grand
Marnier cake" and "very good croissants and brioches";
there's "yummy quiche too"; dissenters (a minority) find it
"boring" and "overpriced."

Pasadena Baking Co. | 24 | 23 | 20 | M |
• 29 E. Colorado Blvd. (bet. Raymond & Fair Oaks Aves.),
  Pasadena, 818-796-9966
  M-Th 7am-11pm/F 7am-midnight/Sat 8am-midnight/
  Sun 8am-11pm

■ Adjacent to and under the same ownership as the always-
packed Mi Piace, this bakery/cafe offers an "attractive
variety" of sweets that "challenges your decision-making",
plus bread so good "you *can* live by it alone"; "terrific
cappuccino" and outside seating with a fine view of Old
Town help make it "very popular", yet it's "not a madhouse."

Patticakes 🚲✉   27 24 24 E

• *1900 N. Allen Ave. (New York Dr.), Altadena, 818-794-1128*
T-Sat 7:30am-6pm

◪ "No special occasion should be without the artistically decorated cakes" from this Eastside baker renowned for "the ultimate, gorgeous" embellishments; the "wonderful miniature cakes" and "fabulous carrot" variety also score high; however, there are a handful of gripes that "prices have gone up" and orders have been "screwed up."

Pavilions   17 19 17 M

• *See listing in Supermarkets section.*

◪ Thanks to the upscaling of these Vons spin-offs, more than a few shoppers say their baked goods are "excellent for a grocery store" and "better than the competition"; but many decry "commercial stuff" that's just "basic and boring"; still, they're "convenient" and the fact that there's "good parking" is no small matter in car-intensive LA.

Pier Avenue Bakery   25 23 23 M

• *705 Pier Ave. (bet. PCH & Ardmore Ave.), Hermosa Beach,*
310-379-6282
Every day 7am-7pm

■ This new Hermosa Beach bread shop next to Descanso Restaurant (both are operated by the Chez Melange group) is off to a good start with an "excellent variety" of loaves, muffins and biscotti marked by "outstanding quality"; "they have their act together" and "you can taste the difference."

Pierre's Pastry 🚲✉   22 19 21 E

• *1037 Swarthmore Ave. (Sunset Blvd.), Pacific Palisades,*
310-454-4017
T-Sat 7am-5pm

■ A well-known French bakery in the Palisades that's praised for its "decadent", "impressive-looking chocolate cakes", "beautiful white-chocolate wedding cakes" and "great sourdough"; the selection is "limited but fine."

Pioneer Boulangerie   22 21 19 M

• *804 Montana Ave. (Lincoln Blvd.), Santa Monica,*
310-451-4998
M-F 6am-8pm/Sat 7am-7pm/Sun 7am-6pm
• *512 Rose Ave. (2 blocks east of Main St.), Venice,*
310-392-3066
M-F 7am-5pm/Sat 7am-4pm/Sun 7am-2pm

◪ What used to be the best-known French baking company in SoCal (complete with its own Basque restaurant) is down to two shops selling "always-reliable" sourdough bread to those who insist these "loaves and rolls" are still "the best"; but, others cavil that except for breads "you can keep the rest" and it's just "a cut above grocery store bakeries."

Baked Goods

Q | V | S | C |

Price/Costco 🍽
- *See listing in Supermarkets section.*

A large membership warehouse store offering row upon row of adequate to very good baked goods, some of which are made on the premises; you'll find everything from large birthday cakes and humongous muffins to cookies, breads and bagels; but beware, you'll need a large family or freezer to take advantage of the low prices.

–| –| –| I |

Q Bakery/Pastries

26 | 24 | 23 | M |

- *16605 Sunset Blvd. (Marquez), Pacific Palisades, 310-459-3564*
  M 7am-11pm/T-Th 7am-7pm/Sat 7am-6pm/Sun 8am-3pm

■ A "real find" "hidden away in a mini-mall", this Pacific Palisades pastry and bread shop is "getting better and better" with "great desserts at great prices" including "fat-free chocolate macaroons"; in addition to "fabulous", "novel breads" there are "delicious pizzas" too; but be advised: "get there early, or all the best muffins are sold out."

Ralphs Markets

15 | 18 | 16 | I |

- *See listing in Supermarkets section.*

■ The "baked-for-the-masses", "priced-right" goods at this supermarket chain include cakes frosted with "colors not found in nature"; quality and taste are "consistent" but "ordinary", which translates into "run-of-the-mill" at best.

Röckenroll 🚴🍽

24 | 19 | 19 | M |

- *Santa Monica Pl. Mall (bet. 4th St. & Broadway), Santa Monica, 310-587-1115*
  M-Sat 10am-9pm/Sun 11am-7pm

■ This popular sandwich/baked goods stand opened by Hans Röckenwagner in the Food Court in Santa Moncia Place Mall has "so-good" cheese pretzels, "lovely rolls" and "incredible eggplant sandwiches" on "wonderful breads"; service lags behind quality but most have no complaints, and "now they have nonfat goodies too – thank you Hans!"

Röckenwagner 🚴

26 | 21 | 22 | E |

- *2435 Main St. (north of Ocean Park Blvd.), Santa Monica, 310-399-6504*
  T-F 11:30am-2:30pm/6pm-10pm/Sat 9am-2:30pm/ 5:30pm-10pm/Sun 9am-2:30pm/5:30pm-9:30pm

■ Home of Hans Röckenwagner, father of the "best" Mittel Europa baked goods, this Santa Monican's "sumptuous breads" are "La Brea's only competition", especially the "great" seven-grain rolls and a "Rudolph Steiner health bread" that tastes too good to be healthy; ginger scones are "favorites" and the brownies are "orgasmic", as are the restaurant's breakfast bread-and-cheese plates.

ROSEBUD CAKES 🚲🖨   27 | 26 | 25 | E
- *311 S. Robertson Blvd. (bet. Olympic & Wilshire Blvds.),*
  Beverly Hills, 310-657-6207
  T-Sat 10am-5pm

■ "Beautiful to look at", "heaven to taste" – so goes the flowery chorus of praise for this Beverly Hills shop's "pricey but delicious" cakes; each "elegant" creation at this "classy act for the yuppie crowd" is "always a masterpiece."

Rose Cafe   21 | 20 | 18 | M
- *220 Rose Ave. (Main St.), Venice, 310-399-0711*
  M-F 7:30am-10pm/Sat 8am-10pm/Sun 8am-5pm

◪ A longtime Venice "meeting place" that's a "favorite showcase of desserts" and still has "the best tarte Tatin" according to fans; its "decadent chocolate cakes from the '80s" are now joined by very '90s "fat-free, sugar-free carrot-pineapple muffins"; however, critics say that "appearances deceive" and "quality and service have gone downhill."

Southern Bakery 🖨   – | – | – | I
- *LAX Mini Mall, 5535 W. Manchester (Aviation Blvd.),*
  Inglewood, 310-568-0593
  M-Sat 11am-7pm/Sun noon-5pm

In a mini-mall not far from LAX, this storefront is home to some of the best cobblers and pies around; servings range from single portions for just pocket change all the way to massive pies that feed your family and the one next door; flavors include all the right fruits, a lemon chess pie that can't be beat and good chicken pot pies as well.

Sweet Lady Jane 🚲   27 | 25 | 23 | E
- *8360 Melrose Ave. (Kings Rd.), W. Hollywood,*
  213-653-7145
  M-Sat 8:30am-11:30pm

■ "Always too crowded", this West Hollywood "postage stamp" of a bake shop has surveyors pining for its "unusual but classy" cakes with "distinctive flavors", including a "lovely lemon meringue tart" and "cheesecake that's better than sex"; even those who complain about "snooty service" seem to agree "SLJ is pricey but worth it for every crumb."

Trader Joe's   22 | 22 | 21 | I
- *See listing in Supermarkets section.*

◪ "Gourmet eaters and cooks on a budget" like these "LA mainstays" for their "good variety" of "dependable" cookies, cakes and "dense, heavy breads", even though "baked goods aren't their specialty"; the "cheesecake is frozen but almost as good as my wife's" and the "mudpie is always a wow"; this Joe provides "surprisingly fine quality for mass-produced baked goods."

Viktor Benes/Mamolo's ⊟♿ 24 23 21 M
● *8718 W. Third St. (2 blocks east of Robertson Blvd.), LA,*
  310-276-4884
  M-Sat 6am-6pm
  For additional listings, see Gelson's and Mayfair Markets,
  and Vicente Foods in the Supermarkets section.
■ Mostly located in upscale supermarkets, this "European-
style bakery" is "everybody's fave" for "yummy" "alligators
you can sink your teeth into"; the "breads and croissants
are good" but it's the sweets that fans flock for, especially
the much-praised "killer" chocolate cakes; "no artificial
ingredients" means "products are nutritious and delicious."

Weby's Bakery 21 21 20 M
● *12131 Ventura Blvd. (Laurel Canyon Blvd.), Studio City,*
  818-769-6062
  M-Sat 7am-7pm/Sun 7am-5pm
◪ This longtime Valley favorite is under "new ownership",
which makes many say "it's not what it used to be"; but,
it's still a source for "whipped cream strawberry cake",
"giant cookies" and "a cake in the shape of a huge burger."

Wild Oats Market ♿ 24 23 22 M
● *603 S. Lake Ave. (California St.), Pasadena, 818-792-1778*
● *1425 Montana Ave. (15th St.), Santa Monica, 310-576-4707*
  Every day 8am-10pm
◪ There's a "nice selection from Il Fornaio and La Brea
Bakery" at these "friendly" health fooders that have "one
of the finest supermarket bakery departments"; staples
include "good bagels and muffins" and beansprouters
love the "variety of healthy items", but the unreconstructed
say "all that bran gets stuck in my teeth."

Zen Bakery ⊟ 20 18 19 M
● *10988 Pico Blvd. (Sepulveda Blvd.), West LA,*
  310-475-6727
  M-F 7am-4pm/Sat 7am-2pm/Sun 8:45am-2pm
◪ Muffins and breads "that taste healthy" are the specialty
here, and in cases such as the "excellent blueberry bran
muffins", many also say "yummy"; a lot of the goods are
"the sort of stuff Dr. Kellogg prescribed in The Road to
Wellville", which may explain comments such as "tasteless"
f unpretentious down-to-earth quality."

Zov's Bakery 27 24 24 M
● *Enderle Ctr., 17440 E. 17th St. (Yorba), Tustin, 714-838-9495*
  M & T 7am-2:30pm/W-Sat 7am-8pm
■ An impressive Orange County bakery attached to Zov's
Bistro that's "worth a special trip" for "excellent-quality"
baked goods that "actually taste as good as they look",
including "great focaccia"; even those who lament that
this "jewel of Orange County" is "too small and crowded"
still "use it for special treats."

Candy & Nuts

Yes, we know that Los Angeles has been called the land of fruits and nuts. That's cute. But this is also the land of some excellent candy stores and terrific places to buy nuts. The latter are well liked for being a natural product that's virtually devoid of cholesterol, though not of fat. And in a city where life isn't always that sweet, a good box of superbly crafted chocolates is much appreciated, especially as a sort of unofficial currency in the entertainment biz. The higher you are on the food chain, the bigger the box of See's Chocolates you get, and it's said you get a box of Teuscher Chocolates when your firm grosses $100 million.

Top Quality
- *28* Teuscher Chocolates
     Edelweiss Chocolates
- *27* Littlejohns Toffee
- *26* Lee Gelfond Chocolates
     Comparte's of California

Top Variety
- *27* Edelweiss Chocolates
- *26* See's Candy
     Garvey Nut House
- *25* Lee Gelfond Chocolates
     Teuscher Chocolates

Top Service
- *25* Teuscher Chocolates
     Lee Gelfond Chocolates
     Edelweiss Chocolates
     See's Candy
- *24* Bit of Switzerland

Best Buys
     See's Candy
     Trader Joe's
     Littlejohns Toffee
     Edelweiss Chocolates
     Lee Gelfond Chocolates

Q	V	S	C

Atelier de Chocolat   ▽ | 27 | 24 | 24 | E |
- *Malibu Country Mart, 3835 Crosscreek Rd. (PCH), Malibu, 310-456-0201*
  M-F 11am-6pm/Sat 11am-10pm/Sun noon-5pm
- *442 E. Main St. (California & Oak), Ventura, 805-648-5937*
  M-Sat 10am-5pm/Sun noon-4pm

■ "I don't even like chocolate and this place makes me drool" sums up this duo's European-style chocolates and treats such as "chocolate–peanut butter graham crackers" that are "favorite" along-the-beach treats for Colony celebs and ordinary Ventura folk alike; as Malibu resident Barbra would say, it all goes down "like buttah."

Comparte's of California | 26 | 22 | 23 | E |
- *912 S. Barrington Ave., Brentwood, 310-826-3380*
  T-Sat 10am-6pm
- *Mail order: 800-213-6485*

■ A "longtime favorite" source for dried fruits, "chocolate-covered fruits" and fruit cakes that can be "shipped around the globe", this ultimate Brentwood "mom-and-pop candy shop" is also renowned for its "chocolate-covered matzo for Passover" and boxes that make "nice party gifts"; "grandmother loved it" and the tradition continues.

Del Rey Nut Co., The 🚴🏍️   24 | 25 | 20 | M
(fka Iliffili Gourmet Nuts)
* *4943 McConnell Ave. (1 block south of Culver Blvd.),
  Marina del Rey, 310-823-6887/800-833-1223
  M-F 8am-4pm*

■ The "best buy in gourmet nuts" might just be at this
Marina del Rey shop with a "great selection" of "fresh",
"excellent" varieties – "when you need anything, they
have it"; it's a real find, "if you can find them."

EDELWEISS CHOCOLATES 🚴✉️   28 | 27 | 25 | E
* *444 N. Cañon Dr. (bet. Little Santa Monica Blvd. &
  Brighton Way), Beverly Hills, 310-275-0341
  M-F 10am-6pm/Sat 10am-5:30pm*

■ Highest rated for quality of the nonchain candy shops, this
Beverly Hills landmark, dating back to 1942, is an "institution"
beloved for its "novelty chocolates", "wonderful chocolate
truffles" and "chocolate-covered cherries"; the flavors are
"heavenly" and "there's always a treat" to be found at this
"friendly mom-and-pop operation", and though prices aren't
cheap, "the smells are free."

Garvey Nut and Candy 🚴✉️🏍️   24 | 26 | 19 | M
* *6416 Flotilla St. (½ block west of Garfield), City of
  Commerce, 213-725-0352, 800-427-6873 (CA only)
  M-F 8am-4:30pm*

☑ "Everything looks great" at this "wholesale supplier" in
far-off Commerce that sells a "good selection of nuts and
candy" to the public in bulk quantities; the setting is like
an "old-fashioned candy store" but some say the illusion
is ruined by "crude, rude" service.

Godiva Chocolatier 🚴✉️   26 | 23 | 24 | VE
* *Beverly Ctr., 131 N. La Cienega Blvd. #725, LA,
  213-651-0697/310-946-3482
  M-F 10am-9pm/Sat 10am-8pm/Sun 11am-7pm*
* *Century City Marketplace, 10250 Santa Monica Blvd.
  (bet. Ave. of the Stars & Constellation Blvd.), Century City,
  310-277-6154
  M-F 10am-9pm/Sat 10am-9pm/Sun 11am-6pm*
* *7th St. Marketplace, 735 S. Figueroa St. (7th St.),
  Downtown LA, 213-624-8923
  M-F 10am-7pm/Sat 10am-6pm/Sun 11am-5pm*
* *Mail order: 800-946-3482*

☑ The "clever packaging" of "excellent but overpriced"
chocolates ("get a second mortgage") is a hallmark of this
popular chain that delivers "candy almost as good as the
hype"; loyalists insist this "chocolate delight" is "better than
the best" and "you get what you pay for", but a few heretics
dismiss it as "too waxy" and best "for those who want to
spend more and get less"; N.B. mail-order available only
Christmas through Mother's Day.

Candy & Nuts

Q V S C

Grand Chocolate Pizza Inc. ▽ 23 22 24 E
- 400 S. Beverly Dr., Beverly Hills, 90212, 310-858-7787
  M-F 9:30am-5pm
- Mail order: 800-475-7787

■ Exclusively mail order, this venture has "no competition in the world" according to fans of its "hilariously exciting" namesake specialty: chocolate pizzas that come in five sizes, with varieties like cappucino break and ultimate passion; it's a "brilliant" "gift idea", even if some say the pizza "looks great, but only tastes fair."

Hadley's Fruit Orchards 23 25 18 M
- 48980 Seminole Dr. (Frwy. #110, Cabazon exit), Cabazon, 909-849-5255
- 6115 Paseo Del Norte (Frwy. #15, Palomar Airport Rd. exit), Carlsbad, 619-438-1260
  Every day 8am-9pm
- Mail order: 800-854-5655

■ The Cabazon branch is a "mandatory oasis" on the way to and from Palm Springs, where it's "fun to buy too much" for both the glitterati and busloads of tourists heading to the nearby Morongo Indian Bingo Parlor; "great dates", "killer date shakes", dried fruits and other "fattening foods" produce "a sugar buzz like no other" and "make the drive home happier"; the Carlsbad branch is newer.

Heminger's Fudge & Chocolate ▽ 24 21 21 E
Company
- 42 E. Colorado Blvd. (bet. Fair Oaks & Raymond Aves.), Pasadena, 818-793-2444
  M 10am-6pm/T 10am-7pm/W & Th 10am-9pm/ F & Sat 10am-11pm/Sun noon-9pm
- Mail order: 800-653-8343

■ Though this Pasadena fudge shop had only a few visits from surveyors, those who've been report "interesting varieties" of "quality fudge" and staffers who are "always willing to give a taste"; N.B. if you're hot and thirsty, try a frozen cappuccino slushie.

LA Nut House 23 24 20 M
- LA Produce Market, 1601 E. Olympic Blvd., Bldg. 200 (bet. 8th St. & Alameda Blvd.), Downtown LA, 213-623-2541
  M-F 2am-2pm
- 14952 Valley View (north of #I-5 Frwy.), La Mirada, 310-926-2331
  M-F 9am-5pm
- Mail order: 800-653-8343

■ With "more nuts than a mental institution", this venerable Downtown Produce Market standby sells only in bulk, making it a good place to "stock up for the holidays"; it's "not fancy but nice" and as for the staff, patrons "love them guys"; the La Mirada branch offers similar goods.

LEE GELFOND   ⎡26⎤⎡25⎤⎡25⎤⎡E⎤
CHOCOLATES, INC. ✇✉
- *275 S. Robertson Blvd. (bet. Wilshire & Olympic Blvds.), Beverly Hills, 310-854-3524*
  M-F 9am-5pm/Sat & Sun by appointment

■ A high-end, "special-order" chocolate emporium that offers what some call the "best in individualized service"; a "very accommodating, responsive owner" creates "great novelties" and "terrific custom work" for her well-heeled Beverly Hills clientele; this is "candy as art."

Littlejohns English Toffee ✉ ⎡27⎤⎡21⎤⎡23⎤⎡M⎤
- *Farmer's Market, 6333 W. 3rd St., stall 432 (Fairfax Ave.), LA, 213-936-5379*
  M-Sat 9am-6:30pm/Sun 9:30am-5pm

■ "English toffee that melts in your mouth" is made before your eyes at this six-decades-old Farmer's Market landmark; besides the "best-in-the-world" toffee, other "great stuff" includes "handmade" peanut brittle, mints, chocolate-covered marshmallows and honeycomb – "yum yum."

Magee's Nuts ✇✉   ⎡–⎤⎡–⎤⎡–⎤⎡M⎤
- *Farmer's Market, 6333 W. Third St. (Fairfax Ave.), LA, 213-938-4127*
  M-Sat 9am-6:30pm/Sun 10am-5pm

Not so much a place to go for sweets and nuts as a Farmer's Market institution (it was one of the original stands in this venerable tourist oasis); you'll find edible nostalgia here in the form of nuts and candy mixes that have long gone out of style, prepared the way it was done way back when.

Robin Rose Ice Cream   ⎡25⎤⎡23⎤⎡21⎤⎡M⎤
- *215 Rose Ave. (Main St.), Venice, 310-399-1774*
  Every day noon-10pm

■ Though best known for ice creams (especially the "very creamy" chocolate-raspberry truffle and "rich" rose petal), this "class act" also scores high for "good chocolates", which the owner also serves gratis at the traffic school she runs (only in LA!); there are "terrific candy apples" too.

Rocky Mountain Chocolate   ⎡23⎤⎡22⎤⎡21⎤⎡M⎤
Factory ✇✉
- *Grand Central Market, 317 S. Broadway (3rd & 4th Sts.), Downtown LA, 213-626-2524*
- *Arco Plaza, 505 S. Flower St. (Figueroa St.), Downtown LA, 213-624-6491*
- *Wells Fargo Court, 330 S. Hope St. (bet. 3rd & 4th Sts.), Downtown LA, 213-687-0351*
  M-F 10am-6pm

☑ Though far from the Rockies, this sweet trio has locals lining up for "chocolate-covered strawberries", "sea foam" and "the best caramel apples"; a minority say "don't waste your calories", but more report "good quality at good prices" and staff that's "eager and quick to please."

See's Candy 📠 25 | 26 | 24 | M |

- 3431 S. La Cienega Blvd. (Jefferson Blvd.), LA, 310-559-4919
- South Bay Galleria, 1815 Hawthorne Blvd. (Artesia Blvd.),
  Redondo Beach, 310-371-6855
- 8613 S. Sepulveda Blvd. (Manchester Ave.), Westchester,
  310-645-8070
- Beverly Ctr., 121 N. La Cienega Blvd. (Beverly Blvd.), LA,
  310-657-1010
- 113 The Plaza Pasadena, Colorado Blvd. (bet. Marengo
  & Los Roblos), Pasadena, 818-795-8596
- Valley Plaza Shopping Ctr., 6529 Laurel Canyon Blvd.
  (1 block north of Victory), N. Hollywood, 818-761-4061
- Westside Pavillion, 10800 Pico Blvd. (bet. Westwood Blvd.
  & Overland St.), West LA, 310-470-2973
- Crenshaw Plaza, 3650 W. Martin Luther King Blvd.
  (Crenshaw St.), LA, 213-296-0013
- Manhattan Village Shopping Ctr., 3004 Sepulveda Blvd.
  (bet. Marine & Rosecrans), 310-545-1126
- Shops at Palos Verdes, 550 Deep Valley Dr. (bet. Indian
  Peak St. & Deep Valley Dr.), Rolling Hills Estates,
  310-541-6275
- Century City Marketplace, 10258 Santa Monica Blvd.
  (bet. Century Park W. & Avenue of the Stars), Century City,
  310-277-9228
- 1301 Wilshire Blvd. (Euclid), Santa Monica, 310-395-2022
- Los Altos Ctr., 2129 Bellflower Blvd. (Stearns St.), Long
  Beach, 310-597-5189
- 21706 Hawthorne Blvd. (Carson St.), Torrance, 310-370-0521
- Stonewood Shopping Ctr., 203 Stonewood St. (Firestone
  & Lakewood), Downey, 310-862-8074
- 24333 Magic Mountain Pkwy. (McBean St.), Valencia,
  805-259-2186
- Media Ctr. Mall, 201 E. Magnolia, Burbank, 818-559-7442
- 17340 Ventura Blvd. (bet. Balboa & Whiteoak Sts.),
  Encino, 818-995-0491
- 1812 Montebello Town Ctr. (bet. Paramount Ave. & San
  Gabriel Blvd.), Montebello, 213-728-7291
- 2159 Glendale Galleria (bet. Colorado Blvd. & B'way),
  Glendale, 818-247-2433
- 3641 E. Foothill Blvd. (Rosemead Blvd.), Pasadena,
  818-351-0121
- Eastland Ctr., 2753 E. Garvey Blvd. (Citrus & Barranca Sts.),
  West Covina, 818-331-1216
- 2098 S. Atlantic Blvd. (Riggin), Monterey Park, 213-887-4880
- Del Amo Fashion Mall (Carson St.), Torrance, 310-370-1252
- Alhambra Shopping Ctr., 914 E. Valley Blvd., Alhambra,
  818-281-7733
- North Hills Shopping Ctr., 16844 Devonshire Blvd.
  (Balboa Blvd.), Granada Hills, 818-363-9320
- Whittwood Mall, 15635 Whittwood Ln. (bet. Scott Ave. &
  Sanna Gertrudis), Whittier, 310-943-8713

See's Candy (Cont.)
- *238 Puente Hills Mall (bet. Colima & Azusa Sts.), City of Industry, 818-964-0660*
- *23 Lakewood Ctr. Mall (bet. Candlewood & Del Amo), Lakewood, 310-531-6284*
- *9839 Paramount Blvd. (Florence), Downey, 310-928-2912*
- *Sherman Oaks Fashion Sq., 14006 Riverside Dr. (Hazeltine & Woodman Aves.), Sherman Oaks, 818-783-2622*
- *1133 Foothill Blvd. (Berdugo Blvd.), La Cañada-Flintridge, 818-790-7022*
- *Topanga Plaza, 6600 Topanga Canyon Blvd. (Victory Blvd.), Canoga Park, 818-883-9114*
- *Santa Anita Fashion Park, 400 S. Baldwin Ave., Arcadia, 818-446-4970*
- *Northridge Fashion Ctr., 9301 Tampa Ave., Northridge, 818-885-1505*
- *Fashion Plaza, 1200 W. Covina Pkwy. (bet. Vincent & Sunset Blvds.), W. Covina, 818-960-2224*
- *San Fernando Combo, 19301 Vanowen St. (Tampa Blvd.), Reseda, 818-708-9971*
  All locations 9am-6pm except for mall branches, which follow mall hours.
- *Mail order: 800-347-7337*

■ See's may not rank at the very top numerically, but it's number one in the hearts of millions of Angelenos for whom it's "the epitome of the holidays", the place to go for Valentine's Day gift boxes or anytime the urge for "basic, great chocolate" strikes; with shops all over, it's a "tradition that's nice to have around" and there's "always a free sample" to be enjoyed, making even adults feel like "a kid in a real candy store."

TEUSCHER CHOCOLATES &⬲⊟   28 | 25 | 25 | VE
- *9548 Brighton Way (Camden Dr.), Beverly Hills, 310-276-2776 M-Sat 10am-6pm*

■ The town's top-rated chocolates – "elegant", "gorgeous" and "delectable" "works of art" – are provided at the Beverly Hills branch of this worldwide chain; it's a "class act" "for the rich" who can not only "dream about the champagne truffles" but actually afford the "splurge."

Trader Joe's   22 | 21 | 21 | I
- *See listing in Supermarkets section.*

■ Known as much for "astoundingly good value" as for "fine quality", this chain is "always an adventure" for those who like to forage in warehouse-like settings for such "best bargains" as "huge candy bars", "chocolate-covered coffee beans", Belgian chocolates, fruit jellies, nuts and dates; "great merchandising and packaging" makes the sweet "guilty pleasures" even more irresistible.

Ultimate Nut & Candy Co. ♿✉   22 | 22 | 20 | M

- *Farmer's Market (3rd St. & Fairfax Ave.), LA, 213-938-1555*
  Every day 9am-7pm
- *Century City Marketplace, 10250 Santa Monica Blvd.*
  (bet. Century Park E. & Century Park W.), Century City,
  310-788-0734
  M-Th, Sun 10am-9pm/F & Sat 10am-10pm
- *10665 Vanowen (Clybourn), Burbank, 818-766-5259*
  M-F 8am-4:30pm
- *Mail order: 800-767-5259*

▣ Supporters say this "always-reliable" minichain provides the "ultimate taste for the ultimate nut lover", including the "best caramel corn with nuts"; dissenters say it "feels like the K-Mart of chocolatiers" and is "nothing special"; still, it's fine "for pig-outs" and helps set a "standard for quality sweets" at reasonable prices.

Caterers

Given that Los Angeles is the Entertainment Capital of the universe, it goes without saying that entertaining is a big thing here. There's probably no city this side of the Seine where caterers are more sought out or have more power than in LA. The studios and networks are endlessly trying to outdo each other when it comes to putting on events worthy of the rise and fall of the Roman Empire.

But while there's no question that catering in Southern California is big business, it's also a small business: there are plenty of firms that will put on a remarkable dinner for you when the boss is coming over, or whenever something special is needed. The price range: from affordable to very insane. As with everything in Hollywood, even the sky isn't always the limit.

Top Quality
- 28 Gai Klass
- 27 Kitchen for Exploring
     LA Celebrations
- 26 Along Came Mary
     Duck Duck Mousse

Top Variety
- 27 Gai Klass
- 26 Kitchen for Exploring
- 25 Along Came Mary
     LA Celebrations
     Rococo

Top Service
- 27 Gai Klass
- 26 Kitchen for Exploring
- 25 Someone's in the Kitchen
- 24 Along Came Mary
     Rococo

Best Buys
- Kitchen for Exploring
- Gai Klass
- El Cholo Catering
- Someone's in the Kitchen
- Along Came Mary

Q	V	S	C
26	25	24	E

Along Came Mary ✍
- *5265 W. Pico Blvd. (Cochran Ave.), LA, 213-931-9082*
  M-F 9am-6pm

■ "One of the hottest" of LA caterers, this "show biz" fave is famous for over-the-top theme events (they do many opening night bashes for studios); their work "always grabs one's attention" thanks to "great ingenuity" in both food (Regional American to ethnic) and presentation; this "gem" "deserves its reputation" and, based on the number of votes it receives, is the caterer most known to our reviewers.

Ambrosia ✍ | – | – | – | E |
- *1717 Stewart St. (bet. Olympic Blvd. & Colorado Ave.),*
  Santa Monica, 310-453-7007
  M-F 9am-5pm

Popular special event and catering firm known for its nice presentations and "variety" of "creative", "good food" for large-scale parties; it has even catered Super Bowls, but critics find the fare less than "ambrosial" at times.

American Gourmet, The ⌷   ▽ 27 | 28 | 27 | M
● *3816 Albright Ave. (Venice Blvd.), LA, 310-391-8413*
  M-F 9am-5pm
■ "Great value for the money" is offered by a Westside
caterer that admirers liken to a "close friend who cares"
and "keeps current" with entertaining trends; cuisine
choices include Chinese, Indonesian, Peruvian, African
and Spanish, but whatever the genre, "excellent food"
and "creative displays" are constants.

Bombay Cafe   – | – | – | M
● *12113 Santa Monica Blvd. (Bundy Dr.), West LA,*
  310-820-2070
  By appointment only
LA's top-rated Indian restaurant is also one of its most
accomplished catering operations, with one of the partners
devoted exclusively to that facet of the business; it offers
a wide assortment of dishes, Indian and otherwise, all
created with an emphatic sense of spicing and a high
level of creativity.

California Celebrations ⌷   ▽ 24 | 23 | 24 | E
● *4051 Glencoe Ave. (Washington Blvd.), Marina del Rey,*
  310-305-8849
  M-F 8am-5pm
■ A "consistently good" caterer with a large entertainment
and corporate clientele that can handle anything from
"office occasions" to large-scale sit-down dinners; the
emphasis is on California cuisine, with International touches
as desired; an in-house art director and staff that's easy to
deal with are two more reasons why it's deemed "top-notch."

Cook's Gathering, The ⌷   – | – | – | M
● *2190 Belmont Ave. (Stearns), Long Beach, 310-494-6615*
  By appointment only
Tim McGrath, former executive chef at Columbia Bar &
Grill and a popular cooking teacher, has become a sought-
after "rent-a-chef" and caterer who prepares California
fare for a steadily increasing list of appreciative clients;
his specialties are intimate gatherings and personalized
menus for weddings, teas and other social functions for
up to 200 people.

Cynthia's   – | – | – | M
● *8370 W. Third St. (1½ blocks east of La Cienega Blvd.),*
  LA, 213-658-7851
  M-F 11am-3pm/5pm-11pm/Sat 5pm-11pm/Sun 5pm-9pm
This small caterer with a cult following (especially among
nearby studios and production houses) is known for her
quirky Americana cuisine, including a world-class fried
chicken, as well as her ebullient personality; there's a
restaurant next to her catering shop for those who want
to taste before they choose.

DC3 Rest. & Catering $\boxed{-}$ $\boxed{-}$ $\boxed{-}$ $\boxed{M}$
- *2800 Donald Douglas Loop N. (Ocean Park Blvd.),
  Santa Monica, 310-399-2323
  M-F 9am-5pm*

This Nouvelle American restaurant with a sizable following
uses its large open space and private rooms for events
overlooking Santa Monica Airport, with parking and the
Museum of Flying next door; anything from rap parties to
high-school reunions get off to a flying start here.

Duck Duck Mousse $\boxed{26}$ $\boxed{24}$ $\boxed{24}$ $\boxed{E}$
- *Victorian Banquet Facility at Heritage Sq., 2640 Main St.
  (Ocean Park Blvd.), Santa Monica, 310-392-4956
  M-F 9am-5pm*

■ "Great name, great reputation", and by most accounts
most clients are "very impressed" with this cheerful,
innovative catering operation; located in the Victorian at
Heritage Square in Santa Monica, it offers 14,000 square
feet of party space on three elegant floors, with a patio
and easy parking; also available for off-site events.

El Cholo Catering $\boxed{23}$ $\boxed{21}$ $\boxed{23}$ $\boxed{M}$
- *1121 S. Western Ave. (bet. Pico & Olympic Blvds.), LA,
  213-737-7718
  M-F 9am-5pm*

■ Run by one of LA's most famous and venerable Mexican
restaurants, this service can handle all the details for a
"wonderful" at-home fiesta – all you do is "have a peach
margarita and enjoy"; with "tasty" food ("fantastic" fajitas,
"great green corn tamales"), "fun" presentations and
"efficient" service, it "shines" at "low cost": it's "*el mejor.*"

Elite Cuisine $\boxed{24}$ $\boxed{22}$ $\boxed{22}$ $\boxed{E}$
- *7119 Beverly Blvd. (½ block west of La Brea Ave.), LA,
  213-930-1303
  Sun-Th 11am-11pm/F 7am-4pm*

■ "Tasty for glatt kosher" is the reaction of many who've
sampled this Westsider's wide variety of "consistently
good", "festively presented" fare, including "delicious
noodle and potato kugel", "good baba ghanoush" and white
corn salad; the only reservation: some find it "expensive
for what you get."

GAI KLASS 🏠 $\boxed{28}$ $\boxed{27}$ $\boxed{27}$ $\boxed{E}$
- *10335 W. Jefferson Blvd. (bet. Indian Wood Rd. &
  Raintree St.), Culver City, 310-559-6777
  M-F 9am-5pm*

■ "A delight to work with", "always lovely", "brilliant" are
typical raves for SoCal's top-rated caterer, a prestigious firm
that has created events ranging from simple to elaborate
for some of LA's largest corporations and most affluent
individuals; costs can add up, but it's "worth every penny"
for "fabulous" food and "caring", "gracious" service;
"simply the best, dollar for dollar."

Judy's Cuisine & Catering ▽ 19 | 21 | 19 | E
- *129 N. La Brea Ave. (bet. Beverly Blvd. & First St.), LA,
  213-934-7667*
  M-Th 10:30am-6pm/F 8am-4pm/Sun 1pm-9pm

▣ Catering bar mitzvahs, weddings and other events for
groups up to 1,200, this kosher caterer with a penchant
for Chinese dishes earns plaudits for "the best matzo ball
soup in town" and other "very good" cooking that tastes
"homemade"; a few doubters say it's just "ok."

Kai's European Catering – | – | – | M
(fka West & West)
- *620 Moulton Ave. (N. Main St.), LA, 213-221-9204*
  M-F 9am-5pm

The catering division of Cafe Berlin at the Brewery Arts
complex on LA's eastern edge dishes up eclectic menus
(and popular bento box–style lunches) for city hall honchos,
Downtown lawyers and other corporate types, as well as
for the more than 350 artists and art-related businesses
that call the Brewery home.

Kensington Caterers ⊟ ▽ 26 | 25 | 26 | M
- *3300 S. Robertson Blvd. (National Blvd.), LA, 310-836-7272*
  M-F 9:30am-5:30pm

▣ This highly rated operation emphasizes California cuisine
with a light touch and can accommodate requests for nonfat
items, which no doubt pleases its many fashion industry
clients; "impeccable service and organization" are
hallmarks and some say it's especially adept at small parties.

KITCHEN FOR EXPLORING 27 | 26 | 26 | E
FOODS, THE
- *1434 W. Colorado Blvd. (Ave. 64), Pasadena, 818-793-7218*
  M-F 8am-6pm

▣ "Everything is done with style" say admirers of this
Pasadena gourmet takeout/gift shop that also offers full
catering services; "fabulous" food (California with ethnic
touches) and "classy presentation" explain why guests at
their events always "want their name"; "you can leave it
all in their hands" and be assured of a "first-class" affair.

L.A. Caterworks – | – | – | M
- *6506 Arizona Ave. (Sepulveda Blvd.), Westchester,
  310-337-0014*
  M-F 8:30am-6pm/weekends by appointment

This large party planning and special event firm specializes
in Californian cuisine but will customize any meal with
International as well as low-fat and vegetarian dishes; their
broad-based client list includes many entertainment industry
giants such as Columbia Pictures, MCA and HBO, as well
as such diverse enterprises as the LA Marathon, City of
Hope and Macy's/Bullock's.

L.A. Celebrations!   27 | 25 | 24 | E

- *1716 S. Robertson Blvd. (Airdrome), LA, 310-837-8900*
  M-F 10:30am-5pm

■ "Marvelous, creative presentations" and "delicious" eclectic food make for events "to cherish"; owner Andrea Bell can create magical events for two to 2,000, including kids' parties and Hollywood openings; fans say they're "the best with meats" and "make pretty pastries", but they're "expensive"; they even grow their own herbs and flowers.

La Cuisine ⌷   24 | 24 | 23 | E

- *2869 S. Robertson Blvd. (3 blocks north of National Blvd.),*
  LA, 310-837-8445
  M-F 9am-5pm

■ You'd expect a firm that's catered for the likes of Julia Child, Ronald Reagan and Prince Charles to be "la crème de la crème", and that's how many surveyors view this "top-of-the-line" operation; "less commercial and more traditional" than some, it specializes in regional country French and Italian cuisine; considering the quality, it's relatively "reasonably priced."

Market Catering and Event Planning   – | – | – | M

- *3502 Aviation Blvd., LA, 310-374-4425*
  M-F 9am-5pm/Sat 9am-3pm

"Well priced", "very accommodating" and "easy to work with" describes this South Bay caterer that does corporate events, premieres, food styling and more; their custom-designed menus feature a blend of Californian, Italian and Asian accents and the mix works: "guests love every dish."

More Than a Mouthful   ▽ 23 | 23 | 23 | M

- *743 S. Lucerne Blvd. (6 blocks east of Highland Ave.),*
  LA, 213-937-6345
  M-F 9am-5pm

■ This LA caterer has been around since 1978, offering eclectic fare of "excellent quality", "lovely service" and a "fantastic setting" thanks to their status as in-house caterer at the historic Ebell theater of Los Angeles (they also cater off-site events); fans say they "handle large parties well" and whip up the "best chicken and sea bass in the city."

Parties Plus   20 | 21 | 21 | E

- *963 E. 12th St. (bet. Central Ave. & Stanford St.), LA,*
  213-624-7101
  M-F 8:30am-5:30pm

◪ One of the busiest caterers in town, this firm says it can handle events for up to 10,000 (perfect if catering a Lakers game); they're "great for business parties", providing it all: from location finders to full decor and Californian-fusion cuisine, but doubters detect a "tendency to do it by rote."

Patina Catering　　　　　　　　　　- - - E
- *5955 Melrose Ave. (west of Cahuenga Blvd.), LA,*
  213-467-1628
  M-F 9:30am-5:30pm

The catering arm of Joachim Splichal's top-rated Patina,
Pinot and Cafe Pinot restaurants, offering his remarkable
contemporary French-Californian cooking in your home or
at the venue of your choice; it's an excellent way to impress
clients and relatives and feed yourself well in the process.

Restaurant Associates　　　　　　　- - - M
- *135 N. Grand Ave. (bet. First & Temple Sts.), Downtown LA,*
  213-972-7318
  M-F 9am-5pm

The new resident caterer at the Music Center also operates
NYC's well-respected SeaGrill and the food concession for
NYC's Lincoln Center and Carnegie Hall; with an exec chef
coming from the Ritz-Carlton Laguna Niguel and refurbished
banquet facilities, Music Center affairs may finally become a
draw for food lovers; P.S. they also cater off-site.

Rick Royce Premier BBQ　　　　25 19 23 M
- *10916 W. Pico Blvd. (west of Westwood Blvd.), West LA,*
  310-441-7427
  Every day 9am-9pm

■ For "gourmet BBQ", surveyors tout this popular rib and
chicken specialist with a new West LA restaurant where
you can sample the goods; run by an affable owner who
shows up at just about every charity event in town, its
events are known for being "good fun" with "lots of
personality", and the BBQ sauce is so tasty that one
fanatic dreams of "bathing in it and licking it off myself."

Rococo ⌂　　　　　　　　　　25 25 24 E
- *6734 Valjean Ave. (Vanowen St.), Van Nuys, 818-909-0990*
  M-F 9am-5pm/by appointment only

■ Serving the West Coast from San Diego to Santa Barbara,
this catering service has been around for 28 years and is
still acclaimed for being "consistently good", "wonderfully
creative" and a "great value"; with "interestingly prepared"
Eclectic fare and "always professional" service, they're
especially "good for large groups."

Soiree Catering/K.P. & Co.　　　　- - - M
- *4105 E. Broadway (Belmont), Long Beach, 310-987-2199*
  M-F 8am-5pm
- *3037 S. Bristol St. (Segerstrom St.), Santa Ana, 714-754-4405*
  M-F 8am-4pm

■ A well-regarded caterer with locations in Long Beach
and Orange County offering everything from the most
elegant dishes to ribs by their Ranch Hands BBQ division;
adept at a variety of International cuisines, they're
considered "creative geniuses" by admirers who also
appreciate the fair tab.

Someone's In The Kitchen   25 25 25 E
• *5973 Reseda Blvd. (Oxnard St.), Tarzana, 818-343-5151*
  M-F 9am-5pm and by appointment
◪ "Joann Roth really takes care of her clients" say admirers
of this well-known San Fernando Valley firm, whose owner is
a constant presence at charity events; expect "beautiful
displays" and a staff that's "attentive to needs"; a few critics
find the food "bland", but most call it "major league all the
way"; call ahead for an extensive menu of take-out meals
and dishes.

Somerset Caterers Inc.   25 24 24 E
• *8982 National Blvd. (Robertson Blvd.), LA, 310-204-4000*
  M-F 8:30am-5pm
■ Caterer for the LA County Museum of Art, this tony
operation is "always outstanding and willing to match
your ideas"; they "cook anything", from classic Americana
to ethnic fare, and most find it all "excellent, especially for
large parties"; costs can add up, but it's one of "the best."

Wonderful Parties, Wonderful   ▽ 27 26 27 E
Foods ⊟
• *10848 Washington Blvd., Culver City, 213-933-6211*
  By appointment only
■ "Don Ernstein is a magician", and though he just released
a lavishly illustrated book of recipes that "gives all his
secrets away", you still need his touch if you want your
event to have "flair" and "sophistication"; offering "beautiful
presentations" of "very creative" Eclectic fare, he "knows
what he's doing" and "could teach Martha Stewart" a
trick or two.

Caviar & Smoked Fish

Caviar and smoked fish aren't regarded as necessities in Los Angeles – at least not in the way that cappuccino and low-fat muffins are de rigueur for living well hereabouts. But even so, both are readily available and perfectly prepared in our many excellent delis and fine food and wine shops, thanks in part to the influence of LA's constantly growing Russian and Persian populations. Now there are circles in which caviar is finally being understood as a way of life – what would a studio party be without them? LA's smoked fish supply has also been given a boost thanks to the arrival of one of New York's most famous smoked fish purveyors, the remarkable Barney Greengrass, situated high atop Barneys New York, of all places – now you can buy a suit with a side.

Top Quality
29 Aristoff Caviar
27 Homarus Lox
26 Caviarteria
    Bristol Farms
25 Wally's

Top Variety
24 Aristoff Caviar
    Ron's Market
    Caviarteria
    Homarus Lox
23 Bristol Farms

Top Service
25 Gelson's Markets
24 Wally's
    Bristol Farms
    Aristoff Caviar
23 Caviarteria

Best Buys
    Homarus Lox
    Surfas Inc.
    Ron's Market
    Bristol Farms
    Wally's

Q	V	S	C
29	24	24	VE

ARISTOFF CAVIAR & FINE FOODS, INC. 🚲 ▤
(fka Caviar & Fine Foods, Inc.)
- *321 N. Robertson Blvd. (1 block north of Beverly Blvd.), W. Hollywood, 310-271-0576*
  M-F 9:30am-5pm/Sat 10am-noon
- *Mail order: 800-332-7478*

■ Top-rated for caviar, this small West Hollywood shop ennobled its name after moving from its original Melrose Place locale; it has "wonderful caviar" that's "competitively priced" and an "extremely helpful staff" who "know" their wares; along with a tasting room, there's also a "chic little dining room" that's "like a Parisian hideaway" – the place to go to "really impress."

Barney Greengrass �🖾   – | – | – | E
- *Barneys New York, 9570 Wilshire Blvd. (bet. Camden & Peck Drs.), Beverly Hills, 310-777-5877*
  M-F 7:30am-7pm/Th 7:30am-8pm/Sat 9am-7pm/
  Sun 9am-6pm
- *Mail order: 212-724-4707*

This branch of one of NY's smoked-fish icons sits atop Barneys New York next to the Armani men's boutique, and has what may be LA's best selection of smoked finery and caviar, including beluga, osetra and sevruga from Russia and China plus American sturgeon and salmon roe; the scrambled eggs with Nova and sturgeon (best on the patio with a view of Beverly Hills) is known to bring tears to the eyes of agents from nearby William Morris, contradicting the belief that ten percenters can't cry.

Bel-Air Wine Merchant 🚲   25 | 22 | 21 | E
- *10421 Santa Monica Blvd. (west of Beverly Glen Blvd.), West LA, 310-474-9518*
  M-Sat 10:30am-7pm

◪ A Century City wine shop with a high-end name that nevertheless provides "great deals on Russian caviar" and "excellent buys" on the "highest-quality" smoked salmon; as may be inevitable with caviar merchants, some say you're "never sure you get what you ordered", but loyalists (a majority) declare "I trust them."

Bristol Farms   26 | 23 | 24 | E
- *See listing in Supermarkets section.*

■ This "reliable" chain of top-rated supermarkets brings a taste of "Brooklyn to Palos Verdes" (and South Pasadena and Manhattan Beach as well); shoppers "can't get enough of those baby chubs", "wonderful" smoked whitefish, "great lox" and "not-too-salty Atlantic smoked salmon" that "melts in your mouth"; everything is beautifully displayed with "elegance – like a museum"; however, just don't expect bargains.

Caviarteria of California Inc. 🚲🖾   26 | 24 | 23 | VE
- *158 S. Beverly Dr. (Wilshire Blvd.), Beverly Hills, 310-285-9773, 800-287-9773 (CA only)*
  M-F 9am-6pm/Sat 10am-6pm

■ A branch of yet another NY emporium, this Beverly Hills shop is a major destination for those seeking a serious fix of beluga, sevruga or ossetra, as well as bargain-priced kamchatka ("bottom of the barrel beluga" with slightly broken grains) and one of the best selections around of domestic roe; the "not-too-salty", "always-tasty smoked fish" offerings include a memorable whitefish dip; "when I win the lottery, I'll buy the place."

Caviar & Smoked Fish

Gelson's Markets
24 22 25 E
• *See listing in Supermarkets section.*
▣ There's "good-quality smoked fish" at the deli counters of this upscale chain; though comments on the selection range from "good" to "hardly any variety", it offers "terrific imported Nova", the "best smoked albacore anywhere" and, as one surveyor puts it, "the best caviar my mother-in-law, the Caviar Expert, ever had" (it's from Aristoff); most say "for a supermarket, it's great" – it may cost "a few cents more, but worth it."

Homarus Lox &
27 24 23 M
(fka Dr. Lox)
• *9340 W. Pico Blvd. (1 block east of Beverly Dr.), LA, 310-273-3004*
  M-F 10am-6pm/Sat 8am-6pm/Sun 8am-4pm
■ "Melt-in-your-mouth lox" and "velvet Nova" at "the best prices" draw mavens from all over Los Angeles to the kosher streets of Beverlywood where this tiny mini-mall storefront reigns; it serves the "greatest smoked fish", including "incredible peppered salmon" and "baked salmon to die for", providing a "constant solution to weekend hors d'oeuvres."

Ron's Market &
21 24 16 I
• *5270 Sunset Blvd. (Hobart), Hollywood, 213-465-1164*
  Every day 8am-10pm
▣ This authentically ethnic Eastside market with foods from around the globe "caters to Middle Easterners" and also reminds Eastern European emigrés of home thanks to "inexpensive Russian caviar" and "lots of interesting smoked fish" (and also, alas, "long waits for service"); it's "always a treat to see the crowd", though some shoppers are concerned about the "scary neighborhood."

Surfas Inc. &
25 21 22 M
(aka Van Rex)
• *8825 National Blvd. (bet. Venice & Washington Blvds.), Culver City, 310-559-4770*
  M-F 8am-5:30pm/Sat 9am-5pm
▣ Known for "generally low prices" on "good-quality" caviar and smoked salmon, this restaurant supply house also stocks specialty foods, including the Van Rex line, which used to be available at their now defunct warehouse on Washington; those who knew it pre-move applaud its offerings of "hard-to-get items" with "some great buys", while those who've dropped by the new location grumble that "now they look like a dump" and there's "hardly anything in stock"; perhaps it's still settling in.

Caviar & Smoked Fish

Wally's &⑬☞

25 | 23 | 24 | E

- *2107 Westwood Blvd. (½ block north of Olympic Blvd.), West LA, 310-475-0606*
  M-Sat 9am-8pm/Sun 10am-6pm
- *Mail order: 800-892-5597*

■ Though first and foremost a wine shop, the cheese and caviar section at this Westwood standby provides "excellent quality", "great variety" and "knowledgeable, personal attention", plus "reasonable prices on caviar"; "caviar is caviar, but Wally's is special."

Wine Merchant of Beverly Hills &⑬☞

25 | 22 | 22 | E

- *9701 Santa Monica Blvd. (Roxbury Dr.), Beverly Hills, 310-278-7322*
  M-F 9:30am-6pm/Sat & Sun 10am-6pm

■ "Great stuff" and "good advice" are a winning formula at this "very expensive" wine and specialty shop where the beluga, sevruga and ossetra are "fit for a Russian"; you'll pay "Beverly Hills prices" but "you get what you pay for."

Cheese

It wasn't so long ago that the big decision Los Angelenos faced when buying cheese was choosing between two colors: yellow and white. But in the past 15 years or so, as the culinary sophistication of Southern California has grown, so has our appreciation of fine cheeses, both at the supermarket level (see Supermarkets section) – where a remarkable assortment of both local and imported cheeses can be found these days – and at the specialty store level (see below), where just about any cheese in the known world can be purchased.

It should be noted that for many of us in health-obsessed Southern California, cheese is a special occasion item, despite those posters around town praising the virtues of California cheese. California may be second only to Wisconsin as a U.S. cheese producer, but we still indulge with caution – it can make that bikini look just awful on you.

Top Quality
29 Cheese Store Bev. Hills
27 Say Cheese
    Bristol Farms
25 Wally's
    Gelson's Markets

Top Service
27 Cheese Store Bev. Hills
25 Say Cheese
    Bristol Farms
23 Gelson's Markets
    Wally's

Top Variety
29 Cheese Store Bev. Hills
26 Bristol Farms
24 Say Cheese
    Trader Joe's
23 Gelson's Markets

Best Buys
    Trader Joe's
    Cheese Store Bev. Hills
    Bristol Farms
    Say Cheese
    Gelson's Markets

Q	V	S	C
27	26	25	E

BRISTOL FARMS
• *See listing in Supermarkets section.*
■ Probably the "best selection" of fromage found in any supermarket in town is in this three-store chain's "solid cheese departments" where "you can taste before you buy"; there's "something for every taste and occasion" including a wide assortment of small-producer products and "unsurpassed goat cheese varieties" – "you want it, they got it", but "you pay for it."

CHEESE STORE BEV. HILLS 🚲 ✉ 29 29 27 E
(aka La Fromagerie)
- *419 N. Beverly Dr. (south of Little Santa Monica Blvd.),
  Beverly Hills, 310-278-2855
  M-Sat 9:30am-6pm*
- *Mail order: 800-547-1515*

■ SoCal's top-rated cheese store, this "real European" across from Nate 'n Al's is a "landmark" for fromagoholics, with a "smell that permeates Beverly Drive"; it's a "sensual treat just to walk in the door" of this "cheese nirvana" that provides "superb quality", "incredible variety" (including "unusual" items) and "patient", "expert help"; it's "best if you have bucks", but admirers say that no one should miss this taste of "France in LA"; P.S. "Mickey would love it."

Gelson's Markets   25 23 23 E
- *See listing in Supermarkets section.*

■ For admirers, the cheese at this high-end chain is "almost as good as Bristol Farms", with a "better selection and variety than your average market"; given the many locations, surveyors say it's "convenient" as well as "dependable", and the various sections are "always well stocked, clean and very organized."

Pavilions   20 19 17 M
- *See listing in Supermarkets section.*

◪ "Limited" but "not bad for a supermarket", the cheeses at this upwardly mobile child of Vons span "basic Brie", "buffalo mozzarella" and "pot cheese for Polish pierogies", but otherwise it's "not gourmet" and could use "a better selection of imports", and some find it "overpriced for a supermarket"; all in all, the consensus among surveyors is "pleasant but not inspired."

SAY CHEESE 🚲   27 24 25 E
- *2800 Hyperion Ave. (bet. Rowena St. & Griffith Park
  Blvd.), Silver Lake, 213-665-0545
  Every day 8am-6:30pm*

■ Everything from "classics to esoterics" is provided at this "cheese lover's heaven" in Silver Lake, just north of Downtown; a longtime "favorite" that remains "one of LA's best fromageries", it offers "Roquefort better than Paris", "terrific service" and "excellent value for the dollar"; even if not in the market for cheese, you can "go here to speak French."

Trader Joe's   24 | 24 | 21 | I
• *See listing in Supermarkets section.*
■ Many of the cheeses sold by this chain are bought in bulk from obscure foreign and domestic producers, which makes for "some great" finds and "best buys", especially when it comes to "popular" types like Brie, cheddar, Gruyere and Jarlsberg; there are "good low-fat choices" too, but for the most pleasure "throw away your diet" at this culinary trading post for yuppies on a budget.

Wally's ⬥🖃   25 | 21 | 23 | E
• *2107 Westwood Blvd. (½ block north of Olympic Blvd.),*
  West LA, 310-475-0606
  M-Sat 9am-8pm/Sun 10am-6pm
• *Mail order: 800-892-5597*
■ A Westwood wine shop that also has "terrific gourmet choices" including an "interesting variety" of "top-quality cheeses" and a "friendly staff" to explain it all and help match selections "with wine"; look for "best buys on Brie" and La Brea Bakery bread to serve with the cheese at this "well-rounded, one-stop shop where the goal is pleasing the customer."

Coffee & Tea

Like a computer virus, coffee mania has infected Southern California. It spread here from Seattle and San Francisco, and has become such an obsession we keep expecting to hear of 12-step programs for caffeine addicts in Coffee Drinkers Anonymous.

More than just a beverage, coffee has turned into a way of life, especially on the Westside of town, buzzing with everything from small bohemian coffeehouses where people wearing berets write poetry to terminally trendy coffee chains where tout le monde goes for a daily iced mocha hit (with nonfat milk, of course).

For do-it-yourselfers who like to make their coffee at home, there are a plethora of good options as well, with beans and equipment sold in shops dedicated to the concept that life isn't worth living without a good cup of java, morning, noon and night.

While the number of coffeehouses surpasses the number of tea shops in Los Angeles, places like the Chado Tea Room and Ten Ren Tea Co. offer encyclopedic varieties of tea. Tea, iced and hot, is becoming more popular as new tea shops open throughout the area, making it clear that tea is no longer just for the Brits.

Top Quality
- 28 Graffeo Coffee
- 27 Piacere Espresso Bar
  Ten Ren Tea Co.
  Chado
- 26 Diedrich Coffee (O.C.)

Top Variety
- 29 Chado
- 27 Ten Ren Tea Co.
- 25 Diedrich Coffee (O.C.)
- 24 Starbucks
  Caffe Latte

Top Service
- 26 Graffeo Coffee
- 25 Piacere Espresso Bar
- 24 Ten Ren Tea Co.
  City Roasters
- 23 Chado

Best Buys
- Piacere Espresso Bar
- Ten Ren Tea Co.
- Chado
- Diedrich Coffee (O.C.)
- City Bean Coffee

Q	V	S	C
25	23	22	M

Arrosto Coffee Co. ▤
- *11652 San Vicente Blvd. (Darlington Ave.), Brentwood, 310-207-4802*
  M-Sat 7:30am-10pm/Sun 9am-10pm
- *11070 Santa Monica Blvd. (Sepulveda Blvd.), West LA, 310-473-2774*
  M-Sat 7:30am-10pm/Sun 9am-10pm
- *264 S. Beverly Dr. (bet. Olympic & Wilshire Blvds.), Beverly Hills, 310-274-3176*
  M-Sat 7:30am-10pm/Sun 9am-10pm

Arrosto Coffee Co. (Cont.)
- *2002 Wilshire Blvd. (20th St.), Santa Monica, 310-315-9878*
  M-F 7:30am-10pm/Sat 8:30am-10pm/Sun 9:30-10pm

■ "A hit already", these functional cappuccino/espresso shops are called "a delicious alternative to overcrowded Starbucks"; they "aren't your typical trendy coffeehouses", but they offer "good coffee" ("roasted in small batches"), and "make a mean espresso" plus "great iced mochas" and latte; best of all, there's "no waiting" – "give it a chance."

Bristol Farms   – – – M
- *See listing in Supermarkets section.*

Perhaps the finest supermarket selection of coffees and teas in SoCal is found at this upscale minichain, including a wide assortment of house blends (the Christmas Blend is especially popular); pots of coffee and tea are always waiting for those who want a taste before buying or just a sip as they shop.

Caffe Latte ⬛   26 24 21 M
- *6254 Wilshire Blvd. (Crescent Heights), LA, 213-936-5213*
  M-F 7am-9pm/Sat & Sun 8am-3:30pm

■ It "smells great" at this American cafe on Wilshire where the air is perfumed with the aromas of Kenyan, Tanzanian and Jamaican Blue Mountain beans that are "fresh roasted daily" for "take home" or a cup of "wonderful, strong coffee" at a "cozy" table while "people-watching"; a "nice choice of quality teas" is a plus, but "indifferent service" draws a few knocks.

CHADO TEA ROOM ⬛   27 29 23 M
- *8422½ W. Third St. (2 blocks east of La Cienega Blvd.), LA, 213-655-2056*
  Sun-Th 11am-6pm/F & Sat 11am-9pm

■ This highly rated, "superhip", "magical" tearoom offers a variety of 150 teas and all sorts of paraphernalia – English tea pots, tea bricks, tea infusers and the like; it's a "tea drinker's heaven" where they "let you smell the teas" to help you select; the only downside is the uninspired Mediterranean cafe menu.

City Bean Coffee ⬛   25 23 23 M
- *10911 Lindbrook Dr. (Westwood Blvd.), Westwood, 310-208-0108*
  M-F 6am-8pm/Sat 7am-8pm/Sun 7am-4pm
- *Mail order: 310-824-1340*

◨ An always-busy Westwood coffee bar with some two dozen coffees; "quality is superb" and the blends ("try the Brazilian Natural Dry") are filled with "earthy, complicated aromas and tastes"; predictably, partisans say it's "as good as Starbucks" and serves the "best blended iced mochas in town" – the two main points of comparison when it comes to coffee in LA; a few doubters say "ok, not spectacular."

City Roasters Coffee Company ⊘ | 25 | 23 | 24 | M |
- *8363 Beverly Blvd. (Kings Rd.), W. Hollywood,
213-655-4834
M-Sat 7am-6pm/Sun 8am-5pm*

■ Yes, they "roast their coffee on the premises" at this West
Hollywood beanery/coffee bar next door to the King's Road
Cafe (arguably the best "bohemian" espresso/cappuccino
joint in town); for fans it's "the only place to buy beans" and
is also a hot spot for a "good cup of joe" – "worth a detour."

Cleo & Cucci | 25 | 23 | 23 | M |
- *17 E. Colorado Blvd. (bet Fair Oaks & Raymond Aves.),
Pasadena, 818-440-9282
M-F 8am-11:30pm/Sat 8am-1:30am/Sun 8am-midnight*
- *3213 Glendale Galleria (bet. Colorado & Broadway),
Glendale, 818-552-3592
M-F 9am-9pm/Sat 9am-7pm/Sun 9am-6pm*
- *Sherman Oaks Fashion Sq., 14006 Riverside Dr.
(Woodman Ave.), Sherman Oaks, 818-906-8784
M-F 9am-9pm/Sat 9am-7pm/Sun 10am-6pm*

■ A busy trio of coffeehouses (the Old Town Pasadena
branch is next door to the burgeoning Mi Piace/Pasadena
Baking Company combine) that provides "nice ambiance,
quality and selection" (36 coffee varieties, flavored and
unflavored, plus "bulk teas"); "great" iced mocha and
"wonderful" espresso help make them "ideal places for a
good book or people-watching."

Coffee Baron, The | 23 | 22 | 22 | M |
- *11733 Barrington Ct. (Sunset Blvd.), Brentwood,
310-476-4868
M-Sat 10am-6pm*

■ There are 40 varieties of beans and blends at this smart
Brentwood location that one connoisseur calls "the only
place that uses Colombian beans for espresso roast";
"homely, friendly service" and "reasonable prices" keep
it a "neighborhood" favorite.

Coffee Bean & Tea Leaf 🖃 | 24 | 23 | 22 | M |
- *11698 San Vicente Blvd. (Barrington Ave.), Brentwood,
310-442-1019*
- *445 N. Beverly Dr. (Little Santa Monica Blvd.), Beverly Hills,
310-278-1865*
- *Villa Marina Marketplace, 13420 Maxella (Glencoe),
Marina del Rey, 310-823-0858*
- *1426 Montana Ave. (14th St.), Santa Monica, 310-453-2093*
- *200 Santa Monica Blvd. (2nd St.), Santa Monica,
310-260-0044*
- *Malibu Country Mart, 3835 Crosscreek, Malibu,
310-456-5771*
- *1088 Weyburn Ave. (east of Westwood Blvd.), Westwood,
310-208-8018*
- *The Plaza at West Covina, 112 Fashion Plaza Dr. (west of
Covina Pkwy.), West Covina, 818-814-2240*

Coffee Bean & Tea Leaf (Cont.)
- *The Marketplace, 6471 E. PCH (Westminster), Long Beach, 310-598-2198*
- *135 N. Larchmont (1st St.), LA, 213-469-4984*
- *Sherman Oaks Fashion Sq., 14006 Riverside Dr. (Woodman Ave.), Sherman Oaks, 818-906-0504*
- *The Commons, 146 S. Lake St. (Green St.), Pasadena, 818-440-9744*
- *1001 Gayley Ave. (Weyburn Ave.), Westwood, 310-208-1991*
- *Manhattan Village Shopping Mall, 3008 Sepulveda Blvd. (Rosecrans Ave.), Manhattan Beach, 310-546-3359*
- *Sunset Plaza, 8591 Sunset Blvd., W. Hollywood, 310-659-1890*
- *Laurel Promenade, 12050 Ventura Blvd. (Laurel Canyon Blvd.), Studio City, 818-506-4620*
- *Paseo Nuevo Shopping Mall, 811 State St. (De la Guerra), Santa Barbara, 805-966-2442*
- *Buenaventura Mall, 363 S. Mills Rd. (Lynn Rd.), Ventura, 805-642-7217*
- *Main Pl., 2800 N. Main St. (Chapman Ave.), Santa Ana, 714-542-6990*
- *The Oaks Mall, 278 W. Hillcrest Dr. (Lynn Rd. exit, #101 Frwy.), Thousand Oaks, 805-497-1211*
- *4580 Calle Alto, Camarillo, 805-484-7924*
- *South Coast Plaza, 3333 Bristol (#405 Frwy.), Costa Mesa, 714-549-1766*
  All locations: M-F 6:30am-9pm/Sat & Sun 7am-9pm
- *Mail order: 800-832-5323*

■ For fans, this growing SoCal chain with a cult following is the biggest competition for the Starbucks behemoth; expect lines of yuppies and Xers who praise its "good selection" of beans and teas and worship the "awesome" iced blended mocha (and the somewhat raffish "vanilla" variation) – "give me an iced blended and I can conquer the world."

Coffee Roaster, The   23 | 22 | 21 | M |
- *13567 Ventura Blvd. (1 block east of Woodman Ave.), Sherman Oaks, 818-905-9719*
  M-Sat 7:30am-6pm

☑ "Neighborhood friendly" and "family owned", this Casual Valley coffee spot makes some feel they're in "the owners' own kitchen"; it has "classical music", "flowers on the table" and flavors that may be "too intense for the java novice"; there's good "Harley Davidson–watching, too"; a few say both the coffee and service are "inconsistent."

Diedrich Coffee ▤   26 | 25 | 22 | M |
- *474 E. 17th St. (Irvine Ave.), Costa Mesa, 714-646-0323*
- *Back Bay Court Ctr., 3601 Jamboree Rd. (Bristol), Newport Beach, 714-833-9143*
- *Tustin Plaza Ctr., 13681 Newport Ave. (Main St.), Tustin, 714-832-7030*

Diedrich Coffee (Cont.)
- *27775 Santa Margarita Pkwy. (Los Alisos & Marguerite), Mission Viejo, 714-472-3733*
- *32371 St. of the Golden Lantern (Camino del Avion), Laguna Niguel, 714-443-0044*
- *22621 Lake Forest Dr. (Muirlands), Lake Forest, 714-837-4555*
- *Crossroads Shopping Ctr., 3972 Barranca Pkwy. (Culver), Irvine, 714-559-9125*
  All locations: every day 6am-11pm
- *Mail order: 800-854-5282*

■ Four generations of Diedrichs have been in the coffee business, even owning their own coffee plantation; these days their seven "culinary drive-ups" with "great ambiance" are located all over Orange County, providing "roaster-fresh" "beans from around the world" and "favorite blends" that are "always smooth."

Euro Coffee   23 | 23 | 22 | M
- *Citicorp Plaza, 735 S. Figueroa St. (7th St.), Downtown LA, 213-614-1811*
  M-F 7:30am-7pm/Sat 9:30am-6pm
- *7200 Melrose Ave. (Formosa Ave.), LA, 213-933-7200*
  M-F 7am-7pm/Sat 9am-7pm/Sun 11am-7pm
- *700 S. Fair Oaks Ave. (Frwy. #110), S. Pasadena, 818-799-8669*
  M-Th 7am-7pm/F & Sat 8am-8pm/Sun 8am-5pm
- *8941 Santa Monica Blvd. (San Vicente & Robertson Blvds.), W. Hollywood, 310-246-0828*
  Sun-Th 8am-midnight/F & Sat 8am-2am

◪ A very serious coffee quartet offering 31 varieties; loyal followers call it a "good value" for "consistent" quality and, despite the name, the "best straight American coffee around", but service receives mixed reactions ranging from "they never forget an order" to "service? there is none."

Graffeo Coffee Roasting Co. ▤   28 | 20 | 26 | E
- *315 N. Beverly Dr. (north of Dayton Way), Beverly Hills, 310-273-0817*
- *1260 Bison Ave. (McArthur Blvd.), Newport Beach, 714-644-0393*
  M-Sat 9am-5:30pm
- *Mail order: 800-3667-9499*

■ SoCal branches of a San Francisco landmark, these roasteries fill the air with aromas of its "basic", "hard-core" varieties: "light, dark or half and half – that's it folks!", but as ratings show, that's plenty; there's no brewed coffee served in these true coffee lover's settings, just beans by the pound ready to rush home and grind; "the best for unadulterated coffee."

Il Fornaio 24 | 21 | 21 | M
- *See listing in Baked Goods section.*

■ Though best known for its superb breads, this bakery/restaurant chain also offers "good coffee – of course, it's Italian!"; there's "not a large variety", but the brews are "European-style", meaning "strong", "robust", "with guts" – even the decaf will get you "hyper"; the few gripes it gets are mostly aimed at "overworked, undertrained" staff.

Il Sogno ✍ – | – | – | M
- *863 Swarthmore Ave. (½ block east of Sunset Blvd.), Pacific Palisades, 310-454-6522*
  M-Sat 7am-9:30pm/Sun noon-6pm

A little-known, well-hidden coffeehouse on a side street in the Palisades, where the "wonderful" owners and "smiling, friendly staff" offer 16 varieties to take home or enjoy "under the trees" on the patio; with a "great setting", "good people" and "rich, strong, fresh" coffee, this hideaway is a "favorite" of those who've discovered it.

Kafeneo Coffee House & Roastery ▽ 26 | 23 | 22 | M
- *25364 Crenshaw Blvd. (bet. PCH & Airport Dr.), Torrance, 310-539-1333*
  M-Th 6am-10pm/F 7am-11pm/Sat 9am-11pm/ Sun 9am-10pm

■ Busy South Bay coffee outlet with an exotic international selection of beans (Guatemalan, Ethiopian, Indonesian and more) as well as special 'after-dinner' roasts; the good variety, "helpful staff" and "homey environment in whichf to sit, sip and chat" add up to a "nice joint."

Marina Coffee Roasters 23 | 22 | 17 | M
- *Marina Beach Shopping Ctr., 550 Washington Blvd. (bet. Palawan Way & Via Marina), Marina del Rey, 310-305-7147*
  M-F 5am-9pm/Sat & Sun 6am-9pm

■ "Go for the atmosphere" at this "too-hip"-for-some Marina "bikers hangout" that's "like a bar scene in the early AM"; with five varieties of house-roasted coffee, "terrific latte", a body-builders' menu and breakfast served all day, it's a "great package."

Pasqua Coffee Bars – | – | – | M
- *Civic Center Mall, 217 N. Hill St. (First St. & Grand Ave.), Downtown LA, 213-625-2205*
- *Central Plaza, 3458½ Wilshire Blvd. (Normandie), LA, 213-382-2142*
- *California Plaza, 300 S. Grand Ave. (3rd St.), Downtown LA, 213-687-2155*
- *Pacific Financial Bldg., 800 W. Sixth St. (Flower St.), Downtown LA, 213-489-4263*
- *Roosevelt Bldg., 733 W. Seventh St. (Flower St.), Downtown LA, 213-688-2860*

Pasqua Coffee Bars (Cont.)
- *Security Pacific Bldg., 333 S. Hope St. (3rd St.), Downtown LA, 213-621-4191*
- *Wells Fargo Plaza, 330 S. Hope St. (3rd St.), Downtown LA, 213-620-1945*
- *Wells Fargo Plaza, 400 S. Hope St. (4th St.), Downtown LA, 213-489-4121*
- *Gas Company Tower, 555 W. Fifth St. (bet. Grand & Olive Sts.), Downtown LA, 213-892-0306*
- *Twin Towers, 2049 Century Park E. (Olympic Blvd.), Century City, 310-286-3023*
- *Watt Plaza, 1875 Century Park E. (Constellation), Century City, 310-553-8226*
- *Sun America Bldg., 1999 Ave. of the Stars (Constellation), Century City, 310-557-0785*
  All locations: M-F 6am-5pm

This business district–intensive chain of joe-to-go shops (with branches in San Francisco and New York) keeps the wheels of industry turning with espresso, macchiato, cappuccino, latte and mocha, along with a variety of flavored iced coffee drinks; three varieties of house beans are available by the bag.

Piacere Espresso Bar 27 | 21 | 25 | I |
- *1101 Air Way (north of #134 Frwy.), Glendale, 818-240-7469 M-F 7:30am-5pm*
- *1948 Hillhurst Ave. (bet. Los Feliz Blvd. & Franklin Ave.), Los Feliz, 213-660-0670 T-Sun 7:30am-10pm*

■ An Eastside pair of coffee shops that are among the highest-rated in SoCal thanks to the "best dark roast beans", "true espresso" and "great cappuccinos – never bitter"; carry-home favorites include "good buys on bulk beans" that are "roasted on-premises" and addictive "chocolate-covered coffee beans" – "this place is tops."

Prebica Coffee & Cafe 23 | 23 | 22 | M |
(fka Coffee Emporium)
- *Villa Marina Marketplace, 4325 Glencoe Ave. (Maxella), Marina del Rey, 310-823-4446 Sun-Th 6:30am-10pm/F & Sat 6:30am-11pm*
- *Farmer's Market at the Atrium Court, 401 Newport Center Dr. (Santa Cruz Ave.), Newport Beach, 714-640-6027 ⊟ M-Sat 7:30am-9pm/Sun 7:30am-8pm*

◪ With locations in the Marina and Newport, this aggressive, high-profile operation is definitely going for the gusto, pleasing many who live on and by the water with its "great" "special blends" and "good loose-leaf iced tea"; critics, however, grumble about questionable service and "not memorable" cups of java.

Coffee & Tea

Renaissance Cafe ▽ 26 | 25 | 23 | M
- *234 Forest Ave. (PCH), Laguna Beach, 714-497-5282*
  M-Th 8am-11pm/F & Sat 9am-12:30am/Sun 7:30pm-10:30pm
- *Brea Marketplace, 955 E. Birch St., Brea, 714-256-2233*
  M-W 8am-11pm/Th 8:30am-11:30am/
  F & Sat 8:30am-midnight/Sun 7:30am-10:30pm
- *24701 Del Prado (Golden Lantern), Dana Point,*
  714-661-6003
  M-Th 8am-11pm/F & Sat 8am-11:30pm/Sun 7:30am-10:30pm
- *2959 El Camino Real (Jamboree Rd.), Tustin, 714-832-2233*
  M-Th 6am-11pm/F & Sat 7am-midnight/Sun 7am-11pm

■ A major competitor for the title of best coffee in Orange County, this operation is "spreading caffeine addiction" thoughout the area with "gorgeous mugs" of "consistently good" brews from a daily-changing list of several dozen blends, plus loose and bagged beans and teas to take home; N.B. all locations have nightly live music.

Rosetree Cottage – | – | – | M
- *824 E. California Blvd. (½ block west of Lake Ave.),*
  Pasadena, 818-793-3337

Actually three connected cottages, this small but choice English tearoom sells over 100 types of tea, many imported, including varieties from Fortnum & Mason, Whittard and Jackson of Picadilly, plus accessories; a full cream tea is offered in the afternoons.

Starbucks 24 | 24 | 22 | M
- *428 N. Beverly Dr. (south of Little Santa Monica Blvd.),*
  Beverly Hills, 310-371-1692
- *Rancho Marketplace, 1190 Alameda Ave. (Main St.),*
  Burbank, 818-557-6604
- *300 N. San Fernando (Palm), Burbank, 818-567-0630*
- *Encino Oaks Shopping Ctr., 17308 Ventura Blvd., Encino,*
  818-986-9621
- *Encino Marketplace, 16461 Ventura Blvd., Encino,*
  818-906-3951
- *114 N. Brand Blvd. (bet. Broadway & Wilson), Glendale,*
  818-547-3694
- *5251 E. Second St., (Covina), Long Beach, 310-987-5043*
- *10911 Pico Blvd. (west of Westwood Blvd.), West LA,*
  310-470-8863
- *Beverly Connection, 100 N. La Cienega Blvd., LA,*
  310-289-7815
- *1161 Westwood Blvd., Westwood, 310-208-6505*
- *11707 San Vicente Blvd. (Barrington Ave.), Brentwood,*
  310-207-4202
- *3900 Cross Creek Rd. (east of PCH), Malibu, 310-317-4515*
- *233 Manhattan Beach Blvd. (Highland), Manhattan Beach,*
  310-545-2709
- *4264 Lincoln Blvd., Marina del Rey, 310-578-6832*
- *15300 Sunset Blvd., Pacific Palisades, 310-573-0177*
- *575 S. Lake Ave. (California), Pasadena, 818-795-0918*

Starbucks (Cont.)
- *3699 E. Foothill Blvd., Pasadena, 818-351-9994*
- *103 W. Colorado Blvd., Pasadena, 818-577-4622*
- *1749 S. Elena (Ave. J), Redondo Beach, 310-540-9080*
- *46 Peninsula Ctr. (bet. Hawthorne Blvd. & Silver Spur), Rolling Hills Estates, 310-544-3942*
- *206 N. Larchmont (south of Beverly Blvd.), LA, 213-469-1081*
- *7624 Melrose Ave. (Stanley Ave.), LA, 213-652-9690*
- *Brentwood Village, 131 Barrington Ave. (1 block south of Sunset Blvd.), Brentwood, 310-472-7119*
- *Torrance Crossroads Shopping Ctr., 24427 Crenshaw Blvd. (Lomita Blvd.), Torrance, 310-530-2034*
- *2265 Huntington Dr. (San Marino Ave.), San Marino, 818-683-0807*
- *2671 Main St. (1 block south of Ocean Park Blvd.), Santa Monica, 310-392-3559*
- *701 Montana Ave. (7th St.), Santa Monica, 310-394-8020*
- *1334 Third St. Promenade, Santa Monica, 310-260-9947*
- *2525 Wilshire Blvd. (26th St.), Santa Monica, 310-264-0669*
- *308 Wilshire Blvd., Santa Monica, 310-451-9626*
- *14622 Ventura Blvd. (1 block west of Van Nuys Blvd.), Sherman Oaks, 818-501-6535*
- *12170 Ventura Blvd. (1 block west of Laurel Canyon Blvd.), Studio City, 818-762-9368*
- *18668 Ventura Blvd. (Reseda Blvd.), Tarzana, 818-345-0060*
- *6 Del Amo Fashion (Hawthorne Blvd.), Torrance, 310-214-7932*
- *970 E. Garvey Ave. S. (Vicente Ave.), West Covina, 818-917-7019*
  Hours vary according to location; please call to check.
- *Mail order: 800-782-7282*

☑ "Help! they're everywhere" – and judging from high surveyor response just about everyone goes to this Seattle-based "phenomenon" that jump-started the caffeine craze on the West Coast and is now SoCal's dominant coffee chain; it takes some flak for being "a bit of a mill" and for "attitude" ("it's only coffee, guys"), but it has "amazing consistency" and quality that's deemed "remarkable for a chain"; in sum, "high concept, great follow through."

TEN REN TEA CO. ▣   27 | 27 | 24 | M
- *726 N. Hill St. (Ord & Alpine Sts.), Chinatown, 213-626-8844*
- *154 N. Valley Blvd. (Del Mar), San Gabriel, 818-288-1663*
- *111 Garvey Ave. (Garfield Ave.), Monterey Park, 818-288-2012*
  Every day 8:30am-7pm

■ Top-rated for tea in SoCal, this posh yet functional Chinatown shop (with siblings) doesn't serve tea, but sells it in a setting that would work just as well for fine jewelry; the "greatest oolongs in the world" are part of an "excellent selection" of more than 100 types (shipments arrive monthly from Taiwan); there's also "lovely and exquisite tea equipment", making this the "Tiffany for tea drinkers."

Trader Joe's | 21 | 21 | 21 | I |
- *See listing in Supermarkets section.*

■ As with every product sold at this rambling chain, the coffees tend towards the quirky but good, at very reasonable prices, making them a "best buy in bulk heaven" – "expect the unexpected" at this "low-rent alternative for boutique" beans; you "can't beat the price and quality" on items like "Kona coffee that's cheaper than it is in Kona."

Urth Cafe ▽ | 29 | 27 | 24 | I |
- *8565 Melrose Ave. (2 blocks west of La Cienega Blvd.), W. Hollywood, 310-659-0628*
  M-F 6:30am-10pm/Sat 6:30am-midnight
- *Mail order: 800-657-9001*

■ Highly respected, if little-known, "organic" coffee and tea shop, with beans from the only eight coffee fincas (ranches) in Central America to use organic methods; though few surveyors mention taste, many appreciate the organic nature of the coffee, and there are also kind words for the "genuinely good-hearted", "friendly" staff at this "charming place" with "nice gift packs."

Cooking Schools

Though restaurant-going is a way of life for many Southern Californians, there are still many food lovers who like to know how to do it themselves, and not just in the microwave. So not only do we have a wide variety of fine cooking schools in the area (be sure to check out additional classes at local high schools and community colleges), but with typical SoCal panache, they have turned into a rather high form of entertainment, with local and visiting chefs of great renown sharing their skills with anxious acolytes. That you may or may not ever make the dish that Julia or Jacques taught you isn't the point; that you saw them do it very much is.

Top Quality
- *27* Jean Brady
  Bristol Farms
- *26* Robert Mondavi
  Let's Get Cookin'

Top Service
- *27* Jean Brady
  Robert Mondavi
- *24* Bristol Farms
- *23* Let's Get Cookin'

Top Variety
- *26* Let's Get Cookin'
- *25* Bristol Farms
  Jean Brady
- *23* Robert Mondavi

Best Buys
- Jean Brady
  Bristol Farms
  Let's Get Cookin'
  Robert Mondavi

Q	V	S	C
27	25	24	M

Bristol Farms Cooking School
(fka Bristol Farms Cook 'N' Things)
- *606 Fair Oaks Ave. (Frwy. #110), S. Pasadena, 818-441-5588*
  M-Sat day & evening classes, call for schedule

■ This "excellent" cooking school is located in a cookware shop next to one of SoCal's top gourmet markets; it offers an "interesting", "offbeat" program taught by local instructors as well as "famous chefs" and authors; most find the classes "informative", though a few claim they're "more a social event than an education."

–	–	–	I

Cuisine Sur La Mer
- *919 Manhattan Ave. (south of Manhattan Beach Blvd.), Manhattan Beach, 310-374-3103*
  M-Th evenings only, call for schedule

A seaside school located in a cozy cookware store in the heart of Manhattan Beach that offers reasonably priced avocational classes with such titles as Dark Chocolate Fantasies, Low-Fat Dinner Party and French Seafood Specialties, all taught by local instructors.

Cooking Schools

O | V | S | C

Epicurean School of Culinary Arts

20 | 19 | 17 | E

- *8759 Melrose Ave. (Robertson Blvd.), LA, 310-659-5990*
  M-Sat day & evening classes, call for schedule

☑ Reactions vary widely to this long-established school across the street from Morton's and Eclipse; supporters say it's a "pro class" for "serious cooks", with "very good chef training"; others find it a "big disappointment" and suggest "more hands-on training" and less "attitude."

Home Economics

– | – | – | M

- *6499 E. PCH, Long Beach, 310-430-3967*
  T-Sat daytime & evening classes, call for schedule

Located in a store that carries "cookware, bath items, gifts and whimsy", this school's curriculum is coordinated by popular LA cooking teacher and chef Tim McGrath, with both day and evening classes taught almost exclusively by a staff of local teachers.

JEAN BRADY COOKING SCHOOL ⊞

27 | 25 | 27 | M

- *680 Brooktree (Sunset Blvd.), Santa Monica, 310-454-4220*
  W evening & Th day classes, call for schedule

■ Jean Brady (partner with *Zagat Survey* co-editor Karen Berk in the Seasonal Table Cooking School) operates SoCal's top-rated school out of her Rustic Canyon home; the "very informative" classes are all taught by Jean along with occasional high-profile guest instructors like Jacques Pepin, Paula Wolfert and Nancy Silverton; the "casual" setting makes it "like learning in your own kitchen" and one fan "still uses her recipes from a course 20 years ago."

L.A. Trade Technical College, Culinary Arts & Baking ⊞

▽ 24 | 24 | 22 | I

- *400 W. Washington Blvd. (Grand Ave.), LA, 213-744-9500*
  M-Th 7am-1:30pm

■ You get the "biggest bang for your dollar" at this "great trade school", a "best-kept secret" that's been teaching professional wanna-bes for more than half a century; courses are "very thorough with the basics" and especially "good for cake making and decorating."

Let's Get Cookin'

26 | 26 | 23 | E

- *4643 Lakeview Canyon Rd. (Agoura Rd.), Westlake Village, 818-991-3940*
  M-Sun day & evening classes, call for schedule

■ "The best chefs from all over" ensure that students learn to "cook in different languages" at this decade-old school; while the space may be "a little too small", most think it's "worth the drive" to the Los Angeles/Ventura County border for a "good variety" of "no-nonsense" courses taught by "people who really love cooking"; P.S. a professional program is offered, along with classes for kids.

Cooking Schools ░Q░ ░V░ ░S░ ░C░

Los Angeles Culinary Institute ░22░ ░19░ ░18░ ░E░
- *L.A. Equestrian Ctr., 480 Riverside Dr., Burbank,*
  818-840-1313
  M-Sun day & evening classes, call for schedule

☑ Master chef Raimund Hofmeister's dream to create an LA Culinary Institute of America (in this case at the Equestrian Center – polo and pollo?), is still reorganizing after an early bankruptcy; former students praise the "excellent", "professional" hands-on training in "technical skills for classic cooking", but others seem unaware that it's up-and-running again.

Peggy Rahn Cooks ⊄ ▽ ░24░ ░23░ ░25░ ░M░
- *484 Bellefontaine St., Pasadena, 818-441-2075*
  M-F evening classes, call for schedule

■ Peggy Rahn, food and travel writer for the *Pasadena Star-News* is a "wonderful cook and teacher with a great sense of humor"; students "want more classes" because they "love her presentation and style."

Robert Mondavi Wine and ░26░ ░23░ ░27░ ░E░
Food Center
- *1570 Scenic Ave., Costa Mesa, 714-979-4510*
  Evening classes, call for schedule

■ This "classy" SoCal outpost of the Napa Valley winery offers both cooking classes with "good chefs" and wine seminars "with great wine tastings"; most judge it "excellent", though there are "too many black-tie affairs."

Seasonal Table, The ⊄ ░–░ ░–░ ░–░ ░M░
- *Victorian at Heritage Sq., 2640 Main St., Santa Monica,*
  310-472-4475
- *Mailing address: 12618 Homewood Way, LA, 90049*
  M-Th evening classes/Sat classes, call for schedule

Recently opened by *Survey* co-editor Karen Berk and respected teacher Jean Brady, this Westside school offers classes and special events with local chefs, authors and other food personalities and emphasizes seasonal cooking; customized corporate and private group cooking classes are an added specialty.

Southern California School of ░–░ ░–░ ░–░ ░E░
Culinary Arts
- *1420 El Centro St. (bet. Fremont & Fair Oaks Blvd.),*
  S. Pasadena, 818-403-8490
  M-Sat 7am-6pm, call for schedule

This independent, not-for-profit professional school, established in 1994, is located in its own building on a South Pasadena side street and has a continuing education department, featuring classes for the home cook taught by staff instructors.

Store For Cooks, A   ▽ 25 22 22 M
* 30100 Town Ctr. Dr. (Crown Valley Pkwy.), Laguna Niguel,
714-495-0445
M-Sat day & evening classes, call for schedule
■ A "small", "innovative" OC operation run by "friendly
people" with cleverly conceived courses under titles like
"Lunch and Learn" (weekly courses at noon on a pair of
dishes) and "Dine and Dash" (a one-hour evening class
for those "on the run"), along with full-menu classes by
local chefs.

Tasting Spoon, The ⊅   – – – M
* 520 Washington Blvd., #816, Marina del Rey,
310-306-8851 (mailing address only)
Call for days & times
This "very personal" small school offers "consistently
good" classes in basic subjects like Soups and Desserts,
Chicken and Fish, and Herbs, taught in private homes in
Van Nuys and Huntington Beach; culinary trips and tours
are also offered.

UCLA Extension – Hospitality/   22 21 20 E
Food Service Management
* 10995 Le Conte Ave., Rm. 515, Westwood, 310-206-8120
M-Sat day & evening classes, call for schedule
■ "Fantastic avocational courses" as well as professional
certificate programs are offered here under the aegis of
UCLA's Adult Education arm by a "good faculty" but with
"poor kitchen facilities"; the consensus is "excellent but
expensive" – "I would have felt ripped off but for the quality
of the staff"; many of the classes are held off campus in
private homes and public facilities.

Upper Crust Cooking School   – – – E
* 73-540 El Paseo (bet. Portola Ave. & Hwy. #74), Palm Desert,
619-568-1998
Sun-Th day & evening classes (Nov & Jan-April), call
for schedule
"Creative and fun" classes are "always full" at this Desert-
area cookware shop where a "wonderful variety of visiting
chefs" teaches both day and night during the season.

Village Kitchen Shoppe   – – – M
* 147 N. Glendora Ave. (Foothill Blvd.), Glendora,
818-914-7897
M-Th evenings, lunchtime mini-classes, call for schedule
Located in a Glendora cookware store, this well-established
school with a small-town ambiance features classes with
local teachers and famous chefs; most sessions are held
in the evening, except for the popular two-hour lunch-and-
learn classes that are taught by the ebullient mother and
daughter team who own the store.

Cooking Schools

Village, The

19 | 17 | 19 | M

(fka Everywoman's Village)
- *5650 Sepulveda Blvd., Van Nuys, 818-787-5100*
  M-Sat day & evening classes, call for schedule

☑ Healthy, alternative classes such as Vegan Cooking I and II, Eat More Weigh Less and Low-Fat Moroccan are offered at this facility that students say "needs a face-lift"; it's "well priced" and the quality of instruction is generally "good" though some say "inconsistent."

Zov's Bistro – Guest Chefs at the Bistro

_ | _ | _ | E

- *17440 E. 17th St. (Frwy. #55), Tustin, 714-838-8855*
  Call for days & times

"Good chefs" from SoCal and beyond teach "excellent" classes at this popular Californian–Middle Eastern bakery and restaurant; it's pricey but students say "it's worth it."

Cookware & Supplies

We like designer kitchens in Southern California with lots of granite and stainless steel. And we like to fill these state-of-the-art spaces with the best of the best when it comes to pots and pans, whisks and knives. Fortunately, the task is made easy thanks to the area's wide variety of exceptional cookware suppliers. From big chains and department stores to smaller privately owned shops, they do everything from supplying just the right paring knife to wheeling in a Wolf range and Traulsen refrigerator. In case you want to know what to do with all this fancy equipment, there's a host of cookbook sources to choose from with The Cook's Library as a top choice.

Top Quality
29 Jordano's
28 Standard Cutlery
 Williams-Sonoma
27 Larry's Shop

Top Service
26 Friedman
25 Standard Cutlery
 Larry's Shop
 Jordano's

Top Variety
28 Jordano's
26 Gloria's
 Cookin' Stuff
25 Standard Cutlery

Best Buys
 Friedman
 Gloria's
 Larry's Shop
 Jordano's

Q	V	S	C
24	24	18	M

Avery Kitchen Supply 🚲
- *836 Traction Ave. (bet. 2nd & 3rd Sts.), Downtown LA, 213-624-7832*
 M-F 8am-4pm

◪ Ratings remain solid for this industrial Downtown Warehouse that used to be one of LA's "best sources" for restaurant-quality kitchenware; some say that it has experienced a "comedown" (perhaps due to downsizing); most still believe it's "worth a drive" for "an education" in "serious gear"; "if they don't carry it, it doesn't exist."

21	23	19	M

Bed Bath & Beyond
- *Beverly Ctr., 142 S. San Vicente Blvd. (bet. Beverly Blvd. & 3rd St.), LA, 310-652-1380*
- *11801 W. Olympic Blvd. (bet. Barrington Ave. & Bundy Dr.), West LA, 310-478-5767*
- *12555 Ventura Blvd. (Whitsett Ave.), Studio City, 818-980-0260*
- *19836 Ventura Blvd. (bet. Corbin & Winnetka Aves.), Woodland Hills, 818-980-0260*

Bed Bath & Beyond (Cont.)
- *Loehmann's 5 Points Plaza, 18641 Main St. (Beach Blvd.), Huntington Beach, 714-842-0068
  M-Sat 9:30am-9:30pm/Sun 11am-6pm*

■ "Everything you need" is "under one roof" at this everyday consumer's "paradise", a chain of massive stores with "lots of bargains" that turn otherwise reasonable humans into shopping obsessives; a "mecca for cheap thrills", it's best for name-brand pots, pans, utensils, knives and gadgets, with a "helpful sales staff" to guide you.

Bob Smith's Restaurant Equipment   ▽ 22 | 20 | 19 | M
- *1890 E. Walnut St. (2 blocks east of Allen, south of #210 Frwy.), Pasadena, 818-792-1185/213-681-9172
  M-F 8:30am-5pm/Sat 10am-2pm*

■ "Quality cookware at good prices" is found at this "very accommodating" Eastside outlet; it proudly claims to have everything from A to Z under one roof, making it "great for offbeat gifts and strange utensils."

Bristol Kitchens   27 | 25 | 24 | M
(fka Bristol Farms Cook 'N' Things)
- *606 Fair Oaks Ave. (#110 Frwy.), S. Pasadena, 818-441-5588
  M-F 8am-9pm/Sat & Sun 8am-7pm*

■ This "gourmet's delight" adjacent to the Bristol Farms store in South Pasadena offers a "limited" but "intriguing" selection of kitchenware and gift items "that no one else carries"; there's a demonstration kitchen for visiting chefs, plus "exceptional service" and "great parking"; in sum, it's "cookware heaven" but "prices are in the clouds too."

Broadway ▱   20 | 19 | 14 | M
- *Broadway Plaza, 750 W. Seventh St. (Flower St.), Downtown LA, 213-628-9311*
- *Balwin Hills Plaza, 4101 Crenshaw Blvd. (King St.), LA, 213-293-5151*
- *Panorama City, 8333 Van Nuys Blvd. (Roscoe Blvd.), Van Nuys, 818-893-7811*
- *Los Altos Mall, 2100 Bellflower Blvd. (Stearns St.), Long Beach, 310-596-3333*
- *Del Amo Fashion Ctr., 21800 Hawthorne Blvd., Torrance, 310-371-4681*
- *Whittwood Mall, 15600 Whittwood Ln. (Whittier Blvd.), Whittier, 310-943-7211*
- *W. Covina Fashion Plaza, 1200 W. Covina Pkwy. (Pacific & Sunset Blvds.), W. Covina, 818-962-3611*
- *Topanga Canyon Shopping Ctr., 21851 Victory Blvd. (Topanga Canyon Blvd.), Canoga Park, 818-883-8311*
- *Century City Shopping Ctr., 10250 Santa Monica Blvd., Century City, 310-277-1234*
- *Stonewood Shopping Ctr., 500 Stonewood St. (Lakewood & Firestone), Downey, 310-923-9331*

Broadway (Cont.)

- *500 Los Cerritos Mall, Cerritos, 310-860-0411*
- *2500 Northridge Fashion Ctr. (bet. Nordhoff & Plummer), Northridge, 818-885-7377*
- *200 Puente Hills Mall (Azusa & Colima), City of Industry, 818-965-8383*
- *Pasadena Plaza Mall, 400 E. Colorado Blvd. (Los Robles), Pasadena, 818-796-0411*
- *Santa Anita Fashion Mall, 400 South Baldwin Ave. (Huntington Dr.), Arcadia, 818-445-5711*
- *Fox Hills Mall, 6200 Slauson Ave. (Sepulveda Blvd.), Culver City, 310-390-8911*
- *2100 Glendale Galleria (bet. Broadway & Central), Glendale, 818-240-8411*
- *Hawthorne Mall, 12200 Hawthorne Blvd. (El Segundo Blvd.), Hawthorne, 310-973-2611*
- *Sherman Oaks Fashion Sq., 14060 Riverside Dr. (Woodman & Hazeltine Aves.), Sherman Oaks, 818-995-8991*
- *Santa Monica Pl., 315 Colorado Ave. (bet. Ocean Ave. & 4th St.), LA, 310-393-1441*
- *Beverly Ctr., 142 S. San Vicente Blvd. (Beverly Blvd.), LA, 310-854-7200*
- *The Oaks Mall, 350 W. Hillcrest Dr. (bet. Moorpark & Lynne Rd.), Thousand Oaks, 805-497-6915 General Hours: M-F 10am-9pm/Sat 10am-6pm/Sun 11am-6pm*
- *Mail order: 800-626-4800*

☑ Thanks to a recent chainwide attempt to upscale their kitchenware, this popular department store offers a wide array of designer cookware, along with weekly demos by local chefs; while prices are decidedly "retail" there are "good bargains at sale time"; the downside: "no sales people around" when you need them; N.B. at press time, the future of Broadway stores is in question due to a proposed merger with the parent company of Macy's/Bullock's.

Bullock's 🖃   23 | 20 | 16 | M

- *Beverly Ctr., 8500 Beverly Blvd. (La Cienega Blvd.), LA, 310-854-6655*
- *401 South Lake Ave. (Del Mar Ave.), Pasadena, 818-792-0211*
- *10861 Weyburn Ave. (east of Westwood Blvd.), Westwood, 310-208-4211*
- *Del Amo Fashion Ctr., 21600 Hawthorne Blvd. (Carson St.), Torrance, 310-370-8511*
- *Northridge Fashion Ctr., 9301 Tampa Ave. (bet. Nordhoff & Plummer Sts.), Northridge, 818-885-6611*
- *W. Covina Fashion Plaza, 1200 W. Covina Pkwy. (#10 Frwy.), W. Covina, 818-960-3611*
- *Century City Shopping Ctr., 10250 Santa Monica Blvd., Century City, 310-556-1611*
- *Media Ctr. Mall, 445 N. First St. (bet. San Fernando Rd. & Magnolia St.), Burbank, 818-841-2100*

Bullock's (Cont.)
- *Woodland Hills Promenade, 6150 N. Topanga Canyon Blvd.,*
  Woodland Hills, 818-313-8844
- *Seventh St. Market Mall, 925 W. Eighth St. (Figueroa),*
  Downtown LA, 213-624-9494
- *Manhattan Village Shopping Ctr., 3400 Sepulveda Blvd.*
  (Rosecrans Ave.), Manhattan Beach, 310-546-5525
- *The Oaks Mall, 220 W. Hillcrest Dr. (Lynne Rd., off*
  #101 Frwy.), Thousand Oaks, 805-496-4444
  General hours: M-F 10am-9pm, weekend hours vary by
  location
- *Mail order: 800-622-9748*

☑ One of the top bridal registry stores, with a computer to
track what has and hasn't been bought; as is often the case
with department store cookware sections, there are "great
prices on sale items", but the staff can be "hard to locate"
and "don't know cooking"; still, this is a "staple" for those
in need of high-tech toasters, rice steamers and the like;
N.B. Bullock's will soon be changing to Macy's.

Chef's Store, The   – | – | – | M |
- *836 Traction Ave., Downtown LA, 213-617-2963*
  M-F 8am-5pm
- *Internet: http://www.chefs-store.com/chef/*
- *E-mail: chef@chefs-store.com*

A supply store for the professional and home chef featuring
up-to-date information and interactive ordering of kitchen
equipment, tableware and specialty items obtainable on
the Internet.

Cookin' Stuff   26 | 26 | 22 | M |
- *22217 Palos Verdes Blvd. (Sepulveda Blvd.), Torrance,*
  310-371-2220
  M-Sat 10am-6pm/Sun noon-5pm

■ What some call the "ultimate cookware selection" is
found at this highly respected South Bay shop; a "total
dream warehouse of kitchen toys", it's the "best place" to
go for "hard to find items" since it carries "everything you
can think of, plus more"; the staff is "experienced" but not
everyone finds them helpful.

Cook's Library, The   29 | 28 | 26 | M |
- *8373 W. Third St. (2½ blocks east of La Cienega Blvd.),*
  LA, 213-655-3141
  M 1pm-5pm/T-Sat 11am-6pm

■ After you've stocked up on cookware elsewhere head
here, to one of the country's best cookbook shops, for
inspiration to use it all; it's a "treasure trove" of tomes "no
one else ever heard of" (but don't expect discounts); owner
Ellen Rose brings in authors for lectures and signings at
this "filled-to-the-brim", "clubby" books-only "retreat" that's
good for "food eavesdropping."

Crate & Barrel ✉   ⎡24⎤⎡24⎤⎡21⎤⎡M⎤
- *Century City Marketplace, 10250 Santa Monica Blvd., Century City, 310-551-1100*
- *75 W. Colorado Blvd. (1 block west of Fair Oaks Ave.), Pasadena, 818-683-8000*
- *Topanga Plaza, 6600 Topanga Canyon Blvd. (Vanowen St.), Canoga Park, 818-346-3900*
- *South Coast Plaza, 3333 Bristol, Costa Mesa, 714-957-1800*
- *Main Pl., 2800 N. Main St., Santa Ana, 714-547-1300 General Hours: M-F 10am-9pm/Sat 10am-6pm/ Sun 11am-6pm*
- *Mail order: 800-323-5461*

■ A "bridal registry must", this chain offers "trendy, upbeat good buys" to an upscale clientele that doesn't mind the downscale prices; fans say they have the "best selection" — "if you don't find it in the store, you will in the catalog"; the fact that "attractive people" shop here doesn't hurt.

Cuisine Sur La Mer   ⎡–⎤⎡–⎤⎡–⎤⎡M⎤
- *919 Manhattan Ave. (south of Manhattan Beach Blvd.), Manhattan Beach, 310-374-3103 M-Sat 10am-6pm*

This small, neighborhood store in Downtown Manhattan Beach supplies pots, pans and kitchen accessories to beach dwellers who don't want to go far for supplies before they stoke their grills.

FRIEDMAN MICROWAVE OVENS 🚲   ⎡27⎤⎡25⎤⎡26⎤⎡M⎤
- *17312 Ventura Blvd. (Louise Ave.), Encino, 818-501-0794 M-F 10am-5:30pm/Sat 10am-5pm*
- *5515 Stearns Ave. (Bellflower Ave.), Long Beach, 310-598-7756 M-Sat 10am-5:30pm*

■ A "complete" source for microwave ovens and cookware, this discount chain is known for its "terrific variety", "knowledgeable" service and "low cost"; it was one of the first places to take microwaving seriously, offering classes and answering questions such as 'can we dry our poodle in one?' and 'how do you hard boil an egg in a microwave?' (you can't and you don't); expect to be "completely satisfied."

Gloria's Cake Decorating Supplies   ⎡25⎤⎡26⎤⎡22⎤⎡M⎤
- *3755 Sawtelle Blvd. (1 block north of Venice Blvd.), Mar Vista, 310-391-4557 M-F 10am-6pm/Sat 10am-5pm*

■ "Real pros" go to this "adult toy store" to buy cake making and decorating supplies "not easily available elsewhere" (they have candy-making items as well); despite a "funky" location in Mar Vista that's "too cramped", this is still "the only place" for creative cake concocters: "every idea you come up with, they can help."

Jane's Cakes and Chocolates ▭   _ | _ | _ | M

- *Zwick's Plaza, 2331 Honolulu Ave. (bet. Ocean View Ave.*
  & Wickham), Montrose, 818-957-2511
  T, W, F, Sat 10am-5pm/Th 10am-8pm
- *Mail order: 800-262-7630*

Tucked into a courtyard in an out-of-the-way location, this
15-year-old specialty store carries a good variety of quality
baking and candy equipment and hard-to-find supplies,
which are also available by mail order; cake decorating
and candy making classes are held on a regular basis.

Jordano's Marketplace   29 | 28 | 25 | E

- *614 Chapala St. (Cota St.), Santa Barbara, 805-965-3031*
  M,W,F,Sat 10am-6pm/T & Th 10am-7:30pm/Sun 11am-5pm

■ Top-rated for cookware quality, this shop is some two
hours north of LA but the "trek is worth it"; though the
cooking school is closing, the store still earns universal raves
as a "fantasyland for foodies" with a "terrific selection" in
"beautiful surroundings" – no doubt the reason that Julia
Child can often be found in Santa Barbara; it's "costly", but
"an addiction" usually is.

Kake Kreations   ▽ 27 | 28 | 25 | I

- *21835 Sherman Way (1 block east of Topanga*
  Canyon Blvd.), Canoga Park, 818-346-7621
  M-F 10am-5:30pm/Sat 10am-5pm

■ "Everything for the cake and candy maker" can be found
at this "very crowded", "inexpensive" San Fernando Valley
emporium; "informative service" helps patrons locate items
in the "fully-stocked" store, where the inventory includes
"every shape of cake mold made."

Larry's Shaver Shop   27 | 22 | 25 | M

- *631 Wilshire Blvd., Santa Monica, 310-393-3291*
  M-F 9am-5pm/Sat 9am-6pm

■ The name doesn't reveal that this is a cookware source,
but fans hail this "shop with an edge" for its "great knives
and equipment" and wonder how such an "old-fashioned",
well-kept "secret got on the list"; "they have it all and repair
it all" at the "best place in LA to get blades sharpened."

Lechter's   18 | 22 | 17 | I

- *Sherman Oaks Fashion Sq., 14006 Riverside Dr.*
  (Woodman Ave.), Sherman Oaks, 818-990-5737
- *Northridge Fashion Ctr., 9301 Tampa Ave. (Nordhoff St.),*
  Northridge, 818-993-8029
- *Topanga Plaza, 6600 Topanga Canyon Blvd. (Vanowen St.),*
  Canoga Park, 818-340-7335
- *212 Santa Monica Pl. (Third St. Promenade), Santa Monica,*
  310-393-8684
- *Westside Pavilion, 10800 W. Pico Blvd. (Westwood Blvd.),*
  West LA, 310-441-1690
- *The Galleria at South Bay, 1815 Hawthorne Blvd.,*
  Redondo Beach, 310-371-4695

Lechter's (Cont.)
- *145 The Plaza, Pasadena, 818-568-2970*
- *S. Anita Fashion Park, 400 S. Baldwin Ave., Arcadia, 818-574-0517*
- *2068 Montebello Town Ctr. Dr., Montebello, 213-726-3088*
- *W. Covina Fashion Plaza, 1200 W. Covina Pkwy. (#10 Frwy.), W. Covina, 818-814-0770*
- *119 Los Cerritos Ctr. (bet. South St. & Gridley Ave.), Cerritos, 310-809-5888*
- *120 Puente Hills Mall, City of Industry, 818-912-8417*
- *201 E. Magnolia, Burbank, 818-848-7537*
- *Media City Ctr., 200 Lakewood Ctr. Mall, Lakewood, 310-630-1228*

Hours vary according to location; please call to check.
◪ Despite average ratings, a large number of responses indicates that sooner or later everyone goes to this "lowbrow" chain of kitchenware stores offering "basic supplies" and a big "selection of gadgets"; the "help" may "need help", but you get "lots for little" at this "McDonald's of cookware."

Let's Get Cookin'   26 | 21 | 22 | E
- *4643 Lakeview Canyon Rd. (Agoura Rd.), Westlake Village, 818-991-3940*
  M-Sat 10am-6pm

■ "What experienced and professional chefs want" is what's found at this "well-stocked" combination cooking school and cookware shop, a "gem of a store" "in the boonies" that sells items "for use, not just show"; the "friendly" staff is "knowledgeable and helpful" and they also have "a lovely selection of gourmet foods"; just don't go looking for bargains; P.S. they also cater.

Robinsons-May ▣   20 | 18 | 15 | M
- *Crenshaw Plaza, 4005 Crenshaw Blvd. (Martin Luther King Jr. Blvd.), Baldwin Hills, 213-298-7541*
- *Lakewood Ctr. Mall, 5100 Lakewood Blvd. (Del Amo), Lakewood, 310-633-0111*
- *Laurel Plaza Shopping Ctr., 6150 Laurel Canyon Blvd. (Oxnard St.), N. Hollywood, 818-766-4111*
- *Galleria at South Bay, 1801 Hawthorne Blvd. (Artesia Blvd.), Redondo Beach, 310-370-2511*
- *Topanga Plaza Shopping Ctr., 21900 Vanowen St. (Topanga Canyon Blvd.), Canoga Park, 818-883-7211*
- *Westside Pavilion, 10730 W. Pico Blvd. (Overland Ave.), West LA, 310-475-4911*
- *Eagle Rock Plaza Mall, 2828 Colorado Blvd. (#2 Frwy.), Eagle Rock, 213-258-8303*
- *Fox Hills Mall, 6050 Sepulveda Blvd. (Slauson Ave.), Culver City, 310-390-8811*
- *Sherman Oaks Galleria, 15301 Ventura Blvd. (Sepulveda Blvd.), Sherman Oaks, 818-986-8110*

Robinsons-May (Cont.)
- *The Shops at Palos Verdes, 580 Deep Valley Dr. (Hawthorne Blvd.), Rolling Hills Estates, 310-544-0222*
- *1900 Montebello Town Ctr. (Montebello Blvd.), Montebello, 213-721-1081*
- *Seventh St. Market Mall (Figueroa St.), Downtown LA, 213-683-1144*
- *Northridge Fashion Ctr., 9301 Tampa Ave. (bet. Nordhoff & Plummer), Northridge, 818-772-1800*
- *Stonewood Mall, 9066 Stonewood St. (bet. Lakewood & Firestone Aves.), Downey, 310-862-2880*
- *Valencia Town Ctr., 26450 McBean Pkwy. (Valencia Blvd.), Santa Clarita, 805-287-5911*
- *W. Covina Fashion Plaza, 1111 W. Covina Pkwy. (#10 Frwy.), W. Covina, 818-962-5400*
- *2198 Glendale Galleria (bet. Orange & Central Aves.), Glendale, 818-247-2600*
- *9900 Wilshire Blvd. (west of Santa Monica Blvd.), Beverly Hills, 310-275-5464*
- *300 Los Cerritos Mall (#605 Frwy.), Cerritos, 310-860-8555*
- *400 Puente Mall (#60 Frwy. & Azusa Ave.), City of Industry, 818-965-5941*
- *Santa Anita Fashion Park, S. Baldwin Ave. (#210 Frwy.), Arcadia, 818-445-8000*
- *103 Santa Monica Pl. (Third St. Promenade), Santa Monica, 310-451-2411*
- *Del Amo Mall, 21760 Hawthorne Blvd. (Carson St.), Torrance, 310-542-5941*
- *The Oaks Mall, 200 W. Hillcrest Dr. (Lynne Rd.), Thousand Oaks, 805-497-6821*
  M-Th 10am-9pm/F 10am-10pm/Sat 10am-8pm/ Sun 11am-7pm
- *Mail order: 800-633-1224*

☑ Like other department store chains, this one (formed by a merger between upscale Robinsons and the downscale May Company) stocks an "average", rather "boring choice"; it's worth it if you catch one of the "great sales" but don't expect to catch a salesperson – they're "never around."

San Marino Hardware   25 | 23 | 23 | E |
- *2134 Huntington Dr. (½ block west of Sierra Madre Blvd.), San Marino, 818-282-6536*
  M-Sat 9am-5:30pm

■ One of the last of the "old-fashioned" hardware stores, this "hidden jewel" with a "great hometown feeling" in old-money San Marino carries everything from paint and pruning shears to a "surprisingly good" selection of pots and pans; they're "accommodating" and "will order special items"; it may be "eccentric" but "you'll never leave empty-handed."

STANDARD CUTLERY & SUPPLY
28 25 25 E

- *9509 Santa Monica Blvd. (west of Rodeo Dr.), Beverly Hills, 310-276-7898*
  M-Sat 8:30am-5:30pm

■ A prime supplier of blades, this small, crowded "tradition" in the midst of upscale Beverly Hills, right off Rodeo Drive, is run by a "knowledgeable" owner who'll share cutlery lore with you as he works; though not cheap it's a "favorite" – the kind of place to bring the family's "Thanksgiving knives" for sharpening before carving the bird.

Star Restaurant Equipment & Supply Co. ⬲
24 24 18 M

- *6178 Sepulveda Blvd. (1 block south of Victory Blvd.), Van Nuys, 818-782-4460*
  M-F 8:30am-5:30pm/Sat 10am-4pm

■ "Shop with restaurateurs" at this longtime Valley cookware supply house that deals mostly with the trade; it may not be fancy, but this "utilitarian" outlet is a "treasure chest" where "a make-believe chef can go crazy"; service varies from "nice" to "not real helpful."

Store For Cooks, A
- - - M

- *30100 Town Ctr. Dr. (Crown Valley Pkwy.), Laguna Niguel, 714-495-0445*
  M-F 10am-6pm/Sat 10am-5pm

This "small" but "fun store with friendly people" has supplied a good selection of gourmet pots, pans and kitchen gadgetry to an appreciative Laguna Beach–area clientele for well over a decade.

Surfas Inc.
- - - M

- *8825 National Blvd. (bet. Venice & Washington Blvds.), Culver City, 310-559-4770*
  M-F 8am-5:30pm/Sat 9am-5pm

This massive warehouse store carries a full line of restaurant supplies (cookware, equipment, china, cutlery and so on) along with Van Rex and other lines of specialty food products; friendly service and competitive prices are pluses that balance the dismal look and sometimes understocked inventory.

Thee Cutlery
- - - M

- *Manhattan Village Mall, 3200 Sepulveda Blvd. (Rosecrans Blvd.), Manhattan Beach, 310-545-5718*
  M-F 10am-9pm/Sat 10am-7pm/Sun noon-6pm

Hidden away in a major shopping mall, this relatively unknown store offers a fine selection of most major knife brands (i.e. Henckel, R. H. Forschner, Trident & F. Dick); the knowledgeable owner also dispenses cutlery advice and does sharpening.

Village Kitchen Shoppe $\triangledown$ $\underline{25}$ $\underline{23}$ $\underline{26}$ $\underline{M}$
- *147 N. Glendora Ave. (1 block north of Foothill Blvd.),*
  Glendora, 818-914-7897
  M-Sat 10am-5:30pm

■ "Why are all the best places in the boonies?" moans one
admirer of this "wonderful, delightful" cookware shop in
faraway Glendora (way east of Pasadena); still, it's "worth
a visit" since they offer a "hell of a presentation" of "cute
items" that are "not your typical stuff"; what's more, "they'll
order special request items."

WILLIAMS-SONOMA 📧 $\underline{28}$ $\underline{24}$ $\underline{25}$ $\underline{E}$
- *317 N. Beverly Dr. (north of Dayton Way), Beverly Hills,*
  310-274-9127
  M,T,W,Sat 10am-6pm/Th 10am-8pm/Sun noon-5pm
- *1112 Glendale Galleria, Glendale, 818-241-0154*
  M-F 10am-9pm/Sat 10am-8pm/Sun 11am-7pm
- *Beverly Ctr., 131 N. La Cienega, LA, 213-652-9117*
  M-F 10am-9pm/Sat 10am-8pm/Sun 11am-6pm
- *146 S. Lake Ave., Pasadena, 818-795-5045*
  M-Sat 9:30am-8pm/Sun 12pm-5pm
- *The Shops at Palos Verdes, 550 Deep Valley Dr., Rolling*
  Hills Estates, 310-541-9545
  M-F 10am-9pm/Sat 10am-6pm/Sun 11am-6pm
- *395 Santa Monica Pl., Santa Monica, 310-451-7633*
  M-Sat 10am-9pm/Sun 11am-6pm
- *Woodland Hills Promenade (Topanga Canyon Blvd.),*
  Woodland Hills, 818-887-4355
  M-F 10am-9pm/Sat & Sun 10am-6pm
- *Sherman Oaks Fashion Sq., 14006 Riverside Dr.*
  (Woodman Ave.), Sherman Oaks, 818-981-1044
  M-F 10am-9pm/Sat 10am-7pm/Sun 11am-6pm
- *Santa Anita Fashion Park, 400 S. Baldwin Ave., Arcadia,*
  818-294-9401
  M-F 10am-9pm/Sat 10am-6pm/Sun 11am-6pm
- *The Oaks, 480 W. Hillcrest Dr. (Lynne Rd. exit, off*
  #101 Frwy.), Thousand Oaks, 805-495-3632
  M-F 10am-9pm/Sat 10am-7pm/Sun 11am-6pm
- *Mail order: 800-541-2233*

■ Arguably the store that started the trend towards upscale
pots and pans, this "always excellent" gourmet cookware
chain is one of the "best in the business", with a "big
choice of great stuff" displayed in "beautiful" surroundings;
a standard-bearer for the genre, it's a "cook's Disneyland"
where the goods are "top of the line" (ditto prices) and
the salespeople actually "know how to cook."

Delis

From groaningly large deli trays to a bagful of bagels and lox for a weekend brunch, the delis of Los Angeles keep locals very well fed with a taste of the old country—albeit one that's often transmogrified into the flavors of a new land. This may be the only place in the world where delis serve breakfast pizzas, plus Chinese and Mexican food. But not to fear—they do a good job with corned beef and pastrami too. And don't forget the pickles and the sour tomatoes. On the other hand, some folks from the East might say "you gotta be kidding!"

Top Quality
26 Brent's
   Langer's
25 Nate 'n Al's
24 Pico Kosher
22 Greenblatt's

Top Variety
26 Brent's
24 Nate 'n Al's
   Jerry's Famous
23 Langer's
22 Junior's

Top Service
23 Brent's
21 Langer's
   Nate 'n Al's
19 Pico Kosher
   Solley's

Best Buys
Brent's
Langer's
Nate 'n Al's
Pico Kosher
Jerry's Famous

Q	V	S	C
–	–	–	M

Art's Deli &
• *12224 Ventura Blvd. (Whitsett Ave. & Laurel Canyon Blvd.), Studio City, 818-762-1221*
  M-F 6:30am-11pm/Sat 6:30am-midnight/Sun 6:30am-11pm
After falling down and catching fire in the Northridge earthquake, Art's is back; the store is bigger than before but Art himself is trimmed down, though he still ensures that the brisket, corned beef, pastrami and various deli platters ordered as takeout by many nearby studios provide a hearty taste of New York in Studio City.

–	–	–	E

Barney Greengrass &
• *Barneys New York, 9570 Wilshire Blvd. (bet. Camden & Peck Drs.), 310-777-5877*
  M,T,W,F 7:30am-7pm/Th 7:30am-8pm/Sat 9am-7pm/ Sun 9am-6pm
• *Mail order: 212-724-4707*
Though most customers eat in at this trendy Beverly Hills smoked fish shop, the deli counter prepares a wide range of take-out salmon, sturgeon and sable for those who don't mind walking past the Armani men's department in Barneys carrying a bag redolent of bagels and lox; at least the prices fit right in.

84

Billy's Restaurant & Bakery 🚴   – | – | – | M
- *216 N. Orange St. (1½ blocks north of the Glendale Galleria), Glendale, 818-246-1689*
  Every day 7am-8:30pm

One of the few delis on the Eastside of Los Angeles County, with an old-fashioned take-out counter manned by grouchy meat slicers who look as if they just arrived from Brooklyn; they also know how to spread chopped liver and pour chicken soup and keep locals well supplied with schmaltz.

BRENT'S DELI 🚴   26 | 26 | 23 | M
- *19565 Parthenia St. (Corbin Ave.), Northridge, 818-886-5679*
  Every day 6am-9pm

■ "Out of the way" but "worth driving to", this Northridge "oasis in earthquake country" is an "old-style", "NY"-like noshery with a busy, efficient take-out counter, providing massive platters that help earn it the No. 1 rating in LA's highly competitive world of corned beef and pastrami; it's in the back of a mall where "crowds" are a constant and "sardonic waitresses" "bring back memories."

Broadway Deli 🚴   19 | 20 | 17 | E
- *1457 3rd St. Promenade (Broadway), Santa Monica, 310-451-0616*
  M-Th 7am-midnight/F 7am-1am/Sat 8am-midnight/ Sun 8am-1am

☑ With decent ratings and "good celebrity-watching", this high-profile Santa Monican's big take-out section offers everything from cheese and pâté to pastry and bagels; it's "good before or after a movie", but otherwise critics say it "doesn't cut the mustard" and is "too white bread" – "3,000 miles from Broadway, and it shows."

Canter's 🚴   18 | 22 | 16 | M
- *419 N. Fairfax Ave. (Beverly Blvd.), LA, 213-651-2030*
  Every day 24 hrs

☑ The countermen are legendary at this fabled "blast from the past" deli where you "don't go for the food" as much as for "the atmosphere"; it's an "institution" that "attracts all walks of life" who need "a place to hang out"; besides, "they're open all night" – "you can't beat the heartburn at 3 AM", when on-deadline screenwriters come in for takeout.

Citi Deli 🚴   ▽ 18 | 21 | 19 | M
- *International Jewelry Ctr. Bldg., 550 S. Hill St. (bet. 5th & 6th Sts.), Downtown LA, 213-629-0910*
  M-Sat 8am-3:30pm

☑ "Whatever they do, they do well" say fans of this "best-kept secret" in the Downtown jewelry mart; it caters lots of office meetings in the jewelry and fashion districts, pleasing most with "good breakfasts" and a "mixed cold-cuts plate" that may be "the best deal in town"; this noshery also has cachet because it's run by Bobby Trager, who cut his deli teeth at NY's fabled Carnegie; doubters find it "average."

Factor's Deli 🚴   19 | 21 | 18 | M

- *9420 West Pico Blvd. (Beverly Dr.), LA, 310-278-9175*
  M-Sat 6am-9:30pm/Sun 7am-9:30pm
- *1315 Third St. Promenade (bet. Arizona Ave. & Santa*
  Monica Blvd.), Santa Monica, 310-393-2323 🏠
  Every day 11am-11pm

◪ An "ok neighborhood deli" with "good but not great"
food – odd, as it's located in the deli-savvy Beverlywood
area (with a small self-service branch in Santa Monica);
many compare it favorably to the midrange LA delis
(Junior's, Jerry's, Stage), calling it "good for what it is", but
not up with the Big Boys when it comes to classic corned
beef; the West Pico branch delivers many a platter to nearby
Century City businesses.

Fox Deli/LA Fresh 🚴   16 | 18 | 17 | M

- *11819 Wilshire Blvd. (1 block west of Barrington Ave.),*
  West LA, 310-479-0177
  M-Sat 7am-9:30pm/Sun 8am-9pm

◪ A former Good Earth restaurant that is now half healthy-
salad spot and half "nondescript" deli; "big portions" and
"good prices" help, but critics say it's "too caught up in
being healthy to be really good"; still, it has a "good locale"
and the counter does a fair-sized take-out business and
delivery of trays to Wilshire Boulevard offices.

Fromin's Restaurant & Deli 🚴   18 | 20 | 18 | M

- *1832 Wilshire Blvd. (19th St.), Santa Monica, 310-829-5443*
- *17615 Ventura Blvd. (east of White Oak Ave.), Encino,*
  818-990-6346
  Every day 7am-9:30pm

◪ "Dependable" but "dull" Santa Monica and Encino delis
that some find as "warm and friendly as a subway car";
nevertheless, these "popular", "funky neighborhood places"
"maintain themselves" with moderate prices, "good potato
pancakes and soups" (matzo ball, chicken and cabbage),
"humongous sandwiches" and "the best roast turkey" –
which is why they're often called on to cater staff meetings
in nearby offices.

Greenblatt's 🚴   22 | 22 | 19 | M

- *8017 Sunset Blvd. (bet. Crescent Heights & Fairfax*
  Ave.), Hollywood, 213-656-0606
  Every day 9am-2am

◪ A "very good, not great" Hollywood Hills deli that's
combined with one of "LA's best wine shops"; "excellent"
chicken soup and "orgasmic" turkey and roast beef
sandwiches are strengths, but eat-ins find that "ordering
at the deli case before being seated" is "a drag"; celebs
and wanna-bes up nearby Laurel Canyon beat the "system"
by calling for delivery, but they also drop in to this cafeteria-
like setting to enjoy the "great late-night scene."

Delis

Jerry's Famous Deli 🚴

21 | 24 | 18 | M

- 8701 Beverly Blvd. (1 block west of San Vicente Blvd.), LA, 310-208-3354
- 12655 Ventura Blvd. (1 block east of Coldwater Canyon Ave.), Studio City, 818-980-4245
- 16650 Ventura Blvd. (bet. Balboa & Hayvenhurst Aves.), Encino, 818-906-1800
- 13181 Mindanao Way (Frwy. #90), Marina del Rey, 310-821-6626
  Every day 24 hrs

◨ An aggressively expanding chain that now has 24-hour branches all over town, some with valet parking; the encyclopedic offerings (from brisket to pizzas) draw mixed reviews: foes cite "inconsistent" fare and "spotty" service, while fans call the eats "better than most", especially the "delicious" soups and "weighty" sandwiches; delivery to Cedars from the Beverly Boulevard branch means you can recover from your bypass with a corned beef sandwich.

Junior's Deli 🚴

20 | 22 | 18 | M

- 2379 Westwood Blvd. (½ block north of Pico Blvd.), West LA, 310-475-5771
  M-Th 6:30am-11pm/F 6:30am-midnight/Sat 7am-midnight/ Sun 7am-11pm

◨ A love-it-or-hate-it experience; critics claim this Westsider is on "a slow road downhill" and say its "high-tech look" makes it resemble "a hospital commissary"; but loyalists swear by "old standbys" from "fab latkes and blintzes" to "always fresh, good and dependable" cold cuts, bagels and lox; the take-out counters are in the front of the restaurant, and it does a good business catering events in the 'hood.

Langer's 🚴

26 | 23 | 21 | M

- 704 S. Alvarado St. (7th St.), LA, 213-483-8050
  M-Sat 8am-4pm

■ The bad news is that everyone complains about this Downtowner's "scary", "nerve-racking" location; the good news is that the food is so "superb" that it's "worth taking a bullet for the pastrami" and other terrific deli fare; typical raves include "LA's best by far", "superb", "gets better every time"; takeout is a popular option, and if you call ahead they'll be waiting with your order as you drive by.

Nate 'n Al's 🚴

25 | 24 | 21 | M

- 414 N. Beverly Dr. (bet. Little Santa Monica & Dayton Way), Beverly Hills, 310-274-0101
  Every day 7:30am-8:45pm

■ The failure of billionaire Marvin Davis' Carnegie Deli, on the same block as Nate 'n Al's, underscored the popularity of this Beverly Hills "classic"; expect a long wait at the take-out counter where half of Hollywood gets bagels, lox, brisket and chopped liver; at tables, movers and shakers kibitz with the "longtime" waitresses, schmingle and enjoy the "best" chicken soup, whitefish and more; it's true "quality."

Pico Kosher Deli 🚲
24 19 19 M

• 8826 W. Pico Blvd. (Robertson Blvd.), LA, 310-273-9381
  Sun-Th 9am-8:30pm/F 9am-2:30pm

■ LA's leading genuine kosher (not kosher-style) deli, this
small storefront near Beverlywood is where mavens advise
going "if you're serious" for the "finest corned beef on rye",
"great chicken" and "the best potato salad ever"; everything
about it is the "real magilla" ("love those pickles in the tuna
sandwich") including the fast take-out service from the
doorside counter.

Solley's Restaurant & Deli 🚲
19 22 19 M

• 4578 Van Nuys Blvd. (bet. Moorpark & Riverside Drs.),
  Van Nuys, 818-905-5774
• 21857 Ventura Blvd. (½ block east of Topanga Canyon Blvd.),
  Woodland Hills, 818-340-0810
  Sun-Th 6:30am-midnight/F & Sat 6:30am-1am

☑ "Nice, homey" delis that are "always busy and noisy"
with "garlicky pickles" on the tables and food that's
"consistently decent", though rarely better than that;
whether they take out or eat in, critics groan about "awful
service" ("Solley needs to get back to watching the
store") and sniff that it's "deli for the novice" – "my wife
loves this place."

Stage Deli 🚲
19 20 16 E

• 10250 Little Santa Monica Blvd. (Ave. of the Stars),
  Century City, 310-553-3354
  Sun-Th 7:30am-10pm/F & Sat 7:30am-midnight

☑ While NY's Carnegie crashed in Beverly Hills, this Seventh
Avenue clone survives, thanks partly to its location in
pedestrian-busy Century City, amidst the 'legal ghetto' (it
feeds many LA entertainment lawyers) and opposite a busy
multiplex; the stagestruck like its "large portions" of "decent
to excellent food", but critics term it a "white-bread deli"
"for tourists", though it does have "NY attitude" – for
better or worse.

Ethnic Food Sources

This chapter – written by Linda Burum, who knows more about the ethnic markets of Southern California than any other living being – is the very heart and soul of this book. The entire ethnic spectrum is to be found here, on the shelves of several dozen remarkable markets where flavors from around the world perfume the air and offer a taste of the West Coast's culinary future. The incredible depth and variety of the food resources reflected in this section provide convincing evidence that Los Angeles is the first city of the 21st century, and a darned tasty city at that. Please refer to the indexes for listings by specific cuisine, i.e. Japanese, Italian, etc.

Top Quality
- 28 Al Dente/Italian
- 26 Domingo's/Italian
  Yaohan Mkt./Japanese
  C & K/Greek
  Tarzana Groc./Mid. East.

Top Service
- 28 Al Dente/Italian
- 25 Domingo's/Italian
- 24 Monte Carlo/Italian
- 23 Panos Pastry/Mid. East.
  Aloha Grocery/Japanese

Top Variety
- 27 99 Ranch Mkt./Asian
- 26 Koreatown Plaza/Korean
  Ron's Mkt./Int'l
  Al Dente/Italian
- 25 Yaohan Mkt./Japanese

Best Buys
  Monte Carlo/Italian
  Al Dente/Italian
  Domingo's/Italian
  C & K/Greek
  Carrillo's/Mexican

Q	V	S	C
20	25	15	I

Ai Hoa ✍
- *860 N. Hill St. (College Ave.), Chinatown, 213-629-8121*
  Every day 8am-8pm

Shun Fat
- *421 N. Atlantic (Garvey St.), Monterey Park, 818-308-9880*
  Every day 8am-8pm

■ The huge and more modern Monterey Park branch of this pan-Asian duo was taken over by Shun Fat, but it still has "things you never knew existed", making it "an adventure" to visit; the old Ai Hoa remains in Chinatown with stock largely geared to a Vietnamese clientele; critics say the Chinatown branch is "just ok", citing fish that's "not always fresh" and aisles that are "not so clean."

Al Dente   28 | 26 | 28 | M

- *11092 Los Alamitos Blvd. (1 block south of Katella Ave.),
  Los Alamitos, 310-598-1124
  T-Sat 9:30am-6:30pm/Sun noon-4pm*

■ "The owner's a gem" and travels to Italy each year
searching out products and recipes, which is why some
say a trip to this Los Alamitos shop is "like being in Roma";
Italian-trained chef Naomi Silvi, the owner's daughter, is
another reason why the prepared foods are so "very good";
the porcini sauce alone is worth a drive, as are such rare-in-
LA items as Abruzzi-style salamis and scamorza cheese.

Aloha Grocery ⇗   22 | 21 | 23 | I

- *4515 Centinela Blvd. (bet. Washington & Culver Blvds.),
  West LA, 310-822-2288
  M-F 9am-7pm/Wed 9am-6pm/Sat & Sun 9am-5pm*

■ Three times a week owner Hiroshi Uyehara fires up his
soybean grinder to produce "unsurpassed fresh tofu"; the
Hawaiian native honed his technique in Japan – try his old-
fashioned *nigiri tofu* made without solidifiers; Uyehara also
flies in Hawaiian breads, poi and ti leaves, and the shop
makes *lomi lomi* – no wonder one fan says this "friendly"
West LA place is where "all our Hawaiian friends shop."

Alpine Village Market & Bakery   22 | 22 | 19 | M

- *833 W. Torrance Blvd. (bet. Vermont Ave. & Figueroa St.),
  Torrance, 310-327-2483
  M-Th 11am-7pm/F & Sun 11am-8pm/Sat 10am-8pm*

◪ Don't be misled: this "kingdom of kitsch" in its Teutonic
shopping mall setting in Torrance isn't all show; a skilled
wienermeister makes "excellent cold cuts and sausages"
on site and offers some low-fat types; it's a "good source
for European products" and many kinds of German-style
bread, but some warn that you must "fend for yourself
with the no-nonsense German cashiers."

Ann's Dutch Imports   ▽ 23 | 22 | 22 | M

- *4357 Tujunga Ave. (Moorpark St.), Studio City, 818-985-5551
  T-Sat 10am-5pm*

◪ "You don't have to go to Holland, you can buy everything
here" instead: cheeses, cookies, cakes and the 20 or so
types of licorice that the Dutch love; they also love
Indonesian food and this shop is "great for Indonesian
spices"; try the *bumbus*, convenient premixed spice pastes.

A1 Italian Deli 🚲   – | – | – | M

- *348 8th St. (Mesa & Centre Sts.), San Pedro, 310-833-3430
  M-Sat 8am-6pm/Sun 8am-midnight*

A standby in the old-line San Pedro Italian neighborhood
for decades, this market's offerings include hard-to-find
meats such as veal breast and osso buco, produce including
cardoons, rapini and thumbnail-size artichokes, breads
from the Portofino bakery, plus homemade sauces, prepared
dishes, frozen ravioli and more.

Artesia Bakery   <u>–</u> <u>–</u> <u>–</u> <u>M</u>

- *18627 S. Pioneer Blvd., Artesia, 310-865-1201*
  M-F 7am-6:30pm/Sat 6am-6pm

Less than 20 years ago Dutch-owned dairy herds roamed past Pioneer Boulevard, the area now known as Little India; a vestige from that time, this bakery still attracts Dutch from all over the state who flock here at Christmas for hand-molded *speculass*, almond paste–filled pastry wreaths and marzipan candies; there are 30 or so kinds of traditional cookies, and the *rogge* rye bread, *applebollen*, and *honingkoek* (honey cake) will remind you of Amsterdam.

Asian Ranch   <u>–</u> <u>–</u> <u>–</u> <u>I</u>

- *13722 Sherman Way (Woodman Ave.), Van Nuys,*
  818-781-0385
  Every day 9am-8pm

Given the Philippines' history of Spanish domination, Chinese trading and American occupation, it's no surprise that Filipino markets resemble international bazaars; the choice at this Van Nuys site includes Chinese long beans, *bagoong* (fermented fish sauce), *leche flan* and, of course, corn flakes; there's a huge array of whole fish that varies wildly in quality, and any fish can be fried to order in the store.

Baducco's 🚲   <u>25</u> <u>24</u> <u>22</u> <u>M</u>

- *Village Glen Shopping Ctr., 2839 Agoura Rd. (1 block*
  south of Westlake Blvd.), Westlake, 818-991-4670
  Every day 9am-7pm

■ "A pleasant surprise for its out-of-the-way" Westlake Village locale, this Italian deli makes "delicious homemade products" and offers "everything needed to cook Italian": imported and domestic meats and cheeses, fresh egg pastas, ready-to-use pizza dough, a variety of sausages including an uncommon sweet kind without fennel, and wonderful bread that Giuliano Bugialli picks up when in town; it's the "real deal."

Bangkok Supermarket   <u>21</u> <u>23</u> <u>14</u> <u>I</u>

- *4757 Melrose Ave. (2 blocks east of Western Ave.),*
  Hollywood, 213-662-9705
  Every day 9am-9pm

◧ One of LA's oldest Thai markets is "a reliable source of imported products and fresh vegetables", "good seafood" and "exotic herbs and sauces", with a bonus of "great odors"; you're advised to "know what you want because it may not be labeled in English" and service isn't stellar; critics cite "uneven supply" and "not so clean" digs, but "if you're going to cook Thai, you must go here."

Bangluck Supermarket ⌺   <u>22</u> <u>24</u> <u>16</u> <u>I</u>

- *5170 Hollywood Blvd. (3 blocks east of Western Ave.),*
  Hollywood, 213-660-8000
  Every day 9am-10pm

Bangluck Supermarket (Cont.)

- *12980 Sherman Way (Coldwater Canyon Ave.),
  N. Hollywood, 818-765-1088
  Every day 9am-10pm*
- *7235 Reseda Blvd. (Sherman Way), Reseda, 818-708-0333
  Every day 8am-9pm*
- *1670 Indian Hill Blvd. (San Bernardino St.), Pomona,
  909-621-7666
  Every day 9am-9pm*

☑ For admirers, this Thai minichain's "fascinating variety" is "the best this side of Bangkok"; the big Pomona branch, with its "eye-opening" live seafood counters, is generally considered the best, but the other locales are also "good sources" of noodles, spices and more; the adjacent Bangluck-owned Sanamluang Cafes and Chinese BBQs are "a top source for takeout" (except at the no-takeout Reseda branch); service is the weak link.

Bay Cities Importing Co. 🚲   24 24 20 M

- *1517 Lincoln Blvd. (bet. Colorado Blvd. & B'way), Santa
  Monica, 310-395-8279
  M-Sat 7am-7pm/Sun 7am-6pm*

☑ Fans "couldn't live without" what they call the "best Italian source on the Westside", and while a small group of critics claim it's "not what it used to be", new management seems to be making positive change; most would gladly "go out of their way" for its "fresh pasta", "great olives", cheeses, oils and deli fare including terrific cold cuts and the "fattest subs in town at incredible prices"; there are Greek and Middle Eastern items too.

Bezjian's Grocery ⊄   23 24 21 I

- *4715 Santa Monica Blvd. (1 block west of Vermont Ave.),
  Hollywood, 213-663-1503
  M-Sat 10am-7pm/Sun 10am-5pm*

☑ This Armenian-owned Greek–Indian–Middle Eastern deli has been around for 30 years and still wins raves for its "lovely meat pies", dolmas, "amazing olive bread", "good sandwiches" and exotica such as Indian spices and dals; everyone likes the "warm, helpful service", but the growing wide availability of Mideastern foods and the declining neighborhood prompts some to ask: "is it worth the schlep to Hollywood?"

Bharat Bazaar ⊄   23 24 19 I

- *11510 W. Washington Blvd. (1 block west of Frwy. #405),
  Culver City, 310-398-6766
  W-M 11am-7pm*

■ This "fun, well-stocked" Culver City Indian market is "worth a trip just for the aromas", not to mention its supply of hard-to-find "authentic supplies" including spices, baked goods, rice, homemade pickles and more; the owner "gives great advice" and is "always ready to share cooking tips and recipes."

Bombay Spiceland ⇱ $\boxed{22}\;\boxed{23}\;\boxed{20}\;\boxed{I}$
- *8650 Reseda Blvd. (Parthenia St.), Northridge, 818-701-9383*
  T-Sat 11am-8pm/Sun 11am-7pm

■ As close to a supermarket as LA Indian stores get, this San Fernando Valley shop has a "mind-boggling" array of "chutneys, spices and rices", as well as a select choice of fresh herbs and vegetables, plus every bean and lentil known to man; fortunately, those not familiar with the sometimes baffling goods will find the staff "always helpful."

Buu-Dien ⇱ $\boxed{-}\;\boxed{-}\;\boxed{-}\;\boxed{I}$
- *642 N. Broadway (bet. Sunset Blvd. & Ord St.),*
  Chinatown, 213-617-8355
  Every day 8am-7pm

Chinatown's most complete Vietnamese charcuterie, where cold cuts and French-style pâtés are made and sold by the pound or piled into *banh mi* (sub sandwiches); other sandwich filling options include roast chicken and *sieu mai*, and there's an array of authentic snacks such as shredded green papaya salads and *goi cuon*, burritolike rice paper–wrapped rolls.

C&K Importing Co. $\boxed{26}\;\boxed{24}\;\boxed{22}\;\boxed{M}$
- *2771 W. Pico Blvd. (Normandie Ave.), Koreatown,*
  213-737-2970
  T-Sat 9am-7pm/Sun 9am-4pm

■ A "great place for Greek foods", with a deli case packed full of myriad olives, fetas, heavenly halvah and spanakopita, plus a tiny cafe next door offering super souvlaki; quality is "always reliable" and the staff is "helpful", as is the owner who really knows wines and offers them at excellent prices; cooking Ethiopian? you'll also find all the necessities here, including *injera*, the fresh Ethiopian pancake bread.

Carrillo's Tortilleria & Deli $\boxed{24}\;\boxed{22}\;\boxed{20}\;\boxed{I}$
- *1242 Pico St. (bet. Kalisher & Mission), San Fernando,*
  818-365-1636
  M-Sat 6am-6pm/Sun 6am-3pm
- *19744 Sherman Way (Corbin St.), Canoga Park, 818-887-6118*
  M-Sat 8am-8pm/Sun 8am-3pm
- *2836 Cochran St. (Sycamore), Simi Valley, 805-522-8939*
  M-Sat 8am-8pm/Sun 8am-3pm

◪ Some think this family-run minichain of Mexican-American delis and tortillerias makes "the best handmade corn tortillas"; everything is done from scratch, including the ground corn tortilla *masa* which may run out late in the day, so get there early; fans love the "wonderful burritos", "very good takeout" and "inexpensive catering", but a few feel the tamales "aren't as good as they were 10 years ago."

Catalina's Market
▽ 17 | 17 | 15 | I

- *1050 N. Western Ave. (Santa Monica Blvd.), Hollywood, 213-464-3595*
  M-F 9am-7:30pm/Sat 9am-8pm/Sun 6:30am-7pm

▇ Still a source for "Argentine ex-patriots who love to buy their *parillada* (mixed grill) meats" from the boisterous butcher counter at this Latin market that also dispenses "good empanadas", fresh produce, spices and more; still, as ratings suggest, there's room for improvement across the board; in recent times the market has turned distinctly Central American, with a Salvadoran-Guatemalan bakery and many Peruvian goods.

Claro's Italian Mkt.
25 | 23 | 22 | M

- *1003 E. Valley Blvd. (Delta), San Gabriel, 818-288-2026*
- *19½ Huntington Dr. (bet. Santa Anita Ave. & 1st St.), Arcadia, 818-446-0275*
- *101 W. Whittier Blvd. (Euclid Ave.), La Habra, 310-690-2844*
- *322 S. Glendora Ave., W. Covina, 818-918-8818*
- *1095 E. Main St. (Newport Ave.), Tustin, 714-832-3081*
- *1655 N. Mountain Ave. (16th Ave.), Upland, 909-946-2689*
  M,T,Th,F & Sat 9am-6pm/Sun 9am-2pm

▇ "Good smells and good prices" are the hallmarks of this Italian market where "authentic" Parma prosciutto, Parmesan cheese and other "always dependable" fare inspire such comments as "if only my grandmother had seen this store"; granny would have loved the handmade Christmas cookies and modern shoppers like the "very lean sausage" made at this family-run institution where fans say "one whiff and you're hooked."

Continental Gourmet
– | – | – | M

- *12921 S. Prairie Ave. (1 block south of El Segundo Blvd.), Hawthorne, 310-676-5444*
  Every day 9:30am-7pm

An undiscovered Hawthorne gem that bakes its own Argentine-style pastries, makes bread for its Argentine-Swiss sandwiches and has *matambre* and homemade *empanadas* beckoning from the deli; on Saturdays the excellent meat department is often jammed with men buying supplies for their *parillada* (mixed grill BBQ); Guatemalan and Peruvian tamales hint at the store's diverse Latin clientele.

DOMINGO'S
26 | 25 | 25 | M

- *17548 Ventura Blvd. (1½ blocks east of White Oak Ave.), Encino, 818-981-4466*
  T-Sat 9am-6pm/Sun 10am-4pm

▇ Fans say "almost everything is delicious and homemade-tasting" at this Italian shop that's been "family owned and run since it opened"; with a "good selection of pasta, cheese and sausages" and a "helpful, knowledgeable staff", it's one of the "best in the Valley"; the few dissenters who cite "not enough variety" and "run-of-the-mill" deli fare are soundly outvoted.

Dong Loi Seafood ⌂   — | — | — | M
- *13900 Brookhurst St. (Westminster), Garden Grove,
  714-534-1410
  Every day 9am-9pm*

Silvery fish glide in aquariumlike tanks and Dungeness crabs
inhabit floor tubs at this huge and very "authentic" Asian
seafood emporium with "good variety and prices"; freezers
are stocked with such things as ready-to-stir-fry squid and
eel as well as everyday shrimp and striped bass.

Ebisu ⌂   ▽ 24 | 22 | 23 | M
- *18930-40 Brookhurst St. (Garfield Ave.), Fountain Valley,
  714-962-2108
  M-Sat 10am-7pm/Sun 10am-6:30pm*

■ A fish store before it was a supermarket, this Fountain
Valley Japanese source built its name on "superb fresh fish",
with countermen who dress choices to order; the owner's
wife and her staff also cook wonderful takeout; they've also
opened a ramen shop and a bakery/cafe, inspiring the
comment "someday they'll own the whole shopping center."

Elat Middle Eastern Market 🚲   — | — | — | M
- *8730 W. Pico Blvd. (Robertson Blvd.), LA, 310-659-7070
  Sun-F 8am-8:30pm*

One of the largest West LA markets serving the Persian-
Jewish and Israeli communities, this Middle Easterner has a
teeming bazaarlike setting and has well-priced fresh herbs
and bargain produce; you can order fish-heads for gefilte
fish and the deli's myriad Israeli-style salads make for fine
impromptu buffets; exotic breads include Afghan flat bread,
fresh *tonir lavash* and Ashkenazi-style challah.

El Camaguay Market   — | — | — | L
- *10925 W. Venice Blvd. (Veteran Ave.), Venice, 310-839-4037
  Every day 8am-8pm*

Handmade cigars near the cash register, mountains of
plantains and frozen *guayaba* reflect this Venice market's
Cuban roots, but these days its inventory has expanded to
include everything needed for South and Central American
cooking as well – Brazilian *dende* oil, Peruvian *ollucos*,
Salvdoran quesadilla and all sorts of Spanish goods from
jamon serrano to *pimientos horneados*.

El Gallo Bakery ⌂   — | — | — | L
- *4546 Caesar Chavez Ave. (bet. 4th St. & Macdonald Ave.),
  East LA, 213-263-5528
  Every day 6am-9pm*

A huge turnover keeps the *pan dulces* at this well-run
Mexican bakery exquisitely fresh; over 50 styles of sweet
breads include the fancifully shaped *elotes* (corn ears),
novios (sweethearts), *nuez de cocoa* (coconuts) and *zapotes*
(fruits), all made by combining two styles of dough into
different forms; special decorated breads are made for
Christmas and Day of the Dead.

El Gallo Giro 🚴🏻🍴   ▽ 25 ⎥ 22 ⎥ 17 ⎥ I ⎥

- *7148 Pacific Ave. (Florence Ave.), Huntington Park,
  213-585-4433*
  M-Th 8am-8pm/F-Sat 8am-midnight/Sun 8am-10pm
- *142 S. Bristol St. (Edinger), Santa Ana, 714-549-2011*
  Every day 24 hrs
- *260 S. Broadway (3rd St.), Downtown LA, 213-626-6926*
  M-Th 8am-8pm/F & Sat 8am-midnight/Sun 8am-10pm
- *5686 E. Whittier Blvd. (Atlantic Blvd.), East LA, 713-726-1245*
  S-Th 7am-midnight/Fri & Sat 24 hrs
- *11912 Valley Blvd. (Garvey Blvd.), El Monte, 818-575-1244*
  M-Th 8am-11pm/F & Sat 24 hrs/Sun closes 11pm

■ Big and dazzling, these white-tiled emporiums are "where Mexicans eat great Mexican food"; with a restaurant, Mexican-style bakery, meat market, tortilleria and cake shop all under one roof, it's "fun to visit" and offers everything from typical street vendor fare, refreshing *aguas frescas* and real Mexico City–style quesadillas to "the best *tortas*" (sandwiches) and tacos.

El Mercado 🍴   ▽ 19 ⎥ 22 ⎥ 17 ⎥ I ⎥

- *3425 E. First St. (bet. Indiana & Lorena), East LA,
  213-268-3451*
  M-F 9am-8pm/Sat & Sun 9am-9pm

☑ Not the food shopping mecca it once was, this Mexican market's food stalls have mostly been replaced by swap meet–style clothing and cowboy boot vendors; one excellent deli remains, but the real reason to go on weekends is to hear "good mariachi bands."

Empanada's Place 🍴   22 ⎥ 20 ⎥ 20 ⎥ I ⎥

- *3811 Sawtelle Blvd. (Venice Blvd.), Mar Vista, 310-391-0888*
  Every day 11am-8pm
- *6136 Venice Blvd. (La Cienega Blvd.), Culver City,
  310-838-3061*
  M-Sat 11am-6pm

☑ Admirers "love their empanadas to take out or serve at parties", while detractors say the "food has deteriorated in the last few years"; but where else can you get those little pies with over a dozen different fillings?; most consider these Latins a "good experience" and handy for "picnics."

Enbun 🏪🍴   21 ⎥ 19 ⎥ 20 ⎥ M ⎥

- *124 Japanese Village Plaza Mall (bet. San Pedro &
  Central), Little Tokyo, 213-680-3280*
  M-Sat 9am-8pm/Sun 10am-6pm

☑ One of the older markets in Japantown, this store draws mixed reviews on the quality of its fish and some feel it's "overpriced and not well stocked"; still, "it's a good place to pick up a quick fix" if "you're Downtown" and its "small market feel" is nice; there's a "wide variety of utensils" too.

Ernie's European Imports 🖃 <u>_</u> | <u>_</u> | <u>_</u> | <u>M</u>

- *8400 Eighth Ave. (2 blocks off Crenshaw Blvd., north of Manchester Ave.), Inglewood, 213-752-1002*
  M 9am-3pm/T-Sat 9am-6pm

Misplaced in an Inglewood neighborhood that's no longer German, this "jewel of a market" is one of the city's "best-kept secrets", a place to stock up on Mozart liqueur–filled chocolates, double-smoked *geraucherter speck* (bacon) or *swarzwalder landschinken* (Black Forest) ham; at Christmas and Easter, their big seasons, they even offer mail-order catalogs; critics call the fare "too heavy."

Family Pastry ⊟ <u>_</u> | <u>_</u> | <u>_</u> | <u>I</u>

- *715 N. Spring St. (Ord St.), Chinatown, 213-622-5255*
  Every day 7am-5pm

Maybe it's the curry pork cookies that prompted one surveyor to call this simple Chinatown storefront "zany", but the place is well patronized, so the modestly priced dim sum and baked goods are always fresh; you'll find shrimp har gow in glutinous rice wrappers, pork-filled fried dumplings and various steamed and baked buns, but a few detractors feel that "quality has gone downhill."

Food Bag ⊟ <u>_</u> | <u>_</u> | <u>_</u> | <u>I</u>
(aka El Cubano)

- *11350 Victory Blvd. (Tujunga Blvd.), N. Hollywood, 818-506-0911*
  M-F 9am-7:45pm/Sat & Sun 8am-7:45pm

A little bit of Havana (or Miami) in the San Fernando Valley, this cheery supermarket stocks everything for la cocina Cubana: *naranjas agrias* (sour oranges used to marinate meats), *tasajo* (dried beef) *sofrito* in jars, and frozen Cuban tamales; its "good meat section" has American and Latin cuts plus Cuban nostalgia foods like Iron Beer and Malta Hatuey sodas; try the Cuban sandwich bar for a real treat.

Frances Bakery ▽ <u>23</u> | <u>20</u> | <u>21</u> | <u>M</u>

- *404 E. Second St. (Alameda), Little Tokyo, 213-680-4899*
  M-Sat 8am-7pm/Sun 8am-5pm

☑ Given the dearth of excellent French pastry shops in LA, many are pleased to find this Franco-Japanese in Little Tokyo doing "tasty French pastries", "beautiful cakes", "lovely bread" and, "believe it or not, the best croissants in LA", but some are put off by what they call "almost-Tokyo prices."

Friar Tuck Shoppe ▽ <u>22</u> | <u>19</u> | <u>21</u> | <u>M</u>

- *13638 Burbank Blvd. (½ block east of Woodman Ave.), Van Nuys, 818-785-4814*
  Every day 10am-7pm

■ "Where Robin Hood would shop if given the chance"; this "friendly little" Van Nuys place carries a small but "terrific" selection of house-baked British items; the excellent chicken and steak pies to bake fresh at home keep droves of Valley expat Brits (and others) returning.

97

Gallegos Mexican Deli   23 | 20 | 22 | I
- *1424 Broadway (15th St.), Santa Monica, 310-395-0162*
  M-Sat 7:30am-6pm/Sun 7:30am-4pm

■ On the Westside since the 1930s, this "friendly", "inexpensive" Mexican deli/minimart offers "excellent" tortillas made on-site, "really good enchiladas", a variety of freshly made salsas, wonderful "homemade tortilla chips" that are "great for a party" and other "delicious food"; the limited grocery section carries good Mexican cheeses, miniature chorizos and a few other specialty items.

Gastronom 🚲🚫   – | – | – | M
- *7859 Santa Monica Blvd. (Fairfax Ave.), W. Hollywood,*
  213-654-9456
  Every day 9am-9pm

Admirers say it's easy to feel like "a tsar" at this small Russian shop where the deli features everything needed for a showy *zakuska* (appetizer) spread, including assorted smoked fish, various eggplant salads and salmon caviar spooned from gallon containers; it all looks delicious but critics claim "some things are great, others horrible."

Goldilocks Bake Shops &   ▽ 21 | 22 | 20 | M
Restaurant
- *209 S. Vermont Ave. (north of 3rd St.), LA, 213-382-2351*
- *17538 Pioneer Blvd. (Artesia Blvd.), Artesia, 310-924-7679*
- *1559 E. Amar Rd. (Azusa Ave.), W. Covina, 818-964-1811*
  T-Sat 9am-8pm/Sun 9am-7pm

◪ With branches around LA, this successful Manila-based deli/bakery chain is where Filipinos come for their *pan de sal* rolls, amethyst-colored yam pudding and the exotic milk shake *halo halo*; fans call the wares "fun" and "luscious", but detractors "are not impressed or tempted"; the Artesia branch has a restaurant where you can get excellent fresh *lumpia*, the soft Filipino- style egg rolls.

Good Food   – | – | – | I
- *1864 E. Washington Blvd. (Allen), Pasadena, 818-794-5367*
  M-Sat 7am-9pm/Sun 8am-6pm

Almost any ingredient needed for Eastern Mediterranean or Arabic dishes can be found at this funky deli where women in babushkas exchange recipes verbally; all the requisite beans and grains are here, plus unusual fresh veggies and cookware such as molds for *mamoun*, walnut- or date-stuffed cookies with an imprinted design.

Granada Market 🚫   20 | 20 | 19 | M
- *1820 Sawtelle Blvd. (Nebraska), West LA, 310-479-0931*
  M-Sat 9:30am-7pm

◪ This old-line Japanese store is too authentic for those who say the staff has "a little difficulty translating into English"; but, regulars swear by its "small but good selection" of "fresh fish" (it also has meat, produce and more) and love its "nice mom-and-pop feel and helpful, friendly service."

Grand Central Market ✍ 18 25 16 I
• *317 S. Broadway (bet. 3rd & 4th Sts.), Downtown LA,
213-624-2378*
M-Sat 9am-6pm/Sun 10am-5pm
◼ This huge Downtown International food bazaar that's
long been undergoing a face-lift is quite a "cultural
experience" but can be "overwhelming"; each stall offers
something different, and if the pig's head is "hard to take"
for some, the "vendors are a kick", especially "Koreans
who speak perfect Spanish"; foes say "quality isn't great",
but you can still get the city's best *gorditas* at Ana-Maria's,
Latin-style seafood cocktails at Maria's Fresh Seafood,
cooked meats at Roast to Go and much more.

Hawthorne Market – – – M
• *24202 Hawthorne Blvd. (PCH), Torrance, 310-373-4448*
M-Sat 8am-8:30pm/Sun 9:30am-7pm
Afghan-style breads such as the sweet-yeasty *rote*, or
praki-lawaash – tortilla-thin and the size of a small
tablecloth – reflect the owners' heritage (they owned a
department store in Afghanistan before the war); but this
market also caters to Iranians and Indians who use many
of the same ingredients; surveyors appreciate the "good
selection" that includes no fewer than 15 kinds of rice at
"very good prices."

Holland American Market ✍ – – – M
• *10343 Artesia Blvd. (bet. Woodruff & Studebaker),
Bellflower, 310-867-7589*
M-Sat 8am-6pm
LA's oldest and largest Dutch store is one of the last vestiges
of what used to be a Dutch milk-farming community in
Bellflower; in addition to cakes, cookies, cured herring and
cheeses imported from Holland there are loads of giftware,
cookware and a whole line of Dutch-Indonesian groceries.

Hong Kong Market 23 25 14 I
• *18414 Colima Rd. (Fullerton Ave.), Rowland Heights,
818-964-1688*
• *137 S. San Gabriel Blvd. (Las Tunas Dr.), San Gabriel,
818-309-1111*
• *127 N. Garfield Blvd. (near Garvey Ave.), Monterey Park,
818-280-8888*
Every day 9am-10pm
◼ Like many of its patrons, the former Chinatown branch
of this shop moved to the suburbs where, in Rowland
Heights, it opened one of the best Chinese markets
anywhere; the huge San Gabriel Valley sites also have a
"great selection" at "low prices"; a few foes find them
"overwhelming" and most would agree service isn't a
strong point; at the Monterey Park store, specialty vendors
sell baked goods, Chinese teas and exotic pharmaceuticals
from stalls around the perimeter.

Ethnic Food Sources

India Sweets & Spices
21 22 18 I

- *22011 Sherman Way (Topanga Canyon Blvd.),
  Canoga Park, 818-887-0868
  Every day 10am-9pm*
- *9409 Venice Blvd. (Overland Ave.), Culver City, 310-837-5286
  Every day 9am-9pm*
- *1020 Huntington Dr. (Mountain Rd.), Duarte, 818-357-6899
  T-Sun 11am-9pm*
- *18191 S. Pioneer Blvd. (183rd St.), Artesia, 310-809-3191
  Every day 11am-8pm*
- *14441 Newport Ave. (Walnut St.), Tustin, 714-731-2910
  T-Sat 10:30am-9pm*
- *133 E. Palmdale Blvd. (6th St.), Palmdale, 805-273-7339
  Sun-Th 10am-8:30pm/F & Sat 10am-9pm*
- *2643 Vineyard Ave. (Ekinger Rd.), Oxnard, 805-579-8443
  T-Sat 11am-8pm*

☑ All locations of this Indian market/deli are independently owned which may be why the stores vary so; but many fans of the Culver City and San Fernando Valley branches feel they're "user-friendly" with an "outstanding variety of curries", "great takeout" and "hard-to-find goods" all at "bargain" prices; but, some sites could use "a cleanup."

Jordan Market 🚲
– – – M

- *1449 Westwood Blvd. (Ohio Ave.), Westwood, 310-478-1706
  Every day 9am-9pm*

Don't expect an Arabic-style deli with stuffed grape leaves or tabbouleh; instead, this midpriced Westwood Near Eastern market is where butchers cut kebabs to order Persian style and you'll find such goodies as dainty, flower-shaped cookies the size of a dime and bath mat–size tandoor breads; there are also bushy bunches of fenugreek, dill and such; P.S. "the best produce is hidden in the back."

Juanito's Tamales ✂
– – – I

- *4214 Floral Dr. (bet. Easter & Mariana Sts.), City Terrace,
  213-268-2365
  M-F 9am-6pm/Sat 7am-6pm/Sun 7am-3pm*

You can watch the women in Juanito's open kitchen carefully wrapping long slender tamales as though each were a gift; they make "the best in LA", both sweet and savory; at holiday time people buy them by the dozens, so get your order in early.

Koreatown Plaza Market ✂
23 26 18 I

- *928 S. Western Ave. (9th St.), Koreatown, 213-385-1100
  M-F 10am-9pm/Sat 10am-9:30pm*

■ "A Korean Gelson's" set in a polished mauve-and-green-marble shopping mall that rivals the Rodeo Collection; offering everything from "fresh produce" to an array of prepared foods, it's praised for its "attractive presentation" that makes shopping "easy for civilians" taking a "trip into Korean food and merchandise"; yet for all its modernity, it's still "another world."

Kowloon Market 🥡   23 | 23 | 14 | I |
- *750 N. Hill St. (bet. Ord & Alpine), Chinatown, 213-488-0264*
  Every day 9am-8pm

■ Even with all the new competition this venerable Chinatown store still has admirers who advise "ignore the smells" – it's "really good" and has "everything you need for Chinese delights"; "good vegetables and meats" plus excellent canned goods keep customers returning, but given its location across from Ocean Seafood restaurant, "good luck finding parking" at mealtimes.

Kuo's Bakery ▣   – | – | – | M |
- *1430 W. Valley Blvd. (Atlantic Blvd.), Alhambra, 818-458-0688*
- *Mar's Plaza, 141 N. Atlantic Blvd. (Garvey Ave.),*
  Monterey Park, 818-457-8855
- *Hong Kong Market Plaza, 135 S. San Gabriel Blvd.,*
  San Gabriel, 818-285-8588
- *Diamond Sq., 818 E. Garvey Ave. (bet. Rosemead &*
  San Gabriel Blvds.), Rosemead, 818-571-8800
- *1220 S. Golden West Ave. (Duarte), Arcadia, 818-821-4888*
- *18743 Pioneer Blvd., Artesia, 310-860-8608*
- *1631 Azusa Ave. (Colima Ave.), Hacienda Heights,*
  818-854-5818
- *3800 Barranca Pkwy. (Culver), Irvine, 714-551-8255*
- *Mail order: 800-828-1689*
  Every day 9am-9pm

With its 800 phone number and beautiful color catalog, this Taiwanese-owned bakery chain is up-to-date, but its famous traditional Chinese moon cakes and green bean pastries are based on ancient recipes; its western cakes are "beautiful" as well, though the supply is a bit "limited."

La Adelita 🥡   – | – | – | I |
- *5812 Santa Monica Blvd. (Western Ave.), Hollywood,*
  213-465-6526
  Every day 6am-10:30pm
- *1287 Union Ave. (Pico Blvd.), LA, 213-487-0176*
  Every day 6am-10pm

The Hollywood branch of this Latin deli has a block-long counter brimming with homestyle Mexican and Central American dishes; at both you'll find *pupusas* and crisp fried plantain strips served with beans and cultured cream, whole roast turkeys sliced to order for *tortas*, and banana leaf–wrapped Central American tamales; but it also has detractors: "handmade tortillas good, prepared food bad."

La Azteca 🥡   – | – | – | I |
- *4538 Cesar Chavez (4th St.), East LA, 213-262-5977*
  M-F 7am-5pm/Sat & Sun 6am-3:30pm

Hand-formed "great fresh tortillas" are this nondescript shop's claim to fame; the flour tortillas made with purified lard thrill fans who disdain the machine-made variety; you can also buy their fresh *masa preparada* and homemade tamales or they'll whip up a burrito for you while you wait.

La Española ▭   – | – | – | M

- *25020 Doble Ave. (Vermont Ave.), Harbor City, 310-539-0455*
  M-F 6am-5pm/Sat & Sun 9am-5pm

This Spanish market started out as a tiny extension of a sausage factory where owner Juana Faraone produces such things as *butifarra Catalana, morcilla con arroz*, paprika-laced *sobrasada* and Spanish-style *jamon serrano* to ship nationwide; it's now much enlarged, with a bigger shop and deli offering many more foods and many items to taste; call for a catalog.

L.A. Man Wah ⌑   22 | 24 | 15 | I

- *758 New High St. (Alpine St.), Chinatown, 213-613-1942*
  Every day 8:30am-7pm

■ One of the first big supermarkets in Chinatown still attracts loyalists who call it the area's "best all-purpose, full-service grocer"; live turtles fascinate kids and help make shopping here "feel like an outing in China", so "check your cultural preconceptions" at the door; there's also a "great produce section" and "more sauces than you can imagine."

La Plaza Market   – | – | – | M

- *19239 Roscoe Blvd. (Tampa Ave.), Northridge, 818-701-5005*
  M-Sat 8am-8pm/Sun 8am-7pm

A neighborhood Northridge market chock full of "very good Guatemalan and Mexican stuff"; you'll find Mexican and South American cheeses, house-made Salvadoran and Mexican sausages, frozen *yuca* and fruit purees plus the usual south-of-the-border-style produce.

Liborio Market ⌑🚲   – | – | – | M

- *864 S. Vermont Ave. (9th St.), Koreatown, 213-386-1458*
  Every day 7am-9pm

"No ambiance but a great source" for Cuban and Central American goods; cassava, yuca and banana leaves for wrapping tamales are heaped in the produce area; the shelves dazzle with plantain flour, annatto paste, tropical fruit purees and cans of black beans — mashed and whole; butchers cut meats *a su gusto* and there's a Central American bakery near the door.

Little Saigon Supermarket   – | – | – | I

- *9822 Bolsa Ave. (Brookhurst Ave.), Westminster,*
  714-531-7272
  Every day 8am-5pm

Vanco Foods

- *10932 Westminster Ave. (Euclid), Garden Grove,*
  714-530-2999
  Every day 8:30am-8:30pm

Little Saigon Supermarket has a "good variety" including an excellent mix of Indonesian, Thai, Malay and Chinese items; it's also "very clean", with such modern conveniences as diced or jullienned wok- ready meats and a large take-out snack area; it has a sibling, Vanco Foods, on Westminster.

Los Cinco Puntos 🍴 ⌐–⌐–⌐–⌐ I⌐
- *3300 Cesar Chavez Ave. (Lorena St.), East LA, 213-261-4084*
  Th-T 8am-6pm

Handmade corn tortillas, succulent carnitas and huge mounds of salsas and guacamoles have drawn a devoted clientele here since 1967; do-it-yourselfers still come in to buy tubs of *masa preparada* to make their own tamales at home; they're probably the same ones who buy the whole lamb heads for stew or taco fillings.

Market World ⌐–⌐–⌐–⌐ M⌐
(fka Hanaam)
- *2740 W. Olympic Blvd. (Vermont), Koreatown, 213-382-2922*
  Every day 8am-10pm
- *3030 W. Sepulveda Blvd. (Maple), Torrance, 310-539-8899*
  Every day 7am-midnight

The new Market World in Torrance is larger and spiffier than the older Koreatown branch, but both have a deli area where you can watch the cooks grill savory Korean pancakes and serve take-out orders of *chap-che* noodles; fans think that even the older store is "clean and organized" with "excellent salad greens and a good meat department", but at either, service doesn't always leap the "language barrier."

Miller's Market ▽ ⌐21⌐ 26⌐ 18⌐ I⌐
- *18248 Sherman Way (Etiwanda), Reseda, 818-345-9222*
  M-Th, Sat 8am-8pm/F & Sun 8am-7:30pm

◪ Offering a fairly complete selection of "good Iranian products" and kosher meat that will be increased when the shop's current remodeling and expansion is complete; they stock meaty turkey parts for kebabs, bunches of fresh herbs and other makings for Persian cuisine: sumac, barberries, pomegranate concentrate, dried sour cherries, saffron, sour grape juice and a delightful selection of baked goods.

Mirch Masala 🍴 ⌐–⌐–⌐–⌐ I⌐
- *8516 Reseda Blvd. (Chase), Northridge, 818-772-7691*
  T-Sat 10:30am-9pm/Sun & M 10:30am-8:30pm

It's not the limited grocery section of this Northridge Indian market/cafe that's the main draw, rather, it's a voluptuous array of takeout chat (snacks) that can easily make a meal, such as rotund samosas, fresh onion *bajis*, *pani puri*, mango *lassi* and creamy sweetened cheese desserts such as *dil bahar* and *rasgolla*; besides edible goodies, the shop also has what must be LA's largest choice of Indian movies.

Monte Carlo ⌐25⌐ 25⌐ 24⌐ I⌐
- *3103 W. Magnolia Blvd. (Buena Vista), Burbank, 818-845-3516*
  M-Sat 9am-8pm/Sun 9am-6pm

◼ Enthusiasts love this Burbank Italian store for its "great smells" that "jump start the senses" and "old country atmosphere" that makes you "think you're in South Philly"; most find the "terrific variety" of food to be "excellent and very reasonable", but foes say it's "just ok, only in a pinch."

Mousse Fantasy ⊄ | – | – | – | M |
- *2130 Sawtelle Blvd. (Olympic Blvd.), West LA, 310-479-6665*
  T-Sat 11am-8pm/Sun 11am-6pm

French pastries created for the Japanese palate are lighter and not as sweet as the originals and they're catching on with sweet lovers of every persuasion; raspberry mousse cake, pear charlotte and fruit tarts are delectable here; for a venture into something cross-cultural try Mousse Fantasy's specialty green tea mousse cake or a spaghetti omelet from the cafe menu.

Nijiya Market | 22 | 20 | 19 | M |
- *2130 Sawtelle Blvd. (Olympic Blvd.), West LA, 310-575-3300*
- *2121 W. 182nd St. (Van Ness Ave.), Torrance, 310-366-7200*
- *2533 PCH (Crenshaw Blvd.), Torrance, 310-534-3000*
- *17555 Colima Rd. (Albatross Ave.), City of Industry,*
  818-913-9991
  Every day 10am-9pm

☑ "A bit of Tokyo on Sawtelle", this convenience shop with bento-box meals to go, "good fresh sushi to take home" and "friendly service" is part of a four-store chain; those who think the takeout is only "fair" might want to try the Torrance branches where food is made on the premises and then delivered to the Sawtelle locale.

99 Price Market ⊄ ▽ | 26 | 28 | 18 | I |
- *9221 Bolsa Ave. (Magnolia), Westminster, 714-894-3888*
  Every day 9am-9pm

■ Under the same ownership as 99 Ranch, this large Asian supermarket in Little Saigon offers a "super selection" at low prices; carnivores call it the "Gelson's of Chinese meats", and it also offers "good fish", wonderful herbs, noodles and more; it's like "walking into Saigon" without leaving LA.

99 Ranch Market | 24 | 27 | 16 | I |
- *988 N. Hill St. (Bernard St.), Chinatown, 213-625-3399*
- *Every day 8:30am-8pm*
- *6450 N. Sepulveda Blvd. (Victory Blvd.), Van Nuys,*
  818-988-7899
- *Every day 8:30am-8pm*
- *1300 S. Golden West Ave. (Baldwin St.), Arcadia,*
  818-445-7899
- *Every day 9am-9pm*
- *1340 W. Artesia Blvd. (bet. Normandie & Vermont Aves.),*
  Gardena, 310-323-3399
- *Every day 9am-9pm*
- *140 W. Valley Blvd. (Del Mar Ave.), San Gabriel, 818-307-8899*
- *Every day 9am-10pm*
- *1015 S. Nogales St. (Gate Ave.), Rowland Hts., 818-964-5888*
- *Every day 9am-10pm*
- *651 N. Euclid St. (Crescent Ave.), Anaheim, 714-776-8899*
- *Every day 9am-9pm*

99 Ranch Market (Cont.)
- *15333 Culver Dr. (Deerfield), Irvine, 714-651-8899*
  Every day 9am-9pm

T & T Supermarket
- *771 W. Garvey Ave. (Atlantic Blvd.), Monterey Park,*
  818-458-3399
- *1388 S. Fullerton Rd. (Frwy. #60), Rowland Hts., 818-965-7788*
- *8150 E. Garvey Ave. (San Gabriel Blvd.), Rosemead,*
  818-573-3699
  Every day 9am-10pm

☑ You'll "feel like Marco Polo" at this "Disneyland of Asian foods", a large supermarket chain with all kinds of Chinese and SE Asian goods, including live seafood, "the best veggies" and many "hard-to-find items"; quality, service and variety "vary" by store and it helps to have "a translator", but the staff is friendly and you'll "always find bargains here."

Olson's Deli ✍   ▽ 25 | 20 | 23 | M
- *5660 W. Pico Blvd. (4 blocks east of Fairfax Ave.), LA,*
  213-938-0742
  T-Sat 10am-5pm

■ "A pre-Christmas visit is a tradition" for fans of what some call "the only good Swedish store left", where you'll find a "limited but very good herring selection" and the whole gamut of Scandinavian cheeses such as *Nokkelost*, *Vasterbotten* and *Finnish Lappi,* a small array of homemade items includes Swedish-style pâté, meatballs, potato sausage and *medisterpolse* sausage.

Otto & Sons ✍   _ | _ | _ | M
- *2320 W. Clark Ave. (Buenavista St.), Burbank,*
  818-845-0433
  M-Sat 9am-7pm

Central European bric-a-brac gathering dust on the shelves strikes some as "tacky", but others ignore the setting because LA's only Hungarian deli has a "good variety" of delectables including such hard-to-find items as *fustolt karaj,* a smoked and dried filet mignon, *teli szalami, gyulai kolbasz* and *praszt kolbasz* sausages; the shop makes wonderful sandwiches and carries Hungarian groceries.

Pacific Market ✍   ▽ 21 | 23 | 21 | M
(fka New Meiji Market)
- *1620 W. Redondo Beach Blvd. (bet. Western &*
  Normandie Aves.), Gardena, 310-323-7696
  M-F 9am-8pm/Sat & Sun 8am-8pm

☑ This place once astonished people with its array of Japanese packaged goods, from myriad styles of fish cake and seaweed-wrapped rice crackers to green tea–flavored gum; nowadays folks are less amazed but still praise its "excellent variety and quality", fine fish, "lots of Japanese-Hawaiian" items and "fair prices"; however, views of the produce vary from "excellent" to "not as fresh as you want."

Panos Pastry 🚴   23 | 23 | 23 | M
- *5150 Hollywood Blvd. (1 block west of Normandie Ave.), Los Feliz, 213-661-0335*
- *17145 Ventura Blvd. (Louise Ave.), Encino, 818-783-9361*
- *418 S. Central Ave. (Colorado Blvd.), Glendale, 818-502-0549*
- *10500 Magnolia Ave. (Cerritos), Anaheim, 714-826-4080*
  Every day 8am-8pm

■ Famous for his pastries in Beirut, Panos Zeitlein now owns four locations in Hollywood offering a huge variety of "yummy" Near Eastern sweets, including "unsurpassable", "gorgeous" baklava; fans also love the "honey-dripping *kataif*", French-influenced pastries and fabulous chocolates.

Porto's Cuban Bakery ⌷   – | – | – | M
- *815 N. Brand Blvd. (Lexington), Glendale, 818-956-5996*
  M-Sat 8am-6pm/Sun 8am-2pm

The sights and sounds of Old Havana are embodied in this wonderful Glendale bakery and cafe where patrons line up for garlic-marinated roast pork Cuban sandwiches, meat pies, *papas rellenas* and pastries that include wine-drenched *capuchinos*, rum-soaked *panatella borachas* and fabulous custard and fruit-filled cakes.

Red Ribbon Bake Shop   ▽ 27 | 23 | 20 | M
- *6091 Sunset Blvd. (Gower), Hollywood, 213-465-5999*
- *2550 E. Amar Rd. (Nogales St.), W. Covina, 818-964-9940*
- *11900 South St. (Pioneer Blvd.), Cerritos, 310-402-3304*
- *Del Amo Ctr., 3550 Carson St., Torrance, 310-542-1991*
  M-Sat 10am-7:30pm/Sun 10am-6pm

■ These Manila-style pastry shops are most famous for their "mango cake to die for" and the purple taro *ube* cake that's "worth a drive to try"; other items such as chicken empanadas, *pan de sal* and tissue-wrapped *polvoron* cookies reflect the Spanish influence on the Philippines.

Rincon Chileno Restaurant   ▽ 20 | 21 | 21 | I
& Deli
- *4354 Melrose Ave. (Vermont Ave.), LA, 213-666-6075*
  T-Th 11am-10pm/F & Sat 11am-11pm/Sun 11am-9pm

■ An extension of a Chilean restaurant, this bargain hole-in-the-wall deli is where you can get "great picnic" or eat-at-home foods such as calzone-size beef empanadas, *humitas* (a sort of Chilean tamale) and a corn custard–topped chicken pie, *pastel de chocolo*, that's "delicious."

Ron's Market ⌷   21 | 26 | 16 | I
- *5270 Sunset Blvd. (Western Ave.), Hollywood, 213-465-1164*
  Every day 8am-10pm

◪ This Armenian-owned supermarket is not only a "heaven for Central and SE European immigrants", it's also said to be "like a trip to the Middle East", with an array of Near Eastern and European breads, cheeses, smoked fish; "good deli, sausages and cheap fresh herbs"; foes say this "noisy, crowded" place has "huge bargains but uneven quality."

Royal Gourmet   – – – M
- *8151 Santa Monica Blvd. (Crescent Heights),*
  W. Hollywood, 213-650-5001
  Every day 9am-9pm

This fancy Russian deli has 20 varieties of caviar; most of it's pasteurized, but with its 16 kinds of cold salads, an array of smoked fish, homemade gefilte fish, Russian soups, piroshki, plus freshly baked cakes and cookies, noshers will be kept abundantly indulged.

Safe & Save ⌗   25 22 21 M
- *2030 Sawtelle Blvd. (bet. Santa Monica & Olympic Blvds.),*
  West LA, 310-479-3810
  M-Sat 10am-7pm/Sun 10am-6pm

■ A fixture in the Japantown-West area of Sawtelle with "lots of variety packed into a small store", including "excellent sukiyaki meat", "wonderful fish for do-it-yourself sushi" and good chicken; "friendly people work here" and they're "very helpful to the novice" Japanese cook.

Seafood City   – – – M
- *3660 S. Nogales (La Puente), W. Covina, 818-964-5093*
- *12811 Sherman Way (½ mile north of Laurel Canyon Blvd.),*
  North Hollywood, 818-764-0300
  M-F 8:30am-9pm/Sat & Sun 8am-9pm

A bevy of languages is spoken at this splashy new Filipino-owned market that carries Mexican and Near Eastern products too; fish and seafood, though abundant, can be a gamble – either very fresh or over-the-hill; on the shelves you'll find staples arranged by ethnic group plus an interesting mix of produce and a small Filipino bakery and takeout near the front door.

Silom Thailand Plaza   – – – I
- *5321 Hollywood Blvd. (bet. Western & Normandie Aves.),*
  Hollywood, 213-993-9000
  Every day 10am-10pm

"Cleaner than Bangkok Market with less soul" is one view of this midsized Thai market, but the plaza it's located in, with its Thai video shop and campy restaurant/nightclub, is a clone of modern shopping complexes in Thailand; the food, especially the herb selection, can be lackluster, but the array of Thai curry pastes and seasonings is fun to explore.

Song Long Bakery ⌗   – – – I
- *9433 Bolsa Ave. (Bushard St.), Westminster, 714-531-0792*
  Every day 8am-7pm

What started as a small Vietnamese bakery has evolved into a full-fledged deli; besides baguettes, croissants, stuffed pâté chaud and other baked goods, it offers *banh mi*, submarine-like sandwiches filled with Vietnamese-style pâté and cold cuts (also sold by the pound), exotic snacks in rice paper, sweet coconut milk desserts and more.

107

Sorrento Italian Market | 24 | 25 | 20 | M |

- *5518 Sepulveda Blvd. (bet. Jefferson & Sawtelle Blvds.),
  Culver City, 310-391-7654
  M-Sat 7am-7pm/Sun 7am-4pm*

☑ Devotees call this family-run Italian shop "a Westside treasure" with "a neighborhood feel", "crowded aisles full of finds" and "bargains in fresh take-out" foods; foes say it's "packed so full it's hard to move around", "overrated" and "expensive" with slow service – in sum, "not worth it."

Tarzana Armenian Grocery | 26 | 22 | 22 | M |

- *18598 Ventura Blvd. (Reseda Blvd.), Tarzana, 818-881-6278
  M-Sat 8am-8pm/Sun 10am-5pm*
- *22776 Venture Blvd. (Fallbrook Ave.), Woodland Hills,
  818-225-1854
  M-Sat 8am-10pm/Sun 8am-8pm*

☑ Actually two Middle Eastern shops: the Tarzana original, "owned by the same family for over 20 years", is a market/ deli that has "lots" of items "in a little store"; at the newer, larger place in Woodland Hills there's more emphasis on the restaurant and takeout; both locations "make a mean falafel", "great" rolled lavash sandwiches and what fans call "by far the best hummus" and baba ghanoush in the city.

Tatiana | – | – | – | I |

- *8205 Santa Monica Blvd. (1 block west of Crescent Hts.),
  W. Hollywood, 213-656-7500
  Every day 9am-9pm*

Fans rave that this Russian shop has "the best chopped liver" and "the only knishes worth the title in this city"; other low-cost delights include the *zaftig* stuffed cabbage, baked eggplant with a lemon-garlic mayo and unusual salads like beets flecked with walnuts; while most agree the goods are "highest quality", some cite occasional "poor service."

Tbilisy & Yerevan ⌷   ▽ | 24 | 20 | 19 | I |

- *7862 Santa Monica Blvd. (Fairfax Ave.), W. Hollywood,
  213-654-7427
  Every day 7am-9pm*

■ "What bread is meant to be" say fans of this shop's clay oven–baked Georgian and Armenian breads that include *shotis puri* and "terrific" lavosh; patrons also "love the stuffed eggplant", chicken with *satsivi* (rich walnut sauce) and other Georgian items.

Top Valu ⌷ | – | – | – | I |

- *4700 Inglewood Blvd. (Braddock St.), Culver City,
  310-390-9639*
- *4831 Whittier Blvd., East LA, 213-268-4280*
- *342 S. Whittier Blvd., Boyle Heights, 213-266-1629*
- *2038 E. Tenth St. (Cherry Ave.), Long Beach, 310-438-1062*
- *421 Pacific Ave. (5th St.), Long Beach, 310-437-7866*
- *10819 Hawthorne Blvd., Lennox, 310-671-7988*
- *420 S. Long Beach Blvd., Compton, 310-631-5136*

Top Valu (Cont.)
• *1120 S. Bristol St., Santa Ana, 714-957-2529*
  Every day 7am-10pm
In addition to the usual Mexican supermarket staples
you'll find a good choice of fresh and dried chilies, chorizos,
Mexican-style cheeses, *cremas,* a variety of Mexican
canned goods and meats cut Latin style, all at good
prices; several branches have excellent hot delis.

Tudor House 🍽 23 20 21 M
• *1504 Second St. (Santa Monica Blvd.), Santa Monica,*
  310-451-4107
  M-Sat 10am-6pm/Sun 11am-6pm
◪ This Santa Monica shop and tearoom has "super foods,
just like London", "lovely high tea" and "wonderful scones";
while some cite "best selection of English imports", others
say it "lacks variety" and claim you "have to be a Brit to get
service" because "the staff has a very 'English' attitude."

United Foods ✍ _ _ _ M
• *736 N. Broadway (Alpine), Chinatown, 213-624-3788*
• *419 Alpine St. (Broadway), Chinatown, 213-620-0368*
  Every day 9am-5pm
Whole sides of roast pork and ducks hang in this old-time
Chinatown spot where cooked meats are a specialty; with
advance notice owner Nelson Moy will provide fresh game
birds, venison, or boar, and he also stocks frozen alligator
and possum, which may explain the comment "good for eye-
catching ideas"; they also run a seafood shop on Alpine.

Valley Food Warehouse Inc. _ _ _ M
• *14530 Nordhoff (Van Nuys), Panorama City, 818-891-9939*
  Every day 7am-10:45pm
If you need a fast bite of seviche or a Salvadoran *pupusa*
or want to stock up on Peruvian *pisco* for a *pisco* sour,
Yucatecan *recados* (spice pastes) for *pollo en pibil,* thick
Mexican *jocoque* (like crème fraîche), or some marinated
adobada de res for your barbecue, this pan-Latin has it all.

Van Nuys German Deli _ _ _ M
• *16155 Roscoe Blvd. (Woodley Ave.), North Hills, 818-892-2212*
  T-F 10am-6pm/Sat 10am-5pm
The place may be plain-looking but the "quality is high" and
prices moderate at this well-stocked German deli; sample
the prosciutto-like *knochenschinken,* the fragrant, smoky
nusschinken and the light chicken *sulze.*

Van's Bakery ✍ _ _ _ l
• *San Gabriel Sq., 140 E. Valley Blvd. (Del Mar Ave.),*
  San Gabriel, 818-288-7272
• *9211 Bolsa Ave. (Magnolia Ave.), Westminster, 714-898-7065*
• *14346 Brookhurst St. (Westminster Ave.), Garden Grove,*
  714-839-1666

Van's Bakery (Cont.)

- *121 E. Valley Blvd. (Del Mar Ave.), San Gabriel, 818-571-5845*
  Sun-Th 8am-8pm/F & Sat 8am-9pm

Van's hodgepodge of French *gateaux* look-alikes, Chinese teacakes and weird Southeast Asian banana-coconut milk drinks and puddings reflect Vietnam's ties with its Chinese immigrants and French Colonials; "communication can be difficult" but pointing and smiling works fine; try a French-Vietnamese submarine sandwich loaded with cold cuts.

Vin Hoa   – – – I

- *1241 E. Anaheim Blvd. (Orange Ave.), Long Beach,*
  310-599-3188
- *1145 Long Beach Blvd. (10th St.), Long Beach, 310-436-2332*
  Every day 9am-8:30pm

In the middle of America's largest Cambodian community, Vin Hoa stocks a pan-Asian selection that inspires such comments as "my home" from Asian-loving Southbay cooks; even those not familiar with all the items at this midsized, well-stocked market enjoy shopping here because "they take time to talk with you and explain."

Yaohan 🖃   26 25 20 M

- *333 S. Alameda St. (3rd St.), Little Tokyo, 213-687-6699*
- *3760 Centinela Ave. (Venice Blvd.), Mar Vista, 310-398-2113*
- *21515 Western Ave. (Carson), Torrance, 310-782-0335*
- *515 W. Las Tunas Dr. (Del Mar), San Gabriel, 818-457-2899*
- *665 Paularino Ave., Costa Mesa, 714-557-6699*
  Every day 9:30am-8pm

◪ With five locations in SoCal, each (except the San Gabriel Valley branch) with its own food court of fast-food eateries, these stores are called the "closest thing to Japan in LA" by admirers of their "spectacular selection" and "beautiful presentation" (except the "prepackaged fish"); foes find them "kind of plastic", "too big to get help" and "expensive."

Ye Olde Kings Head Gift Shoppe   22 19 20 M

- *132 Santa Monica Blvd. (2nd St.), Santa Monica, 310-394-8765*
  M-Sat 10am-6pm/Sun noon-5pm

◪ Next to a well-known British pub, this Santa Monica shop is "ersatz English, but fun"; it tends to have "more china than food" and though the tea may be "well priced, not all varieties are on hand"; some find the service a bit "cheeky."

Yie Mei Chinese Pastry 🏴   – – – I

- *Di Ho Shopping Ctr., 736 S. Atlantic Blvd. (4 blocks south*
  of Garvey Blvd.), Monterey Park, 818-284-9306
  Every day 7am-8pm

Taiwanese in style, this Monterey Park bakery is a gold mine of sweet and savory treats including delicious scallion pancakes, pork and green onion turnovers and steamed buns with assorted fillings; prices are modest and baked goods are always "very fresh" – sit in the cafe and order yours with bowls of sweet or savory soy milk.

Fish

With the Pacific Ocean as our backyard, it's not surprising that Southern California has some of the best fish in the world, especially the seafood sold in various ethnic markets, where absolute freshness (as for sushi) is imperative. The impressive supply of fish here also has something to do with our belief that fish is good for you – and if something is good for you, we like to eat it in large quantities. (As Jerry Seinfeld says, "You know why you've never seen a fat fish? Because they eat fish.")

Though fish abounds in LA, you will pay plenty for it at the higher-end establishments. But you don't have to; a journey to any of the Asian markets, e.g. 99 Ranch, Ebisu, Yaohan, will help you find superb seafood at a fraction of the cost.

Top Quality
28 Santa Monica Seafood
 Fish King
27 Bristol Farms
26 Gordon's Market
 Davy's Market

Top Variety
28 Santa Monica Seafood
27 Fish King
26 99 Ranch
25 Gordon's Market
 Davy's Market

Top Service
27 Davy's Market
26 Fish King
 Bristol Farms
25 Gelson's Markets
 Santa Monica Seafood

Best Buys
 Fish King
 Santa Monica Seafood
 Davy's Market
 99 Ranch Market
 Gordon's Market

Q	V	S	C
27	25	26	E

BRISTOL FARMS
• *See listing in Supermarkets section.*
■ The top-rated supermarket fish source, Bristol Farms' four branches have "excellent" seafood sections featuring a "really fresh" assortment that's big enough so shoppers "always find" what they need, aided by a "knowledgeable staff"; they also offer what some call the "best sushi of any market", made in-house; "expect high quality, and expect to pay for it."

–	–	–	M

Captain Kidd's ▣
• *Redondo Beach Marina, 209 N. Harbor Dr. (Beryl St.), Redondo Beach, 310-372-7703*
 Sun-Th 9am-9pm/F & Sat 9am-10pm
Just north of the Redondo Pier, this fish market/restaurant is treasured by locals for its extensive selection of fresh seafood; prices are reasonable, and Captain Kidd's catch is also available prepared-to-go with a choice of charbroiling, grilling, deep-frying and Cajun spicing.

Chalet Gourmet 🚲   24 | 22 | 23 | E
- *7880 Sunset Blvd. (Fairfax Ave.), LA, 213-874-6301*
  M-Sat 9am-9pm
■ Better known for its top grade meats, this Sunset Blvd.
market "for the rich and famous" also has "reliable", "very
fresh", "high-quality" seafood; while shoppers carp about
"high prices", they return for specialties such as the "best
seafood sausage" and because this is "one of the few spots
that sells fish heads and bones for stock and bouillon."

DAVY'S FISH MARKET ↯   26 | 25 | 27 | M
- *9127 Reseda Blvd. (Nordhoff St.), Northridge, 818-886-3955*
  Every day 9am-7pm
■ "Lines can be long" at the "best fish market in the SF
Valley", but a fine selection of "excellent" fresh seafood
and "friendly" service make it "worth the wait"; prepared
takeout includes "fab poached salmon", "great tempura"
and fish 'n' chips; those in the swim of things swear that
shopping here "makes one feel healthy and clean."

FISH KING   28 | 27 | 26 | M
- *722 N. Glendale Ave. (bet. Monterey Rd. & Glenoaks Ave.),*
  Glendale, 818-244-2161
  M-Sat 9am-7pm/Sun 11am-5pm
- *19550 Ventura Blvd. (bet. Corbin & Shirley Aves.),*
  Tarzana, 818-345-1205
  M-Sat 10am-7pm
■ A Valley minichain with a "fantastic" selection of "the
finest, freshest, unfishiest fish around" – "if it swims, they
have it" and "if they don't, they'll order it"; believers say
this piscatorial "paradise" is the "only place to buy fish"
and "worth the drive if you don't live close"; it ranks
second in quality to SM Seafood by just a thin fin.

Gelson's Markets   26 | 23 | 25 | E
- *See listing in Supermarkets section.*
■ With more branches than Bristol Farms, Gelson's ranks
very well among supermarkets thanks to a "big selection"
of seafood that most consider worth "the bucks"; high
scores for service are won by an "always helpful" staff
who "cut to order" and "will shell the jumbo tiger shrimp
for you"; there's also "quality sushi" at these markets
where the fish is "fresh fresh fresh."

GORDON'S FISH MARKET 🚲   26 | 25 | 25 | M
- *9116 W. Pico Blvd. (west of Doheny Dr.), LA, 310-276-6603*
  M-Sat 8:30am-6pm
■ "Neighborhood charm and service" and the "memory of
Ma Gordon" are lures that make this market popular with
the nearby Orthodox Jewish community; there's the "best
lox choices and prices" and "great gefilte fish" dispensed
by "real fishmongers"; this "knowledgeable supplier" is
the "cat's meow" – "never had a fish here I didn't like."

Hughes Markets   21 | 20 | 21 | M |
• *See listing in Supermarkets section.*
☑ Many shoppers view this chain as "an excellent source of good quality fish" – a "reliable" supermarket "best buy" with "very fresh specials"; however, given its size it's perhaps inevitable that "some branches are better than others", and critics sniff about occasional "fishy smells" and too many "prewrapped and frozen" items.

99 Ranch   25 | 26 | 19 | I |
• *See listing in Ethnic Food Sources section.*
■ First-timers exclaim with amazement at this Asian chain's "astonishing array" of "fresh, cheap" seafood, some of it only pennies more than wholesale; it boasts an "unreal selection" of "unusual varieties", including "exotic" shellfish, and much of the stock is "kept alive in tanks"; the downside is that there aren't a lot of people who can answer questions.

Phil's Fish & Poultry   26 | 25 | 24 | E |
• *11640 San Vicente Blvd. (Barrington), Brentwood, 310-820-5853*
  M-F 9am-6:30pm/Sat 9am-5:30pm
■ Known for its many in-store puns (they're phishing for laughs), this former chain is now a single shop but still has a loyal Westsider following who gladly "swim to Brentwood" for the "last and best" of a dying breed; "they stand behind their merchandise" and the "helpful" staff will "bone the fish you catch" and also cook shellfish and poach salmon; "good sourdough bread" and chicken pot pies are bonuses.

Quality Seafood Market   ▽ 21 | 23 | 18 | M |
• *130 Int'l Boardwalk, Redondo Beach, 310-374-2382*
  M-F 11am-7pm/Sat & Sun 10am-8pm
☑ There's a "wide variety of seafood" at this rambling semi-outdoor market by the Redondo Beach Pier that's a major weekend spot for many of LA's international community; fish, crabs and shrimp are cooked to order and often taken to the newspaper-covered tables outside; this may be the "only place on the West Coast with fresh, tasty Ipswich clams", but critics say it's "mediocre."

SANTA MONICA SEAFOOD   28 | 28 | 25 | M |
• *1205 Colorado Ave. (12th St.), Santa Monica, 310-393-5244*
  M-F 9am-7pm/Sat 9am-6pm
• *1700 N. Main St. (Ball Rd.), Orange, 714-921-2632*
  M-F 9:30am-7pm/Sat 9:30am-6pm
■ SoCal's top-rated seafood market for quality ("beautiful") and variety ("unbelievable"), this "SM landmark" (with an Orange outpost) wins raves for its "fresh fish at fair prices with friendly service" – no surprise, since the family that runs it organized the area's fishing fleet earlier this century and today supplies seafood to almost every major restaurant in town; it's a "best source" for raw, smoked and prepared fish, recipes, cookware and more; the only caveat: on busy days shoppers are "packed in like sardines."

Special Foods International ✑ ▽ <u>28</u> | <u>23</u> | <u>23</u> | <u>M</u>

- *6533 S. Sepulveda Blvd. (Centinela Ave.), Westchester, 310-641-2111*
  M-Sat 5am-5pm

■ A tiny shop hidden behind Dinah's Fried Chicken Restaurant north of LAX that's mainly a wholesaler but also retails, offering "great prices on exotic fish", the "best lobsters" and other "really good" shellfish at moderate prices; but service can sometimes be less than gracious.

Tusquella's Seafood   <u>26</u> | <u>24</u> | <u>24</u> | <u>E</u>

- *Farmer's Market, 6333 W. Third St., Stall 138 (Fairfax Ave.), LA, 213-938-1919*
  Every day 7:30am-6pm

■ This Farmer's Market landmark that seems to have "been around forever" is a "local favorite" for "very fresh", "superior quality" fish, including "great petrale when they have it" and "good shrimp if you can't get to Chinatown"; though some charge that "high prices are geared to tourists", fans consider it one of the "best in the city."

Flowers

Some might think that Los Angeles residents have less need of florists than most, since so many of us live in homes surrounded by flowers that grow year-round. But for special occasions, there's something about pulling a begonia out of the ground that just doesn't seem to say, "I love you." Or more importantly, "Thanks for signing me to a three-picture deal." And so the florists of SoCal prosper and thrive, and as the results of this *Survey* attest, they create some pretty amazing bouquets and arrangements to make that wedding or special party the event of the decade.

Top Quality
29 Jacob Maarse
    David Jones
28 Campo dei Fiori
    Solarimum (Bel-Air)
    Silver Birches

Top Service
26 Mark's Garden
    Secret Garden
25 Jacob Maarse
    Campo dei Fiori
24 Silver Birches

Top Variety
27 Jacob Maarse
26 Mark's Garden
    Secret Garden
    Campo dei Fiori
    LA Premiere

Best Buys
    Mark's Garden
    Secret Garden
    Jacob Maarse
    Campo dei Fiori
    LA Premiere

Q	V	S	C

CAMPO DEI FIORI ⚂

28	26	25	E

• *648 N. Martel (Melrose Ave.), W. Hollywood, 213-655-9966*
M-F 9am-8pm/Sat 9am-6pm

■ A "very original", oddly situated shop in the middle of alternative-lifestyle Melrose, where they make "inventive", "extremely pretty" arrangements of "unusual" flowers and plants; the "owners care" – "trust them to deliver the best."

DAVID JONES ⚂

29	25	23	VE

• *450 N. Robertson Blvd. (bet. Melrose Ave. & Beverly Blvd.),*
W. Hollywood, 310-659-6347
M-Sat 8:30am-5pm

■ W. Hollywood's "grand master" produces "beautiful, creative designs" that are "expensive" but in "wonderful taste"; fans gush over "flowers at their finest" that can also be shipped as gifts with food and wine.

Dutch Flower House ⚂

▽ 25	22	24	E

• *12231 Wilshire Blvd. (Bundy Dr.), West LA, 310-820-5229*
M-F 10am-6pm/Sat 10am-5pm

☑ "Charming designs" that are "like old Dutch paintings" are the strength of this "reliable" shop run by "lovely people"; to devotees it's a "favorite on all counts", but a few demur: "good for wreaths only."

Empty Vase ☻ <u>25</u> <u>23</u> <u>22</u> <u>E</u>
- 9033 Santa Monica Blvd. (bet. Robertson Blvd. &
  Doheny Dr.), W. Hollywood, 310-278-1988
  M-Sat 8am-8:30pm/Sun 9am-6pm

The "king of topiary" is also known for "lovely roses"
and "exotic" blooms; while picky types say "good, not
great", you can fill your vase with some "wonderful
arrangements" from this "very pretty store."

Fleurish Fine Flowers & ▽ <u>28</u> <u>29</u> <u>27</u> <u>E</u>
Baskets
- Santa Monica Airport, 3050 Airport Ave. (bet. Centinela
  & Walgrove Aves.), Mar Vista, 310-391-4334
  By appointment only

This "impressive" florist (who does custom work for
movies and TV) creates "inventive and artful arrangements";
high ratings support the praise: "great imagination",
"wonderful" and, even better, "the owner is a love."

Floral and Hardy <u>–</u> <u>–</u> <u>–</u> <u>M</u>
- Beverly Connection, 100 N. La Cienega Blvd. (Beverly Blvd.),
  LA, 310-657-8771
  M-F 8am-11pm/Sat & Sun 8am-10pm
- Encino Marketplace, 16403 Ventura Blvd. (Hayvenhurst
  Ave.), Encino, 818-981-6644
  M-Sat 8am-9pm/Sun 9am-8pm

This surprisingly well-stocked minichain of florist stands
outside supermarkets allows you to bag some roses and
begonias; despite their modest locations, some claim these
are among the best places to buy flowers in town.

Flower Fashions <u>25</u> <u>23</u> <u>23</u> <u>E</u>
- 9960 Santa Monica Blvd. (Wilshire Blvd.), Beverly Hills,
  310-275-0159
  M-F 8am-5pm/Sat 8am-2:30pm

A Beverly Hills tradition where "you pay top dollar – but
their jobs are always perfect"; the "only florist who still
makes candy clowns" is a "talented designer" that "you can
count on", but a few claim it's "not what it once was."

Flower Shop, The ☻ <u>26</u> <u>23</u> <u>24</u> <u>M</u>
- 616 N. Almont Dr. (Melrose Ave.), W. Hollywood, 310-274-8491
  M-F 9am-5pm/Sat 9am-noon

"Excellent quality and service" are the rule at this simply
named W. Hollywood shop, where satisfied recipients praise
"lovely arrangements" created by "truly great designers";
prices are satisfying too.

Growing Wild ☻ <u>28</u> <u>26</u> <u>27</u> <u>M</u>
- 1201 Highland Ave. (12th St.), Manhattan Beach, 310-545-4432
  M-Sat 9am-6pm

Surveyors are wild about this "outstanding", moderately
priced South Bay shop with a "marvelous" staff full of
"innovative ideas"; their "flair for the original" produces
"beautiful arrangements" that "seem to last forever."

Flowers $\boxed{Q}\boxed{V}\boxed{S}\boxed{C}$

JACOB MAARSE ⚡ $\boxed{29}\boxed{27}\boxed{25}\boxed{E}$
- *655 E. Green St. (El Molino Ave.), Pasadena, 818-449-0246*
  M-Sat 9am-6pm

■ The "place to buy flowers when invited to the boss's house", this "fabulous, imaginative" Pasadena "standard" that grows thousands of roses is simply one of "the best", "a delight" with "beautiful Victorian flowers" and a "great eye for detail"; prices are as "breathtaking" as the arrangements.

LA Premiere ⚡ $\boxed{26}\boxed{26}\boxed{23}\boxed{E}$
- *8928 W. Olympic Blvd. (LaPeer Dr.), Beverly Hills, 310-276-4665*
  M-F 7:30am-9pm/Sat & Sun 9am-6pm

■ "Outstanding table arrangements" win raves for this "very creative", service-oriented Beverly Hills florist; recipients praise "magnificent" compositions that "last a long time."

Laurel's Custom Florist ⚡   ▽ $\boxed{28}\boxed{28}\boxed{26}\boxed{E}$
- *7964 Melrose Ave. (Fairfax Ave.), LA, 213-655-3466*
  M-F 9am-5pm/Sat 9am-5pm (by appointment only)

■ What some call "the most talented florist in town" delivers "brilliant" arrangements with "fast", "willing service" that's "worth every cent" (even if it adds up to a lot of cents); "they've done all my windows on Rodeo" says one local merchant who apparently has many windows on Rodeo.

Los Angeles Wholesale Flower Market/Southern California Flower Market, Inc. ✉ $\boxed{-}\boxed{-}\boxed{-}\boxed{M}$
- *754-755 S. Wall St. (bet. 7th & 8th Sts.), Downtown LA, 213-622-1966*
  Market hours: M,W,F 2am-noon/T,Th,Sat 6am-noon

Despite its problem Downtown location, the LA wholesale flower market with vendors that sell to consumers on the side consists of several massive warehouses filled with hundreds of flower purveyors, offering everything at discount prices; P.S. not all flower sellers at the market will sell to the general public – be sure to ask.

Manhattan Fruitier West ⚡✉ ▽ $\boxed{27}\boxed{24}\boxed{26}\boxed{E}$
- *310 N. Vista Ave. (north of Beverly Blvd.), LA, 213-938-4122*
  M-F 9am-5pm

■ A variation on a theme (no flowers for sale here), this shop creates "baskets of fruit that are works of art", based on still life paintings; they have a sizable clientele in the Biz who rave about their "exquisite" arrangements with "prices to match."

Marc Fredericks ⚡ $\boxed{-}\boxed{-}\boxed{-}\boxed{E}$
- *8445 Warner Dr. (bet. National Blvd. & Higuera St.), Culver City, 310-287-2273*
  By appointment only

While not well known to many of our surveyors, this "perfectionist" situated near the Sony Studios wins high praise from fans for "wonderful service" and the "great style" of his "gorgeous", "always fresh" arrangements.

MARK'S GARDEN 🚲   27 | 26 | 26 | M
- *13838 Ventura Blvd. (bet. Woodman & Hazletine Aves.), Sherman Oaks, 818-906-1718*
  M-Sat 9am-7pm/Sun 9am-5pm

■ This Burbank Studios favorite in Sherman Oaks "always does a spectacular job no matter what your price range"; "beautiful spring baskets and exotics" as well as "exquisite" arrangements at "nonastronomical" prices win loyal fans who say: "Mark has never failed us."

Rita Flora 🚲   – | – | – | M
- *468 S. La Brea Ave. (6th St.), LA, 213-938-3900*
  Every day 8am-10pm

Rather Japanese, somewhat minimalist flower store in the middle of La Brea's gallery and restaurant row, with a popular California cuisine cafe next door, allowing that most unusual of experiences – flowers and fine pastry, roses and roasted coffee; it helped introduce the joy of flowers to the cappuccino/espresso crowd.

SECRET GARDEN 🚲✉   27 | 26 | 26 | E
- *221 S. Robertson Blvd. (bet. Wilshire & Olympic Blvds.), Beverly Hills, 310-659-5854*
  Every day 9am-5pm (by appointment only)

■ This "creative" Beverly Hills florist does "spectacular weddings" and always offers a "beautiful variety, not just the standard boring selection"; fans would like this very popular shop to be less busy, warning "if you print this, I'll never forgive you"; sorry.

SILVER BIRCHES/
SYLVIA TIDWELL 🚲   28 | 25 | 24 | E
- *180 E. California Blvd. (Arroyo Pkwy.), Pasadena, 818-796-1431/310-274-9040*
  M-Sat 8:30am-4:30pm

◪ Sylvia Tidwell, known for "exquisite" work and "personalized service", has joined forces with this highly respected Pasadena "competitor of Jacob Maarse"; praised as a "more reasonable alternative" for "special occasions", the shop offers "unusual arrangements" that show the mark of "genius", but a few critics warn they can be "unreliable" and sometimes deliver "attitude for days."

Solarium 🚲   28 | 24 | 24 | VE
- *2922 Beverly Glen Circle (Beverly Glen), Bel Air, 310-475-0401*
  M-F 9am-5pm/Sat 9am-4pm

■ Situated high above Bel Air and Beverly Hills, this is where the beautiful people go for "beautiful orchids" and other "gorgeous flowers"; partisans call it the "most reliable of the pack" with "terrific" service, though as always "you will pay for it."

Flowers

q | v | s | c

Southland Certified Farmers' Markets ⊄
— | — | — | I
• *See listing in Produce Section.*
Some of the freshest flowers around (unless you grow them yourself) can be purchased at the open-air farmers' markets located throughout the Southland; though variety is sometimes limited, you can fill your house with blooms such as orchids, Casablanca lilies, gerbera daisies and lilacs in season at a nominal cost.

Stanley Kirsten &⫐⊟
25 | 24 | 22 | E
• *709 Wall St. (7th St.), Downtown LA, 213-622-3415*
  M-Sat 8am-5pm
▣ Followers have "been a fan of this man for years", praising the "old-time elegance" of his "Victorian" floral arrangements; but critics charge "not consistent" – you get "gorgeous work only if he knows you."

Tommy Farmer's
— | — | — | E
• *2451 Mission St. (Las Flores), San Marino, 818-355-6762*
  By appointment only
This Eastside florist specializes in lavish parties, debutante balls and society weddings; his floral arrangements, incorporating herbs as well as props from his extensive silver and linen collection, reflect his background as a former art designer at Disney.

White Gate Flowers &⫐⊟
— | — | — | E
• *562 N. Larchmont Blvd. (2 blocks south of Melrose Ave.), LA, 213-465-1222*
  T-Sat 8am-4pm
One of the main places where folks in old-money LA buy their roses and petunias is a well-respected shop on busy Larchmont Boulevard that "does a spectacular job" offering "some beautiful ideas", though there are occasional grumbles about service.

Woods, The &⫐
27 | 25 | 22 | VE
• *11711 Gorham Ave. (bet. Barrington & Montana Aves.), Brentwood, 310-826-0711*
  M-F 8am-8pm/Sat 8am-9pm/Sun 9am-6pm
▣ "It's like walking through a garden" in this spacious Brentwood shop that's filled with "the most unique selection anywhere"; for many, the "lovely ideas" and "beautiful presentation" are "like a breath of fresh air", but the bloom wilts a bit for those who complain of "ridiculously high" prices and "snotty attitude."

119

Health/Natural Food

It might come as a surprise to some, but LA has a real love-it-or-hate-it relationship with health foods. Though we're perceived as a city of tofu-gobbling tree huggers, not everyone here thinks that bean sprouts are the answer to all life's woes. Health and natural foods stores do abound, however, often mixing organic produce with antiquarian attitudes that help bring a wonderful sense of the country to the big city, allowing urbanites to buy bulghur and cumin in bulk, along with such necessities as unpasteurized goat's milk cheese. And don't forget the Ethnic Food Sources when you're looking for health food with a foreign accent.

Top Quality
27 Mrs. Gooch's
26 Wild Oats
25 Mother's Market
    Erewhon Market
24 Co-Opportunity

Top Service
24 Mrs. Gooch's
23 Wild Oats
22 Mother's Market
21 Pacific Coast Greens
    Erewhon Market

Top Variety
26 Mrs. Gooch's
25 Mother's Market
    Wild Oats
    Erewhon Market
23 Follow Your Heart

Best Buys
    Mother's Market
    Mrs. Gooch's
    Wild Oats
    Erewhon Market
    Follow Your Heart

Q	V	S	C

Co-Opportunity

Q	V	S	C
24	23	19	M

- *1530 Broadway (16th St.), Santa Monica, 310-451-8902*
  Every day 8am-10pm

■ "Off the beaten path but always crowded", this Westside " '60s throwback" is a "main place to shop for organic and bulk items" thanks to "great quality" and selection; there are "discounts for members" and some rate the produce "better than Mrs. Gooch's", but service ranges from "responsive" to "the grumpiest ever."

Erewhon Natural Food Market

25	25	21	M

- *7660 Beverly Blvd. (5 blocks east of Fairfax Ave.), LA, 213-937-0777*
  M-F 9am-9pm/Sat & Sun 9am-8pm

☑ A "New Age Gelson's", this massive health food market is "in a class by itself" – an "excellent, full-service store" with deli and juice bar, boasting a "broad selection" and a staff that's "informed" about everything from Chinese herbs to seaweeds; but critics "could do without the more-holistic-than-thou" attitude and "scandalous" prices for some items.

Follow Your Heart   24 | 23 | 20 | M |
- 21825 Sherman Way (bet. Canoga Ave. & Topanga
  Canyon Blvd.), Canoga Park, 818-348-3240
  M-Sat 7am-9pm/Sun 8am-9pm
- 19 S. Milpas St. (#101 Frwy.), Santa Barbara,
  805-966-3694
  Every day 9am-8pm

■ "A real gem" of an organic market and restaurant on
the northern edge of the San Fernando Valley where
healthy-ites buy "quinoa in bulk", vitamins, "nonfat items"
and more; it's "great for homeopaths" and there are
"yummy sandwiches and soups" in the cafe; the Santa
Barbara branch is worth a stop if you're in the area.

Granny's Pantry   ▽ 22 | 21 | 19 | M |
- 560 S. Arroyo Pkwy. (California Ave.), Pasadena,
  818-796-8442
  M-F 9am-7pm/Sat & Sun 9am-6pm

■ This friendly natural foods shop in Pasadena has "good
raw milk and eggs", a "large selection of vitamins" and
lots of bulk grains and nuts, all at discount prices; there's
no produce or prepared foods, but "with a name like this,
how can they miss?"

Mother's Market & Kitchen ▭   25 | 25 | 22 | M |
- 225 E. 17th St. (Orange Ave.), Costa Mesa, 714-631-4741
- 19770 Beach Blvd. (bet. Yorktown St. & Adams Ave.),
  Huntington Beach, 714-963-6667
  Every day 9am-10pm
- Mail order: 800-595-6667

■ Among the few organic markets that compare well with
general interest supermarkets, these huge stores "make
you feel healthy just walking down the aisles"; "you name
it, they got it" and it's mostly "unbelievably good" and
reasonably priced; there's also a "cozy" restaurant that's
a "great place to meet a healthy single" mate at the
Huntington Beach location.

MRS. GOOCH'S WHOLE   27 | 26 | 24 | E |
FOODS MARKET ⚲
- 239 N. Crescent Dr. (Dayton Way), Beverly Hills, 310-274-3360
- 826 N. Glendale Ave. (Glenoaks), Glendale, 818-240-9350
- 9350 Reseda Blvd. (Plummer St.), Northridge,
  818-701-5122
- 405 N. PCH (bet. Beryl & Carnelian Sts.), Redondo Beach,
  310-376-6931
- 12905 Riverside Dr. (Coldwater Canyon Ave.), Sherman
  Oaks, 818-762-5548
- 3476 Centinela Ave. (Palms), West LA, 310-391-5209
- 451 Avenida de los Arboles (Moorpark), Thousand Oaks,
  805-492-5340

Mrs. Gooch's Whole Foods Market (Cont.)
- *Tustin Courtyard, 14945 Holt Ave. (bet. Irvine Blvd. & 1st St.), Tustin, 714-731-3400*
  Every day 9am-9pm

■ "The Cadillac" of natural food sources draws a huge response from surveyors who rate it "the best all around" thanks to "top-quality everything"; these "clean, gorgeous" markets offer "beautiful" produce, "good prepared foods", "wonderful" meats, poultry, fish and much more; the bad news? "bring money", and some find it "inconsistent from store to store."

Nature Mart 🖃   21 19 18 M
- *2080 Hillhurst Ave. (2 blocks south of Los Feliz Blvd.), Los Feliz, 213-660-0052*
  Every day 9am-10pm

☑ "Bulk bin" offerings of nuts, cereals, spices and more help make this "small" Los Feliz shop a "wonderful bargain", as do "great buys on natural juices"; it's good for "fresh veggies, remedies and breads" and has "101 kinds of water", but middling service ratings support the claim that it's "poorly run."

Nowhere Natural Foods Market 🚲   – – – M
- *8001 Beverly Blvd. (bet. Fairfax & Crescent Hts.), LA, 213-658-6506*
  M-Sat 9am-10pm/Sun 10am-9pm

An old-line organic shop, next to the very vegetarian Nowhere Cafe, with a big vitamin and mineral department, purely produced produce, and most everything else needed to lead a blameless existence, not far from the corned beef and pastrami seraglios of Fairfax.

One Life Natural Foods   20 20 17 M
- *3001 Main St. (Pier Ave.), Santa Monica, 310-392-4501*
  Every day 9am-9pm

☑ Some say this "neighborhood" Westsider "used to be better", but it still offers "the best, cheapest selection of herbs", both "medicinal and culinary", a "good macrobiotic section" and "very good dried fruits"; prices are lower than at some competitors but the "produce is not as good."

Pacific Coast Greens 🚲   22 20 21 E
- *22601 Pacific Coast Hwy. (½ mile south of Malibu Pier), Malibu, 310-456-0353*
  Every day 9am-8pm

☑ Despite the health consciousness of upscale Malibu, this local organic shop "with good, interesting selections" "always seems somewhat deserted"; the problem may be that the "produce could be better" and prices could be lower; still, supporters "hope they make it."

Papa John's Natural |19| |19| |18| |M|
Market & Cafe
• *5000 E. Second St. (Argonne St.), Long Beach,*
  310-439-3444
  M-Sat 9am-8pm/Sun 10am-7pm
◪ "Just average, nothing special" is the consensus on
this neighborhood market; "informative employees" are a
plus but shelves are "sometimes bare" and produce
"could be better"; the in-store cafe is liked by some while
others say the "food looks better than it tastes."

Quinn's |19| |18| |17| |M|
• *8466 Melrose Ave. (½ block east of La Cienega Blvd.),*
  W. Hollywood, 213-651-5950
• *1864 N. Vermont Ave. (½ block south of Franklin Ave.),*
  Hollywood, 213-663-8307
  M-F 8am-9pm/Sat 8am-7pm/Sun 10am-6pm
◪ One of the oldest health food chains around, dating
back to the Eisenhower Administration; loyalists find it
"convenient" and "surprisingly reasonable" in price, but
dissenters say it's "going downhill", citing "erratic",
"drone" service and "unpredictable inventory"; all in all, it
"hasn't changed since the hippies shopped there", and it
probably should.

Rainbow Acres |21| |19| |19| |M|
• *11665 Santa Monica Blvd. (1 block east of Barrington Ave.),*
  West LA, 310-444-7949
• *13208 W. Washington Blvd. (4 blocks east of Lincoln Blvd.),*
  Marina del Rey, 310-306-8330
• *Marina Waterside Shopping Ctr., 4756 Admiralty Way,*
  Marina del Rey, 310-823-5373
  M-F 9am-9pm/Sat & Sun 9am-8pm
◪ A moderate-sized Westside organic chain that's
"decent for a quick fix"; the "selection is limited" and
critics say it's "zip for produce", but there are "great
closeouts" and "good vitamins"; be advised that service
can be "slow and spacey" – odd with all that ginseng
within reach.

Venice/Ocean Park Food Co-op |20| |18| |17| |M|
• *839 Lincoln Blvd. (Brooks Ave.), Venice, 310-399-5623*
  Every day 9am-9pm
◪ Life hasn't changed a lot out here since Jerry Rubin and
Abbie Hoffman's heyday, and that's also true of this "very
small" co-op where "'60s people still hang, now with
children"; it's "great for bulk items" and the goods are
definitely wholesome and natural: the "apples are ugly –
no alar" and "the worms are still alive"; less groovy is
service that can be "mean."

123

Wild Oats Market   26 25 23 E
- *603 S. Lake Ave. (California), Pasadena, 818-792-1778*
- *1425 Montana Ave. (15th St.), Santa Monica, 310-576-4707*
  Every day 8am-10pm

■ Admirers go gaga over this "classy", "smart-looking" "newcomer" that "radiates energy and health"; it's a "natural foods museum" with the "best bananas in the world, and that's just the start"; whether there really are "individually polished peas" is debatable, but some might feel they should be, given the prices.

Windward Farms   22 17 16 M
- *105 Windward Ave. (bet. Main St. & Pacific Ave.),*
  Venice, 310-392-3566
  Every day 8:30am-7pm

☑ Possibly the best organic market in holistic Venice, this "veggie retreat" is the "perfect country store in the city", "good for seasonal produce" and "convenient on the way home from the beach"; veggies aside, selection is "scanty."

Herbs & Spices

Most people buy their herbs and spices at the supermarket in small, regimented containers. But not all. There are those who prefer to shop for seasonings at stores where the turnover is constant, the quality is first rate, and you can fill a jar with oregano for next to nothing. And when in need of ethnic herbs and spices, nothing beats these fragrant culinary outlets for freshness and variety.

Top Quality
28 Co-Opportunity
26 Bharat Bazaar
25 Bezjian's
24 Erewhon
   Wild Oats

Top Service
22 Co-Opportunity
   Erewhon
   Bharat Bazaar
21 Wild Oats
   Bezjian's

Top Variety
27 Co-Opportunity
26 Bharat Bazaar
   Bezjian's
24 Erewhon
22 Wild Oats

Best Buys
Bharat Bazaar
Co-Opportunity
Bezjian's
Erewhon
Wild Oats

Q	V	S	C
—	—	—	M

Ann's Dutch Imports
• *4357 Tujunga Ave. (Moorpark St.), Studio City, 818-985-5551*
   T-Sat 10am-5pm
LA's main "Indonesian source" is heady with the rich smells of Asia and stocked with all the ingredients needed to make *rijstaffel, nasi goreng* and the like, plus "awesome" hot sauces; most consider it a culinary adventure as well as a "great" spice source, but a very few dissenters think that quality could be better.

Bezjian's Grocery ⌷

25	26	21	I

• *4715 Santa Monica Blvd. (1 block west of Vermont Ave.), Hollywood, 213-663-1503*
   M-Sat 10am-7pm/Sun 10am-5pm
■ The best source for Middle Eastern spices in town is this always-busy, Armenian-owned market in the area known as Little Armenia, offering a "wonderful choice" of seasonings plus what may be the biggest choice of olives in town and items such as real Lebanese string cheese; "they have what you need" and the "smells make you want to buy", as do the low prices.

Bharat Bazaar 🚚   26 26 22 I
- *11510 W. Washington Blvd. (1 block west of Frwy. #405), Culver City, 310-398-6766*
  W-M 11am-7pm

■ "The cheapest, high-quality bulk spices this side of Price Club" are what you'll find in this pleasant Culver City Indian shop where a single sniff transports you to Bombay and New Delhi; with a "great selection" and "very helpful" owner, it's judged one of "the best" of its kind: there are also "good buys on betel nuts" and "fresh samosas."

CO-OPPORTUNITY   28 27 22 M
- *1530 Broadway (16th St.), Santa Monica, 310-451-8902*
  Every day 8am-10pm

■ A Westside tradition, this "spice heaven" is top rated in our *Survey* for the quality and variety of its herbs and spices; one of the area's best health food markets, it has an "excellent" selection of bulk herbs that allows you to choose as much or as little as you need; "forget buying a whole jar to use for a one-time recipe" – here you can purchase a pinch and nobody minds.

Erewhon Natural Food Mkt.   24 24 22 M
- *7660 Beverly Blvd. (5 blocks east of Fairfax Ave.), LA, 213-937-0777*
  M-F 9am-9pm/Sat & Sun 9am-8pm

■ This large, popular organic supermarket has a "good selection" of "organic and nonirradiated spices" (for those who worry about such things), along with lots of holistic herbs and many products sold in bulk; with moderate prices and a healthy karma, it's a nice place to buy your basil and parsley.

Herb Products, Co. 🚚 💻   ▽ 26 28 22 I
- *11012 Magnolia Blvd. (bet. Vineland & Lankershim Blvds.), N. Hollywood, 818-984-3141*
  M-F 9am-5:30pm/Sat 9am-5pm

■ A rather unusual San Fernando Valley shop that's "like a pharmacy", where many of the herbs are "medicinal rather than culinary"; even so, cooks will find a full range of spices, plus pure essential oils and some of the best Spanish saffron around, all at "good prices"; you can also "mail order special herbs."

Wild Oats Market 🚲   24 22 21 M
- *603 S. Lake Ave. (California), Pasadena, 818-792-1778*
- *1425 Montana Ave. (15th St.), Santa Monica, 310-576-4707*
  Every day 8am-10pm

■ Highly praised as a health food market, this upscale Pasadena shop also earns applause for its herbs and spices; an impressive supply of bulk items, "good values" and "very helpful personnel" explain its appeal; you can easily "meet most of your basic needs" here.

Ice Cream & Frozen Yogurt

Along with coffee, ice cream may be LA's biggest food obsession. Fortunately, this consuming passion has been rendered acceptable by the growing variety of low-fat and nonfat products that allow us to indulge in, say, a frozen yogurt flavored with cinnamon and espresso without drowning in a sea of gluttonous guilt.

Top Quality
28 Al Gelato
    Ben & Jerry's
27 Eiger
26 Häagen Dazs
    Robin Rose

Top Service
23 Al Gelato
    Fosselman's
22 Ben & Jerry's
    Emack & Bolio's
    Eiger

Top Variety
26 Al Gelato
25 Ben & Jerry's
    Baskin-Robbins
24 Humphrey Yogart
    Fosselman's

Best Buys
Fosselman's
Bigg Chill
Al Gelato
Ben & Jerry's
Ciao Livio

Q	V	S	C
28	26	23	E

AL GELATO 🍽

- *806 S. Robertson Blvd. (bet. Olympic & Wilshire Blvds.), LA, 310-659-8069*
  Every day 10am-midnight

■ Top-rated across the board, this highly authentic Italian gelato shop is as close as LA gets to the legendary Il Gelato of Florence, providing frozen treats that are "the very essence of flavor" (hazelnut, espresso and the like); this is "real Italian gelato served in insane American-sized portions" at prices to match, but then, it always costs more for "the best."

21	25	19	M

Baskin-Robbins 31 Flavors 🍽

- *Locations throughout Southern California; for specific locations and hours, call 800-331-0031*

◪ Plenty of ice-cream lovers "grew up on" this ubiquitous chain's flavors, and while it's "not the most fashionable" place these days, most still consider it a "reliable" "old standby" for "good", "all-American" treats plus newer-fangled items like "delicious cappuccino blasts" and "low-cal, low-fat stuff"; it's "good for kids", but cynics cite "lots of flavors, not much taste" and "poor" service.

Ben & Jerry's ⊟   28 | 25 | 22 | E

- 11740 San Vicente Blvd. (west of Barrington Ave.),
  Brentwood, 310-447-0695
- Del Amo Mall, 3550 Carson St. (behind Mann Theater),
  Torrance, 310-371-6891
- 245 Pine Ave. (next to AMC Theater), Long Beach,
  310-437-1422
- 3824 Cross Creek Rd. (next to Malibu Cinema), Malibu,
  310-456-5337
- 234 PCH (Torrance Blvd.), Redondo Beach, 310-372-7292
- 119 N. Maryland (near Mann Theater), Glendale,
  818-545-0455
- 164 E. Palm Ave. (next to AMC Theater), Burbank,
  818-566-7602
- 14318 Ventura Blvd. (Beverly Glen Blvd.), Sherman Oaks,
  818-789-9951
- 16101 Ventura Blvd., Encino, 818-788-4462
- Century City Marketplace (near AMC Theater), Century
  City, 310-788-9682
- 2441 Main St. (Pico Blvd.), Santa Monica, 310-450-0691
- Hollywood Galaxy Ctr., 7021 Hollywood Blvd. (near
  Chinese Theater), Hollywood, 213-962-4541
- 29041 Agoura Rd. (front of Mann Theater), Agoura Hills,
  818-879-1798
  Sun-Th noon-10pm/F & Sat noon-midnight

■ This top-rated Vermont-based chain helps "lessen the guilt" of indulgence with its pro-environment stance; but its real appeal is "decadent" ice cream that's "overloaded" with butterfat and other bad-for-you good stuff; "fantastic" flavors like "phenomenal Chunky Monkey" and "crunchy, munchy" Cherry Garcia make even Gingrichians sigh "hate their politics, love their ice cream."

Bigg Chill, The ⊟   25 | 22 | 21 | I

- 10850 Olympic Blvd. (Westwood), West LA, 310-475-1070
- 12050 Ventura Blvd. (Laurel Canyon Blvd.), Studio City,
  818-508-7811
  M-F 7:30am-11pm/Sat & Sun 11am-11pm

■ A "bigg thrill, a bigg treat" rave devotees of this duo's "addicting", "always fresh" frozen yogurt in a choice of "interesting flavors"; "tremendous portions" help make it a "best-for-the-buck" buy, so expect "long lines" at both branches of this "favorite, guilt-free" "happening."

C.C. Brown's ⊟   25 | 19 | 21 | M

- 7007 Hollywood Blvd. (Orange Dr.), Hollywood, 213-464-7062
  M-Th 1pm-10pm/F & Sat 1pm-midnight

☑ The oldest ice cream shop in town, this "nostalgic" 1906 "landmark" near Mann's Chinese theater predates the entertainment industry that grew up around it; it's long been hailed for "the best hot fudge sundae in town" (it claims to have invented that dessert), and if critics say "it's better in memory than reality", most agree it's "a classic."

Ciao Livio Gelateria ⊄   ▽ 25 | 22 | 21 | M

- *14550 Ventura Blvd. (Van Nuys Blvd.), Sherman Oaks,*
  818-784-5286
  Sun-Th 10am-10:30pm/F & Sat 10am-midnight

■ An intense fudge flavor called "chocolate death", which really is "to die for", is the main draw at this small Valley ice cream shop; its "wonderful tastes" are also evident in a "nice selection of gelato"; most say "good to excellent."

Cultured Class, The ⊄   22 | 20 | 20 | M

- *8719 Santa Monica Blvd. (bet. La Cienega & San*
  Vicente Blvds.), W. Hollywood, 310-657-8350
  Sun-Th 11am-11pm/F & Sat 11am-midnight

■ Fans consider this small W. Hollywood shop "the original frozen yogurt place" and still "best of the lot because they aerate", yielding "the closest thing to creamy ice cream" and an "addiction that's less dangerous than most"; more than 80 items at the fresh fruit and toppings bar help ward off boredom, but some think service "should be nicer."

Double Rainbow ⊄   24 | 22 | 20 | M

- *1898 Westwood Blvd. (Missouri Ave.), Westwood,*
  310-470-6232
  M-Th 10am-10:30pm/F & Sat 10am-11:30pm/Sun 1pm-9:30pm
- *7376 Melrose Ave. (Martel St.), LA, 213-655-1986*
  M-F 10am-midnight/Sat 10am-1am/Sun 11am-midnight

◪ A San Francisco ice cream/frozen yogurt establishment moved south, where supporters feel it "doesn't get the respect" it deserves as an "SF treasure"; though it earns praise for "high quality" and "yummy" flavors, it's also knocked as "overrated" and "inconsistent", with poor staffing" at times.

Eiger Ice Cream & Yogurt ⊄   27 | 22 | 22 | E

- *124 S. Barrington Pl. (Sunset Blvd.), Brentwood,*
  310-471-6955
  Sun-Th noon-9pm/F & Sat noon-10pm

■ Despite a low-key location on a Brentwood side street, this shop has a cult following of Westsiders who applaud ice cream and frozen yogurt they deem "absolutely the best", "in LA or anywhere"; flavors are "almost too rich", making it well "worth the haul to get there"; it's "expensive" but you're likely to see "lots of celebs", some of whom "can eat a whole ice cream pie at one sitting."

Emack & Bolio's ⊄   25 | 21 | 22 | M

- *625 Montana Ave. (7th St.), Santa Monica, 310-451-1315*
  Sun-Th 9am-11pm/F & Sat 9am-midnight

■ The Santa Monica branch of a Boston-based ice cream shop that claims to have invented Oreo Cookie ice cream; it's judged a "comer" with "great flavors" that just may be "the creamiest and least healthy" around; "you'll never find better peppermint ice cream" and the yogurt is made with "real yogurt cultures."

Fosselman's Ice Cream 🔁   25 | 24 | 23 | M
- *1824 W. Main St. (bet. Atlantic Blvd. & Fremont Ave.),*
  Alhambra, 818-282-6533
  M-Sat 10am-10pm/Sun 11:30am-10pm
■ A half-century-old San Gabriel Valley "old-fashioned
ice cream parlor", with old-fashioned flavors to match –
"excellent fresh peach", the "best dark chocolate",
"wonderful banana splits"; many people "love this place."

Gelato Desserts 🔁   ▽ 24 | 20 | 21 | M
- *13737 Fiji Way (Lincoln Blvd.), Marina del Rey,*
  310-827-8100
  Every day 9am-8pm
■ This small Marina purveyor of ice cream, yogurt and
gelato is where "the Italians all eat, and say it's the real
thing"; the ice cream is "creamy and good", and it also
offers a full line of custom-made cakes and desserts to go.

Häagen Dazs 🔁   26 | 23 | 20 | E
- *11703 San Vicente Blvd. (Barrington Ave.), Brentwood,*
  310-820-1666
- *Manhattan Village Shop Ctr., 3000 N. Sepulveda Blvd.,*
  Manhattan Beach, 310-545-5616
- *Century City Shopping Ctr., 10250 Santa Monica Blvd.,*
  Century City, 310-552-0417
- *Huntington Oaks Shopping Ctr., 666 W. Huntington Dr.,*
  Monrovia, 818-303-2002
- *229 Los Cerritos Mall (#605 Frwy.), Cerritos, 310-402-9669*
- *15302 Sunset Blvd. (Swarthmore), Pacific Palisades,*
  310-230-1132
- *Ross Plaza, 17418 Colima Rd. (bet. Azusa & Fullerton),*
  Rowland Hts., 818-810-2264
- *Santa Anita Mall, 400 S. Baldwin Ave. (#210 Frwy.),*
  Arcadia, 818-445-4437
- *Beverly Ctr., 8500 Beverly Blvd. (La Cienega Blvd.), LA,*
  310-657-8881
- *Ports O'Call Village (bet. Butterfly Ln. & Middle Rd.),*
  San Pedro, 310-547-9653
- *17200 Ventura Blvd. (bet. Louise Ave. & Balboa Blvd.),*
  Encino, 818-385-0257
- *5257 E. Second St., Long Beach, 310-438-0215*
- *1200 W. Covina Pkwy. (bet. Glendora & Covina), W. Covina,*
  818-813-9773
- *10878 Kinross Ave. (east of Westwood Blvd.), Westwood,*
  310-208-6833
- *Paseo Nuevo, 8190 State St., Santa Barbara,*
  805-966-0084
- *Newport Fashion Island Shop Ctr., 401 Newport Ctr. Dr.,*
  Newport Beach, 714-644-3416
- *154 S. Coast Hwy. (Broadway), Laguna Bch.,*
  714-497-5507
- *101 Main St. (east of PCH), Huntington Beach,*
  714-536-7744

Häagen Dazs (Cont.)
- S. Coast Plaza, 3333 Bristol St., Costa Mesa, 714-754-7752
- 1165 Coast Village Rd., Montecito, 805-969-7946
- Brea Mall (Imperial Hwy.), Brea, 714-529-9434
- 74-933 Hwy. 111, Indian Wells, 619-341-6364
  General hours: M-Sat 11am-9pm.
  Call individual locations to check Sunday hours.

■ With branches all over the world, this chain provides what partisans call "a controlled narcotic prescribed by heaven if you're good" – "consistently yummy", "industrial-strength gourmet ice cream" that's worth the "cholesterol disaster" for the likes of "divine chocolate-chocolate chip" and "can't-stop-eating-it rum raisin"; foes find it "too rich" in taste and price, but most can only sigh "wish I liked it less."

Heidi's Frogen Yozurt/ Swensen's $\boxed{-}$ $\boxed{-}$ $\boxed{-}$ $\boxed{\text{M}}$
Ice Cream/Steve's Ice Cream ⌐⌐
- 1511 Montana Ave. (15th St.), Santa Monica, 310-458-2955
  Every day 11am-11pm
- 62 W. Union St. (Fair Oaks), Pasadena, 818-440-9800
  M-Th 11:30am-11pm/F & Sat 11:30am-midnight/
  Sun 11:30am-10pm
- 429 B Shoreline Dr. (opposite Long Beach Convention Ctr.),
  Long Beach, 310-495-0121
  Sun-Th 10am-9pm/F & Sat 10am-10pm
- 5213 E. Second St. (Corona), Long Beach, 310-439-7868
  Sun-Th 10:30am-10pm/F 10:30am-11pm/Sat 10am-11pm
- 18515 Devonshire St. (Reseda Blvd.), Northridge,
  818-368-6262
  Sun-Th 11am-10pm/F & Sat 11am-10:30pm
- 1450 W. 25th St. (Western Ave.), San Pedro, 310-548-7871
  Every day 11am-10pm
- Marriott's Desert Springs Hotel, 78455 Country Club Dr.
  (Cook), Palm Desert, 619-341-2211
  M-Th noon-9pm/F noon-10pm/Sat 11am-10pm/
  Sun 11am-9pm
- 4693 Telephone St. (Main St.), Ventura, 805-642-6933
  M-Th 11am-9pm/F & Sat 11am-9:30pm/Sun 11am-7pm
- 150 Citadel Dr. (Telegraph Rd.), City of Commerce,
  213-889-1979
  M-F 8am-8pm/Sat & Sun 9am-8pm

To fans, this "family-oriented chain" is "a longtime fave" for "good old-fashioned ice cream" and "great chocolate sodas", but detractors say it "used to be better" and is now merely "ok, if that's all that's available"; because of ownership changes, most Heidi's stores are now affiliated with either Swensen's or Steve's Ice Cream.

Humphrey Yogart ⌐⌐ $\boxed{24}$ $\boxed{24}$ $\boxed{21}$ $\boxed{\text{M}}$
- Brentwood Gardens, 11677 San Vicente Blvd.
  (Barrington Ave.), Brentwood, 310-207-2206
- Beverly Ctr., 100 N. La Cienega Blvd. (bet. Beverly & 3rd),
  LA, 310-652-1941

Humphrey Yogart (Cont.)
- *7555½ Melrose Ave. (bet. Fairfax & La Brea Aves.), LA, 213-651-4886*
- *1312 Third St. Promenade (Arizona Ave.), Santa Monica, 310-394-6818*
- *4574 Van Nuys Blvd. (Frwy. #134), Van Nuys, 818-906-2490*
- *18429 Nordhoff St. (Reseda Blvd.), Northridge, 818-886-8078*
- *Triangle Square Shopping Ctr., 1875 Newport Blvd., Costa Mesa, 714-650-3733*
  M-F 10am-11pm/Sat & Sun 10am-midnight

■ Despite the atrocious pun of a name, this minichain offers some of the most "creative" frozen yogurt around; patrons choose between lower-fat sweet or slightly higher-fat tart versions, with mix-ins ranging from Reese's Pieces to espresso and cinnamon; surveyors like the "freedom of choice" and consider it "hands down the best" – "it must be in the mixing machines."

Lappert's ⌘   – | – | – | M
- *29 Pier Ave. (Hermosa Ave.), Hermosa Beach, 310-318-3953*
  Every day noon-9pm

Nestled in beautiful Downtown Hermosa Beach, a block from the ocean, this branch of a fabled Hawaiian chain offers the kind of richly flavored ice cream popularized on Oahu, and now equally cultish in the South Bay; needless to say, macadamia nuts are prevalent in the mixes.

McConnell's of Santa Barbara ⌘   25 | 23 | 21 | M
- *1588 Mission Dr. (Attardag Rd.), Solvang, 805-688-9880*
  Sun-Th 11am-6pm/F & Sat 11am-9pm
- *201 W. Mission St. (De La Vina), Santa Barbara, 805-569-2323*
  Every day 10:30am-midnight

■ This small local chain is hailed by admirers as "best in the West", with "the top vanilla bean in town", the most superb "strawberry ice cream on the planet" and other "amazing" flavors so lush they "coat the roof of your mouth" – "too rich for every day, but what a treat"; their ice cream is also available at such restaurants as Louise's and the Hard Rock Cafe and in markets all over SoCal.

Penguin's Place ⌘   19 | 19 | 19 | I
- *2180 Westwood Blvd. (Olympic Blvd.), West LA, 310-470-2919*
  Every day 10:30am-midnight
- *11146 Palms Blvd. (Sepulveda Blvd.), West LA, 310-391-0571*
  Sun-Th 11am-10:30pm/F & Sat 11am-11pm
- *4710½ Admiralty Way (bet. Lincoln Blvd. & Fuji Way), Marina Del Rey, 310-301-8230*
  Every day 11am-9:30pm

Penguin's Place (Cont.)
- *6502 Spring St. (bet. Mission & Monterey), Long Beach, 310-420-6118*
  Sun-Th 9am-11pm/F & Sat 9am-11:30pm
- *Old Town Hall, 20016 Hawthorne Blvd. (bet. Del Amo Blvd. & 190th St.), Torrance, 310-370-7066*
  Sun-Th 10am-10pm/F & Sat 10am-10:30pm
- *800 S. PCH (Knob Hill), Redondo Beach, 310-540-1333*
  Sun-Th 10am-10pm/F & Sat 10am-11pm
- *815 W. Naomi Ave. (bet Baldwin & Duarté), Arcadia, 818-446-5473*
  Every day 11am-11pm
- *852A E. Alosta Ave. (Citrus Ave.), Azusa, 818-969-5050*
  Sun-Th 11am-9pm/F & Sat 11am-9:30pm
- *16902 Devonshire St. (Balboa Blvd.), Granada Hills, 818-366-1521*
  M-Sat 8:30am-10:30pm/Sun 9am-10:30pm
- *703 Pier (PCH), Hermosa Beach, 310-379-2490*
  Sun-Th 11am-9:30pm/F & Sat 9am-11pm
- *711 Foothill Blvd. (Oakwood Ave.), La Cañada, 818-790-0298*
  M-Th 7:30am-9:30pm/F 7:30am-10pm/Sat 8:30am-10pm/ Sun 9am-9:30pm
- *1103 Fair Oaks Ave. (Oxley), S. Pasadena, 818-799-0643*
  Every day 10am-10pm
- *9840 Topanga Canyon Blvd. (Lassen St.), Chatsworth, 818-998-8883*
  Sun-Th 11am-10pm/F & Sat 11am-11pm
- *405 Silver Spur Rd. (bet. Hawthorne & Crenshaw Blvds.), Rolling Hills, 310-377-9666*
  Sun-Th 11am-9:30pm/F & Sat 11am-10pm
- *9234 Lakewood Blvd. (Gallitin), Downey, 310-862-4489*
  Sun-Th 11am-10pm/F & Sat 11am-10:30pm
- *10879 Los Alamitos Blvd. (Katella Ave.), Los Alamitos, 310-493-3509*
  Every day 10:30am-10pm
- *28901 S. Western Ave. (Capitol), Rancho Palos Verdes, 310-547-1882*
  Sun-Th 11am-10pm/F & Sat 11am-11pm
- *24317 Magic Mountain Pkwy. (McBean Pkwy.), Valencia, 805-253-2304*
  M-F 6:30am-10pm/Sat 10am-11pm/Sun 11am-10pm
- *1344 N. Moorpark Rd. (Janss), Thousand Oaks, 805-495-3440*
  Sun-Th 11am-10pm/F & Sat 11am-11pm
- *3835 E. Thousand Oaks Blvd. (West Lake Blvd.), Thousand Oaks, 805-497-4494*
  Sun-Th 11am-9:30pm/F & Sat 11am-10pm

◪ Seen by some as a good "alternative" to higher-priced yogurterias, this massive chain provides what admirers call "a special treat without a lot of guilt", but detractors rate it "just ordinary" or worse – "tastes fake" with an "aftertaste"; still, "kids like it" and choosing from the "wide variety of toppings" can be "fun."

Robin Rose Ice Cream/Chocolates ⊟   26 23 22 E

- *215 Rose Ave. (Main St.), Venice, 310-399-1774*
  Every day noon-10pm

■ Locals are downright fanatic about this Venice shop's ice cream, especially the oft-cited "rich, rich, rich" raspberry chocolate truffle flavor that's so "addictive" you could easily "gain 20 pounds"; those who venture further find other "imaginative", "well-made", "adult" flavors such as white chocolate and rose petal; "one of LA's best indulgences."

Slender Sweet Shoppe ⊟   – – – M

- *2261 Foothill Blvd. (Ocean View Ave.), La Cañada,*
  818-248-2185
  M-F 10am-8pm/Sat 10am-9pm/Sun noon-8pm

As the name implies, all the ice cream and frozen yogurt found in this shop is fat free, which is why body obsessives "love" it; there's also a "huge variety of sugar-free and low-fat goodies" such as mousse, pies and more, all served by "some of the nicest staff" in an "old-fashioned" setting.

TCBY ⊟   19 17 18 I

- *715 Montana Ave. (bet. Lincoln Blvd. & 7th St.),*
  Santa Monica, 310-395-8388
- *1570 Rosecrans Ave. (bet. Sepulveda Blvd. & Aviation*
  Blvds.), Manhattan Beach, 310-643-9622
- *1872 S. PCH (Prospect), Redondo Beach, 310-543-1299*
- *980 N. Western Ave. (Park Plaza), San Pedro,*
  310-832-5522
- *15110 Rosecrans Ave. (La Mirada Blvd.), La Mirada,*
  714-523-9156
- *1772 Avenida De Los Arboles (Frwy. #23), Thousand Oaks,*
  805-492-2389
- *32525 Golden Lantern St. (Camino Del Avion), Dana Point,*
  714-661-0219
- *9971 Chapman Ave. (Brookhurst), Garden Grove,*
  714-638-4746
- *30301 Street of the Golden Lantern (Marina Hills),*
  Laguna Niguel, 714-363-1454
- *1154 Brookside Ave. (San Mateo), Redlands, 909-335-8988*
  All locations: every day 11am-10pm

◪ The initials stand for "The Country's Best Yogurt", a grandiose claim that some agree with ("delicious", "good and creamy", "the name says it") and others don't ("a little bland", "chemical aftertaste"); still, it's one of America's biggest chains, with branches in many shopping malls and at LAX where you can have a lick "between planes."

Mail Order

Mail order has exploded into such a booming, multimillion dollar industry that we could easily have put together a book based entirely on mail-order sources. In fact, people could do most of their shopping these days – even for food – by catalog, given the inclination and a willingness to pay shipping costs.

Adding to the trend, many local shops now accept mail orders for shipment almost anywhere. We have indicated throughout the book which local establishments provide mail order by placing an envelope symbol next to their name. For a complete list of those stores, see the Mail Order section of the Indexes.

What follows is a highly selective listing of mail-order houses that can bring some of the best of the country's food products and related items right to your doorstep.

Aidell's Sausages
- *1625 Alvarado St., San Leandro, CA 94577-2636,*
  510-614-5450/800-546-5795
  M-F 8:30am-5:30pm EST
Unusual sausages like Thai, Burmese, chicken-apple, creole and smoked duck.

American Spoon Foods
- *1668 Clarion Ave., Petoskey, MI 49770, 800-222-5886*
  M-F 9am-5pm EST
Preserves and chutneys, salad dressings, sugar-free jams and chocolate sauces from Michigan.

Balducci's
- *P.O. Box 10373, Newark, NJ 07193-0373, 800-225-3822*
  Every day 7am-8:30pm EST
A wide assortment of prepared foods, cheeses, meats, fish, coffees, breads, pâtés, dried goods and sauces.

Bridge Co.
- *214 E. 52nd St., New York, NY 10022,*
  212-688-4220/800-274-3435
  M-F 9am-5:30pm/Sat 10am-4:30pm EST
A wide variety of kitchenware, baking tools, porcelain and heavy-gauge cookware at discount prices.

Calyx & Corolla
- *1550 Bryant St., San Francisco, CA 94103,*
  415-626-5211/800-800-7788
  Every day 24 hrs
Fresh and dried flower arrangements with vases, wreaths, and special year of plants/year of fragrance plants program.

Chef's Catalog   M
- 3215 Commercial Ave., Northbrook, IL 60062-1900,
  800-338-3232
  M-F 8am-5pm CST

Major brands of cookware, cutlery, small electrical items
and gourmet tools at discount prices.

Chef's Collection   M
- 10631 SW 146 Pl., Miami, FL 33186-2871, 800-590-2433
  M-F 8:30am-5pm/Sat 10am-3pm EST

Major brands of cookware, cutlery and cooking
accessories at discount prices.

Cold Hollow Cider Mill   M
- P.O. Box 430, Rte. 100, Waterbury Ctr., VT 05677,
  802-244-8771/800-3APPLES
  Every day 8am-6pm EST

Vermont maple syrup, sugar granules, apple cider syrup,
apple butters and jelly.

Community Kitchens   M
- The Art of Food Plaza, Ridgely, MD 21685, 800-535-9901
  Every day 7am-11pm EST

Louisiana products such as gumbo, jambalaya spice and
pre-packaged food mixes.

D'Artagnan   E
- 399-419 St. Paul Ave., Jersey City, NJ 07306,
  201-792-0748/800-DARTAGN
  M-F 9am-6pm EST

French-style specialties like foie gras, confits, terrines,
magrets and Christmas goose.

Dean & DeLuca   VE
- 560 Broadway, New York, NY 10012,
  212-431-1691/800-221-7714
  Every day 9am-5pm EST

A wide assortment of prepared foods, cheeses, meats,
fish, coffees, breads, pâtés, dried goods and sauces.

Demi-Glace Gold   M
- More Than Gourmet, 115 W. Barges St., Akron, OH
  44311, 216-762-6652/800-860-9392
  M-F 8am-8pm EST

Classic veal, chicken, and vegetable stock reductions
(demi-glace) in 1-lb. and 1.6-oz. sizes.

Desserts by David Glass   VE
- 140-150 Huyshope Ave., Hartford, CT 06106,
  203-525-0345/800-DAVID99
  M-F 8am-4pm EST

Cakes, bite-size truffles, chocolate-covered cheesecake,
pumpkin cheesecake; mail order November–March only.

Discovery Kitchens E
- *P.O. Box 6325, Woodland Hills, CA 91367, 818-887-2007/
800-367-6865
M-F 9am-5pm PST*

A wide variety of handpicked and handcrafted food specialty items produced by small, family-owned American businesses.

E.A.T. VE
- *1064 Madison Ave., New York, NY 10028, 212-772-0022
Every day 7am-10pm EST*

Breads, muffins, cookies, cakes, pastries, prepared foods and gift items.

Fraser Morris E
- *1264 Third Ave., New York, NY 10021,
212-288-2727/800-423-3571
M-F 8:30am-7pm/Sat 8am-6pm/Sun 10am-6pm EST*

Large selection of caviar, dried fruits, nuts, teas, frozen appetizers, prepared foods and cheeses.

Freida's by Mail M
- *4465 Corporate Ctr. Dr., Los Alamitos, CA 90720-2561,
800-241-1771
M-F 8am-5pm PST*

Rare and exotic produce, fresh and dried chilies, gift baskets and sampler boxes.

Grace's Marketplace E
- *1237 Third Ave., New York, NY 10021
212-737-0600/800-325-6126
M-Sat 7am-8:30pm/Sun 8am-7pm EST*

A potpourri of Italian-accented specialties: pâtés, olive oils, balsamic vinegars, olives, cheeses, meats, and poultry.

Herb Farm, The E
- *8280 Issaquah-Fall City Rd., Fall City, WA 88024,
206-784-2222/800-866-4372
M-F 9am-5pm PST*

Over 600 varieties of herbs and perennial plants.

King Arthur Flour Company E
- *P.O. Box 1010, Norwich, VT 05055, 800-827-6836
M-F 9am-8pm/Sat 9am-5pm EST*

Specialty flours and home-baking utensils, hard-to-find baking supplies and ingredients.

K-Paul's Louisiana Enterprises E
- *P.O. Box 23342, New Orleans, LA 70183, 504-524-7394/
800-457-2857
M-F 8am-5pm CST*

Chef Paul Prudhomme's seasonings and other Louisiana products such as andouille sausage, tasso ham, New Orleans king cake and sweet-potato pecan pie.

Maison Glass E
- *111 E. 58th St., New York, NY 10022,
212-755-3316/800-822-5564
M-F 7:30am-6pm/Sat 8am-5:30pm EST*

Gourmet pâtés, smoked salmon, caviars, jams and nuts.

Maytag Dairy Farms M
- *P.O. Box 806, Newtown, IA 50208, 800-247-2458
M-F 8am-5pm/Sat 9am-1pm CST*

Handmade Maytag blue cheese, white cheddar, Edam and other Midwest specialty cheeses.

Meadow Farms Country Smokehouse M
- *P.O. Box 1387, Bishop, CA 93514, 619-873-5311
Every day 9am-6pm PST*

Smoked meats, bacon, beef, elk, and buffalo jerky.

Melissa's/Worldwide Produce M
- *P.O. Box 21127, Los Angeles, CA 90021, 800-588-0151
M-F 7am-5pm PST*

Over 300 specialty produce items, including herbs, spices, exotic fruits, mushrooms, chilies and edible flowers.

Mo Hotta-Mo Betta M
- *P.O. Box 4136, San Luis Obispo, CA 93403, 800-462-3220
M-Sat 9am-7pm PST*

Salsas, soups, jalapeño fudge sauce, spices, snacks, specialty gifts and an endless list of hot, jerk and barbecue sauces.

Mozzarella Company M
- *2944 Elm St., Dallas, TX 75226, 214-741-4072
M-F 9am-5pm/Sat 9am-3pm CST*

Homemade Italian and Latin cheeses, including buffalo mozzarella.

Murray's Sturgeon E
- *2429 Broadway, New York, NY 10024, 212-724-2650
M-F 8am-7pm/Sat 8am-8pm/Sun 8am-7pm EST*

A variety of smoked fish and caviar.

North Bay Trading Co. E
- *P.O. Box 129-Castle Rd., Brule, WI 54820-0129,
800-348-0164
Every day 24 hrs*

Canadian lake organic wild rice and wild rice soup.

Omaha Steaks E
- *4400 S. 96th St., Omaha, NE 68103, 800-228-9055
Every day 7am-11pm EST*

Top sirloin, prime rib, filet mignon, roasts, chicken, lamb, pork and gourmet food items.

Oregon Territory Co.   M
- 8065 Southwest Cirrus Dr., Beavertown, OR 97005, 800-247-0727
  Every day 24 hrs

Smoked salmon and turkey breast; desserts and candies; dried fruit, preserves and produce – all grown and prepared in Oregon.

Peet's Coffee   M
- P.O. Box 12509, Berkeley, CA 94712, 800-999-2132
  M-Sat 6am-6pm PST

A wide choice of gourmet coffee beans and ground coffees.

Petrossian   VE
- 182 W. 58th St., New York, NY 10019, 212-245-2217
  Every day 11am-midnight EST

A variety of smoked fish and caviar.

Pinnacle Orchards   M
- P.O. Box 616, Maumee, OH 43537, 800-759-1232
  Every day 9am-8pm CST

Fresh fruit of the month club and holiday gift baskets.

Polarica   E
- 13 Hudson St., New York, NY 10013,
  212-406-0400/800-GAME-4-US
  M-F 8am-6pm EST

Mail order–only restaurant supplier of exotic game; also carries products like rattlesnake, smoked salmon and caviar.

Ronaldo Maia   VE
- 27 E. 67th St., New York, NY 10021, 212-288-1049
  M-F 9:30am-6pm/Sat 11am-5pm EST

Floral arrangements and custom-blended potpourris available in hand-crafted vases and containers.

Russ & Daughters   M
- 179 E. Houston St., New York, NY 10002, 212-475-4880
  M-W 9am-6pm/Th-Sat 9am-7pm/Sun 8am-6pm EST

Smoked fish, salmon, gefilte fish, herring and whitefish.

Sarabeth's Kitchen   E
- 169 W. 78th St., New York, NY 10024, 800-552-JAMS
  M-F 9am-5pm EST

Muffins, scones and sticky buns, along with jams.

Shepherd's Garden Seeds   E
- 6116 Hwy. 9, Felton, CA 95018, 408-335-6911
  M-F 8:30am-5pm PST

Gourmet vegetable, flower and herb seeds, cookbooks and specialty items for gardening and cooking from the garden.

Sonoma Cheese Factory   M
- 2 W. Spain St., Sonoma, CA 95476, 800-535-2855
  M-F 8:30am-5pm/Sat & Sun 9am-6pm PST

Over 19 varieties of Sonoma jack cheeses and other Sonoma select food products.

Sylvia Weinstock `VE`
- *273 Church St., New York, NY 10013, 212-925-6698*
  M-F 9am-5pm EST
Custom bakery specializing in wedding and birthday cakes.

Todaro Bros. `E`
- *555 Second Ave., New York, NY 10016, 212-532-0633*
  M-Sat 7am-9pm/Sun 8am-8pm EST
Italian specialties: veal sausage, prosciutto, Italian
specialty meats and more.

Urbani Truffles `E`
- *2924 40th Ave., Queens, NY 11101, 800-281-2330*
  M-F 7am-7pm EST
Truffles, fresh and dried mushrooms and smoked salmon.

Virginia Diner `M`
- *P.O. Box 310, Wakefield, VA 23888, 800-868-6887*
  M-F 9am-5pm EST
Peanuts, peanut products, gourmet nuts and confections.

Vivande Porta Via `M`
- *2125 Fillmore St., San Francisco, CA 94115, 415-346-4430*
  Every day 10am-10pm PST
Full line of imported and domestic Italian specialty
products, including baked goods, oils, vinegars, flours,
grains, legumes and condiments.

White Flower Farms `E`
- *Rte. 63, Litchfield, CT 06759, 203-496-9600*
  M-F 9am-9pm/Sat 9am-6pm/Sun noon-6pm EST
A wide variety of plants and flowers, including African
violets and daffodil bulbs.

Wine Enthusiast, The `E`
- *P.O. Box 392, Pleasantville, NY 10570, 800-417-7788*
  M-F 9am-5:30pm/Sat 10am-5pm EST
Wine cellars, racks, glassware, accessories and other
wine-related items.

Wolfermans `M`
- *One Muffin Ln., P.O. Box 15913, Shawnee Mission, KS
  66285-5913, 800-999-0169*
  Every day 6am-8pm CST
Specializes in English muffins, but also offers rolls,
crumpets, rugalach, tea breads and brownies.

Zabar's `M`
- *2245 Broadway, New York, NY 10024, 212-787-2000*
  M-F 8am-7:30pm/Sat 8am-8pm/Sun 9am-6pm
Tofu and lox spreads, bagels, breads, smoked fish, caviar,
knishes, chopped liver, pot pies and duckling.

Meat & Poultry

After having been banished from the local diet for a while, beef is back, sausage has turned haute and the noble chicken is the diner's best friend (especially if the skin is removed). Although the supermarket still reigns supreme, more and more Southern Californians are rediscovering the simple joys of going to specialized markets where the butchers are highly skilled and the staff knows a tenderloin from a flank, a poularde from a pullet. The main reason for meat's comeback: there's nothing like the fine flavor that a good hunk of properly cooked protein provides. Even cardiologists enjoy it.

Top Quality
- **29** Schreiner's
  - Superior Meat Co.
  - Owen's Market
  - Bel-Air Meats
- **28** Atlas Kitchen

Top Variety
- **28** Superior Meat Co.
- **27** Bristol Farms
- **26** John Tusquella's
  - Bel-Air Meats
  - Marconda's

Top Service
- **27** Owen's Market
  - Atlas Kitchen
- **26** Bristol Farms
  - European Kitchen
  - Gelson's Market

Best Buys
- Atlas Kitchen
- Schreiner's
- European Kitchen
- Golden West Meats
- Superior Meat Co.

Q	V	S	C
25	23	23	E

Arrow Market 🚲
- *8315 Santa Monica Blvd. (3 blocks east of La Cienega Blvd.), W. Hollywood, 213-654-0934*
  M-Sat 8am-9pm/Sun 9am-9pm

■ A longtime West Hollywood meat purveyor, this "family operation" has a skilled staff that helps customers select "the best frankfurters in LA", "beautiful veal and pork" and other cuts "personalized" to suit individual needs; admirers consider it "the only real butcher" in the area and even note that it's a "wonderful source for dog bones."

28	25	27	M

ATLAS SAUSAGE KITCHEN ⊘
- *10626 Burbank Blvd. (½ block west of Cahuenga Blvd.), N. Hollywood, 818-763-2692*
  T-F 10am-6pm/Sat 9am-5pm

■ "Absolutely, positively the best sausage in town" is what fans find in this North Hollywood shop that dates back to 1945 (prehistoric in Valley terms), selling European-style links including "good bratwurst" and "Irish pork sausage"; regulars rate the quality "better than in Munich", and while that's debatable, it does have a "small-town German" feel and "great service."

BEL-AIR PRIME MEATS &🖃

| 29 | 26 | 26 | E |

- *Beverly Glen Marketplace, 2964 Beverly Glen Circle (Beverly Glen), Bel Air, 310-475-5915*
  M-Th 7:30am-10pm/F & Sat 7:30am-11pm/Sun 8am-10pm

■ Catering to the beef styles of the rich and famous, this "prime de la prime" butcher provides an affluent community with "excellent service and quality" – you "can't get better prime anywhere in town" say devotees, but you'll pay for the honor; the staff knows meat and they know how to sell: "go in for a steak, and before you know it you've bought a side of beef."

BRISTOL FARMS

| 28 | 27 | 26 | E |

- *See listing in Supermarkets section.*

■ Top-rated among supermarket butcher shops thanks to "exceptional quality and variety" plus "plenty of butchers" to help you select "everything from chicken sausage to osso buco"; pluses include "attractive displays", a computer that spits out recipes, and, at least for some lucky folks, "free bones for soup"; "expensive and worth it."

Chalet Gourmet Market &🖃

| 26 | 25 | 23 | E |

- *7880 Sunset Blvd. (Fairfax Ave.), LA, 213-874-6301*
  Every day 9am-9pm

■ Though oft-maligned for high prices, the Chalet is justly praised for its "top-grade beef and veal" carved by a butcher who "knows his stuff"; kudos go to "good cold cuts", "precooked chicken" and "melt-in-your-mouth porterhouse"; it's a good choice when in the mood to "indulge in a steak", but indulge too often and you may "go broke."

Danish American Farms 🖃

| 22 | 25 | 20 | I |

- *16212 Parthenia St. (Frwy. #405), North Hills, 818-893-6334/800-332-6474*
  Every day 8am-9pm

◪ There's "always a long wait" at this sizable North Hills country market in the middle of the San Fernando Valley, but most feel the "meats are worth it" thanks to "always fresh" quality, "great variety" and "good buys"; dissenters say "some things are better than others" and those lines make it too much "like shopping in Poland."

Doheny Kosher &🖃

| 27 | 23 | 25 | E |

- *9213 W. Pico Blvd. (2 blocks west of Doheny Dr.), LA, 310-276-7232*
  M-Th 7am-5:30pm/F 7am-2:30pm

■ Granted, the competition is limited, but this Beverlywood shop ranks as the town's top kosher butcher; known for "trustworthy" quality and service, it's praised for the "best chicken" and brisket, "wonderful roast turkeys" and more; some partisans give it the ultimate seal of approval: "my mother-in-law's choice."

Eschbach's Meat Products 🚲 ▱▽ 27 | 24 | 20 | M

- *18045 S. Western Ave. (182nd St.), Gardena, 310-324-1376*
  M-Sat 9am-6pm

■ An "outstanding", "old-fashioned" German meat market incongruously set in the South Bay version of Little Tokyo, where they'll "custom cut choice meat at surprisingly low prices"; it's especially "good for pork products and sausages" – in short, a "wonderful butcher."

EUROPEAN DELUXE   28 | 25 | 26 | M
SAUSAGE KITCHEN 🚲▱

- *9109 Olympic Blvd. (Doheny Dr.), Beverly Hills,*
  310-276-1331
  M-Sat 6am-6pm

■ How very LA – a fine sausage outlet right next to a popular sushi bar; it's an "excellent source of homemade, flavorful sausage" with "no preservatives", including specialties like "summer veal sausage" that have fans crying "wunderbar!"; "they know what they're doing" at this "delicious" "old favorite."

Farmer's Market Poultry   27 | 24 | 24 | M

- *Farmer's Market, 6333 W. Third St., Stall 216 (Fairfax Ave.),*
  LA, 213-936-8158
  M-Sat 8am-6:30pm/Sun 9am-5pm

■ Poultry is "skinned and deboned at no extra cost" at this fowl stand in the tourist-intensive Farmer's Market; along with the "best" birds, it offers "specialty items like rabbit and squab" and "even Christmas goose", all served by "courteous people"; "want chicken feet? duck breasts?" – odds are they have it and it's "excellent."

Farms, The 🚲   – | – | – | M

- *2030 Montana Ave., Santa Monica, 310-828-4244*
  M-F 8am-8pm/Sat & Sun 8am-7pm

When Fireside Market closed its doors after 35 years in business, Westsiders lamented the loss of its fine butcher; but The Farms, under the same ownership and located down the street, provides the same quality meat and service that Fireside did; N.B. Fireside is relocating to the Brentwood Country Mart under the name Brentwood Farms.

G&K Kosher Meats 🚲▱   25 | 24 | 22 | E

- *9126 W. Pico Blvd. (bet. Doheny & Oakhurst Drs.), LA,*
  310-276-2664
  M-Th 8am-5pm/F 8am-2pm

■ A well-respected kosher market in Pico's Kashruth Gulch, with "fresh", "quality" meats, "friendly service" and "the greatest chicken breasts"; there's "always a long wait", but longtime customers "wouldn't go anywhere else."

`Q` `V` `S` `C`

GELSON'S MARKETS
`27` `26` `26` `E`

• *See listing in Supermarkets section.*

■ The meats are "always fresh" and service is "courteous" and "helpful" at this highly rated supermarket chain with butchers "you can talk to"; it's "pricey" but "primo", with "immaculate" premises, "terrific" variety and quality that's "dependable – no ifs, ands or buts."

Golden West Meats &
`25` `25` `25` `M`

• *2012 Lincoln Blvd. (1 block south of Pico Blvd.), Santa Monica, 310-392-4166*
  M-Sat 9am-5:30pm/Sun 10am-4pm

☑ "Like being in Brooklyn", except it's near the water in Santa Monica, this "real butcher shop" provides "fresh lamb and veal", "tender, low-fat hams" and more; as one admirer puts it, this is where "helpful people sell good-quality meats to your specification" at moderate prices.

Honey Baked Ham 🖃
`26` `17` `21` `E`

• *300 N. La Brea Ave. (Beverly Blvd.), LA, 213-939-6868*
• *5299 N. Sepulveda Blvd. (1 block north of Jefferson Blvd.), Culver City, 310-390-4452*
• *20042 Ventura Blvd. (Winnetka), Woodland Hills, 818-905-5995*
• *4332 South St. (Lakewood Blvd.), Lakewood, 310-634-9711*
• *10157 Reseda Blvd. (Devonshire St.), Northridge, 818-701-5900*
• *480 S. Sierra Madre Blvd. (San Pasqual), Pasadena, 818-792-9627*
• *2635 Wilshire Blvd. (Princeton), Santa Monica, 310-829-4607*
• *2861 PCH (bet. Crenshaw & Hawthorne Blvds.), Torrance, 310-326-7603*
• *20042 Ventura Blvd. (Winnetka Ave.), Woodland Hills, 818-703-8888*
• *859 S. Glendora Ave. (south of Cameron), W. Covina, 818-960-3951*
• *10531 W. Pico Blvd. (1 block west of Beverly Glen), West LA, 310-470-0011*
• *541 N. Glendale Ave. (#134 Frwy.), Glendale, 818-242-0082*
• *2428 W. Whittier Blvd. (2 blocks west of Beach Blvd.), La Habra, 310-694-2114*
• *Granary Sq. Shopping Ctr., 25900 McBean Pkwy., Valencia, 805-255-9000*
• *3959 E. Thousand Oaks Blvd. (Westlake Blvd.), Westlake Village, 805-991-6966*
  Hours vary according to location; please call to check.

■ A "tradition for family events", the namesake specialty of this national chain is famed for its "sugar coating" that partisans just can't get enough of; while the hams are "hard to beat", the smoked turkey is also a "wonderful treat" and it all makes for good "gifts – they ship"; it also has "great ham bones for soup."

Hughes Markets |20| |20| |19| |M|
- *See listing in Supermarkets section.*

☑ To fans, this SoCal supermarket chain is "a cut above the others" for meats, with weekly specials that are "good buys" and "helpful butchers who will customize orders if requested"; foes say quality "varies by store."

Huntington Meats 🖃 ▽ |23| |24| |22| |E|
- *6333 W. Third St., Stall 350 (Fairfax Ave.), LA, 213-938-5383*
  M-Sat 8:30am-6pm/Sun 10am-5pm

■ Huntington Meats offers "some of the best steaks", "marbled and not too lean", plus "good specialty roasts", a "variety of sausages" and more; manned by "old-time butchers who will do it all", the place is "historically great."

J&T European Gourmet 🖃🏷 ▽ |27| |25| |18| |M|
(fka Andrzej)
- *1128 Wilshire Blvd. (12th St.), Santa Monica, 310-394-7227*
  M-F 9am-7pm/Sat 9am-6pm/Sun 10am-4pm

☑ A "mini-trip" to Mittel Europe, this sparkling white, brightly lit shop smokes its own meats, including "the best Polish sausage this side of Chicago" and "subtly seasoned head cheese"; quality is "excellent", but the downside is staff that "shows no concern for customers."

Jody Maroni's Sausage |26| |24| |20| |M|
Kingdom 🏷🖃
- *2011 Ocean Front Walk (Venice Blvd.), Venice, 310-306-1995*
  M-F 11am-sunset/Sat & Sun 11am-8pm
- *City Walk, 1000 Universal Ctr. Dr. (#101 Frwy.), Universal City,*
  818-622-5639
  Every day 10am-11pm
- *1315 Third St. Promenade (south of Arizona Ave.),*
  Santa Monica, 310-393-9063
  M-Sat 11am-11pm/Sun 11am-9pm
- *Mail order: 800-428-8364*

■ LA's most famous sausage-maker, the ubiquitous, gregarious Jody (aka Jordan Monkarsh) has turned sausage into haute cuisine; duck, chicken, lamb, turkey, exotic herbs and spices all go into making these "creative" sausages that fans deem "best in the US"; as "Jody junkies" can attest, they're worth "going off the veggie wagon" for.

Louis Foods 🚲🖃 ▽ |26| |23| |22| |E|
- *451 S. Sierra Madre Blvd. (San Pasqual Ave.),*
  Pasadena, 818-795-4281
  Every day 7am-11pm
- *South Hills Shopping Ctr., 1420 Azusa Ave. (2 miles south*
  of #10 Frwy.), W. Covina, 818-916-2070/800-696-5684
  Every day 7am-10pm

■ A "Pasadena secret without parking problems" but with meat that's "always fresh and flavorful", including the "best prime"; "surprisingly good" quality and "helpful" service are a pleasing combo; the West Covina branch is new.

Q | V | S | C

MARCONDA'S MEAT MARKET ⌷ | 28 | 26 | 26 | E

- *Farmer's Market, 6333 West Third St., Stall 512 (Fairfax Ave.), LA, 213-938-5131*
  Every day 9am-6pm

■ "Fine meat" and "accommodating butchers" have brought customers to this Farmer's Market stand since 1941; "if you can afford it" it's "worth every penny" for the "best liver", "good low-fat ground beef" and other "prime" cuts; some also buy "big marrow bones" for pampered pooches.

Mrs. Gooch's Whole Foods Market 🚲 | 27 | 24 | 25 | E

- *See listing in Health/Natural Food section.*

■ "You don't need to be a health nut" to appreciate the "beautiful displays" of "pure", chemical-free meat and poultry at this natural foods market; with "excellent quality" and "knowledgeable butchers" who'll "go to extra lengths" to please, you clearly "get what you pay for."

Noonan's Ribs 🚲⌷ | 25 | 19 | 22 | M

- *6601 S. Western Ave. (bet. Florence & Gage Ave.), LA, 213-752-0032*
  M-F 8am-4pm/Sat & Sun 8am-noon

■ You can get Noonan's "excellent" baby back ribs at markets all over the city, but aficionados say they're best from "the source" (though it's located in an iffy industrial area); they especially appeal to fans of "dry", "not fatty" BBQ, and the "sauce is A-1" too.

OWEN'S MARKET 🚲⌷ | 29 | 25 | 27 | E

- *9769 W. Pico Blvd. (Roxbury Dr.), LA, 310-553-8181*
  Every day 9am-6pm

■ Catering to the carriage trade, this upscale neighborhood market provides Beverly Hills and Beverlywood residents with "top-quality" beef and steaks, delivered to their door, if desired; to well-heeled regulars it's "like an old-fashioned family butcher" complete with "warm", "personal service."

Pavilions | 20 | 21 | 19 | M

- *See listing in Supermarkets section.*

☑ These upscale spin-offs of Vons have supporters who say they're "fine for everyday shopping", offering "better-than-average" supermarket meat and poultry at "good prices"; but foes say "varying quality" means "you never know what you'll get"; still, they're "convenient", even if "service is sometimes lacking."

Price/Costco | – | – | – | I

- *See listing in Supermarkets section.*

The size of some of the cuts of meat can be intimidating unless you have large numbers to feed, but the quality of the beef, pork and lamb at this food-oriented warehouse store will impress the most picky carnivores; service is not a strong suit – be prepared to butterfly your own lamb and make your own kebabs.

SCHREINER'S FINE SAUSAGE ⌖   29 | 25 | 25 | M

- *3417-19 Ocean View Blvd., Glendale, 818-244-4735*
  M-Sat 9am-5:30pm

■ One of SoCal's top meat markets, this small Glendale shop "smells and tastes like you're in Germany", earning raves for the "best all-veal hot dogs", "good turkey dogs", "excellent Black Forest ham", "awesome smoked pork chops" and "wonderful spareribs"; some consider it the "best German deli in LA."

SUPERIOR MEAT CO. ♿⌖   29 | 28 | 25 | E

- *9533 W. Pico Blvd. (Beverly Dr.), LA, 310-553-8515*
  M-F 6am-4pm

■ Top rated for variety, this wholesaler is used by most of the restaurants in town, but it also sells retail if you buy in bulk and order at least 24 hours in advance; and many do, since it offers some of the "best overall quality meat in LA", or maybe even the "best west of Chicago"; "if you want to cook at home what you order at LA's finest restaurants, come here."

Ventura Kosher Meats ♿   – | – | – | E

- *18357 Ventura Blvd. (Reseda Blvd.), Tarzana,*
  818-881-3777
  M-Th 8:30am-6pm/F & Sun 8:30am-3pm

You don't have to be Jewish to enjoy the excellent glatt kosher meats, poultry and cooked dishes (briskets, stuffed cabbage, knishes and so on) at this popular West Valley butcher; first-timers are advised to shop early to avoid the crowds before the holidays and on Fridays.

Vicente Foods   26 | 23 | 25 | E

- *12049 San Vicente Blvd. (Bundy Dr.), Brentwood,*
  310-472-5215
  M-Sat 9am-9pm/Sun 9am-8pm

◪ Haute yet "homey", this market's meat department is praised by fans as a "good source for unusual cuts" of "excellent quality", but foes deem it "run-of-the-mill with high prices"; they'll handle "special orders" and there's "always an open check-out stand", but "you can't worry about money if you shop here."

Party Rentals*

Sometimes you need the services of a company that can supply everything from extra tables and chairs to dance floors, theme props or extra glasses for a champagne party. That's where party rental firms like those listed below come in.

There are a few things to keep in mind when dealing with these firms. Most have minimums and require a deposit. And though advance notice requirements vary, you should always reserve rented items as early as possible. During the holidays, for example, glassware, plates, chairs and other party equipment are in huge demand. Call a month ahead — it won't be too soon.

Abbey Rents
- *1001 N. La Brea Ave. (Santa Monica Blvd.), LA, 213-466-9582*

A-Packaged Parties
- *6412 Independence Ave. (bet. DeSoto Ave. & Victory Blvd., south of Roscoe Blvd.), Woodland Hills, 818-710-1222*

A-Rental Connection
- *21311 Deering Court (1 block east of Canoga Ave.), Canoga Park, 818-883-7368*

Avery Kitchen Supply
- *836 Traction Ave. (bet. 2nd & 3rd Sts., east of Alameda St.), Downtown LA, 213-624-7832*

Celebrate w/Linen Lenders
- *13830 Ventura Blvd. (2½ blocks west of Woodman Ave.), Sherman Oaks, 818-789-6878*

Classic Party Rentals
- *8476 Steller Dr. (south of National Blvd., east of Hayden Ave.), Culver City, 310-202-0011*

Lady of the Cloths
- *13837 Ventura Blvd. (2½ blocks west of Woodman Ave.), Sherman Oaks, 818-986-2843*

---

* Not listed in Alphabetical Index.

Party Rentals C

L.A. Party Rents E
- 13520 Saticoy St., Van Nuys, 818-989-4300

Pico Party Rents I
- 2537 S. Fairfax Ave. (Washington Blvd.), Culver City, 213-936-8268

Premiere Party Rents M
- 12100 Washington Blvd. (bet. Centinela & Inglewood Aves.), Culver City, 310-391-2552

Regal Rents VE
- 9925 Jefferson Blvd. (bet. Overland Ave. & LaCienega Blvd.), Culver City, 310-204-3382

Unique Tabletop Rentals E
- 15000 Lakewood Blvd. (bet. #105 & #91 Frwys.), Bellflower, 310-529-3632

Party Sites*

When the party or event you're planning requires more space – or more pizzazz – than your home or office has to offer, it's time to look for an outside site. Luckily, Los Angeles has an ample supply of dramatic party sites suited to every size, taste and pocketbook. This section offers a sampling of some of the more interesting locales, including private clubs, mansions, museums, hotels, nightclubs and restaurants. There are lots of other good party sites at art galleries, schools, office building lobbies and even public parks; just use your imagination. And the Los Angeles Conservancy offers for a nominal fee a list of historic sites available for special events.

There are several things to bear in mind. Hotels, restaurants and clubs almost always insist on providing the party food – so, obviously, will catering facilities with their own spaces. Conversely, most other sites will ask you to make your own catering arrangements. Also, remember that some of the more public spaces, such as museums, usually have various restrictions, and to rent space at a private club you usually have to be a member or be sponsored by one – be sure to inquire.

We've included the number of party rooms at each site (**rms**), as well as general capacity (**cap**), type of cuisine (for restaurants) and an idea of cost. Many sites have additional outdoor capacity, so be sure to ask. And bear in mind that the cost estimate is a very rough guideline, because prices are affected by a variety of factors, such as guarantees, group size, contracted services, etc., thus most sites leave a lot of room for negotiation. (Some prices are so flexible that we have marked them with an **N**, meaning negotiate.) Some public spaces, for example, allow unlimited entertaining for corporations that pay a seemingly hefty (but usually tax-deductible) membership fee. Other sites charge a flat fee for space, still others a per-person rate. We suggest you call to find out how each site charges, and shop around extensively.

When dealing with restaurants, hotels or nightclubs, it is wise to reserve a time business is slow. Otherwise you'll be paying for the business they give up as well as the business you give them.

---

* Not listed in Alphabetical Index; capacities are maximum for smallest and largest dining room; check for additional capacity outdoors.

MUSEUMS, HISTORIC HOUSES, ETC. `c`

Adamson House†**/200 cap `M`
• *23200 PCH, Malibu, 310-457-8185*

**Atom Smasher's Neon
Warehouse**/1 rm, 400 cap `M`
• *8650 Hayden Pl., Culver City, 310-559-6177*

Breakers, The/2 rms, 150-230 cap `N`
• *210 E. Ocean Blvd., Long Beach, 310-983-2803*

Brookside Country Club/3 rms, 80-400 cap `M`
• *1133 N. Rosemont, Pasadena, 818-577-4497*

Calabasas Inn/2 rms, 180-300 cap `I`
• *23500 Park Sorrento Dr., Calabasas, 818-222-8870*

Calamigos Ranch/6 rms, 125-350 cap `M`
• *327 Latigo Canyon, Malibu, 818-889-6280*

Calif. Heritage Museum†/1 rm, 125 cap `I`
(fka Santa Monica Heritage Museum)
• *2612 Main St., Santa Monica, 310-392-8537*

Castle Green/3 rms, 50-250 cap `M`
• *99 S. Raymond Ave., Pasadena, 818-792-4444*

Children's Museum†/1 rm, 400 cap `N`
• *310 N. Main St., Downtown LA, 213-687-8801*

Craven Estate†/3 rms, 250 cap `VE`
• *430 Madeline Dr., Pasadena, 818-799-0841*

Crown Rose Mansion/3 rms, 75 cap `I`
• *1247 N. Garfield Ave., Pasadena, 818-791-8387*

Descanso Gardens†**/500 cap `N`
• *1418 Descanso Dr., La Cañada, 818-952-4385*

**Dorothy Chandler
Pavilion/Music Center of LA
County**/multiple spaces, 120-2,500 cap `N`
• *125 N. Grand Ave., Downtown LA, 213-972-7318*

Ebell of Los Angeles, The/4 rms, 125-600 cap `M`
• *4400 Wilshire Blvd., LA, 213-937-6345*

**Gene Autry Western Heritage
Museum†**/various spaces, 225-2,000 cap `M`
• *4700 Western Heritage Way, Griffith Park, 213-667-2000*

**George C. Page Museum† (c/o
Natural History Museum)**/1 rm, 150 cap `VE`
• *5801 Wilshire Blvd., LA, 213-964-6355*

---

† BYO caterer.
**Outdoor facility only.

Party Sites   C

Greystone Mansion†**/200 cap   M
• *905 Loma Vista Dr., Beverly Hills, 310-550-4796*

Hollywood Athletic Club/4 rms, 25-285 cap   M
• *6525 Hollywood Blvd., Hollywood, 213-962-6600*

Hollywood Park/various spaces, 100-1,000 cap   N
• *1050 S. Prairie Ave., Inglewood, 310-419-1529*

Hornblower Dining Yachts/5 yachts, 200 cap   M
• *13755 Fiji Way, Marina del Rey, 310-301-6000*

Ivy Substation/Media Park†/1 rm, 200 cap   I
• *9070 Venice Blvd., Culver City, 310-838-5734*

Japanese Garden, The†/1 rm, 84 cap   I
• *6100 Woodley Ave., Van Nuys, 818-756-8166*

Kidspace Museum/1 rm, 20 cap   I
• *390 S. El Molino, Pasadena, 818-449-9144*

La Venta Inn/various spaces, 175 cap   M
• *796 Via del Monte, Palos Verdes Estates, 310-378-9378*

Long Beach Museum of Art†**/various   E
spaces, 400 cap
• *2300 E. Ocean Blvd., Long Beach, 310-439-2119*

Los Angeles Public Library†/various spaces,   N
25-100 cap
• *Central Library, 630 W. 5th St., Downtown LA,
  213-228-7474*

**Los Angeles State and Country   E
Arboretum†****/300 cap
• *301 N. Baldwin Ave., Arcadia, 818-446-8251*

Los Angeles Zoo†**/5,000 cap   N
• *5333 Zoo Dr., LA, 213-664-1100*

Magic Castle, The/various spaces, 400 cap   N
• *7001 Franklin Ave., Hollywood, 213-851-3442*

Marquis Events/Exclusive charter agent for   N
15 first-class private yachts/150 cap
• *3007 Washington Blvd., Marina del Rey, 310-454-8212*

Merry-Go-Round†/300 cap   I
• *201 Santa Monica Pier, Santa Monica, 310-394-7554*

Museum of Contemporary Art, The/   N
various spaces, 3,000 cap
• *250 S. Grand Ave., Downtown LA, 213-621-1736*

Museum of Flying/various spaces, 1500 cap   N
• *2772 Donald Douglas Loop, N. Santa Monica,
  310-392-8822*

† BYO caterer.
**Outdoor facility only.

Party Sites

C

Natural History Museum†/various spaces,   N
750 cap
• *900 Exposition Blvd., LA, 213-964-6355*

New York Food Co.'s Catalina   M
Room**/500 cap
• *6610 Palos Verdes Dr. S., Rancho Palos Verdes, 310-544-8884*

Olympic Collection, The/5 rms, 120-630 cap   N
• *11301 W. Olympic Blvd., West LA, 310-575-4585*

Orcutt Ranch†**/175 cap   I
• *23600 Roscoe Blvd., West Hills, 818-346-7449*

Oviatt Building†/various spaces, 125 cap   M
• *617 S. Olive St., Downtown LA, 213-622-6096*

Pacific Asia Museum†**/1 rm, 100 cap   M
• *46 N. Los Robles, Pasadena, 818-449-2742*

Paramount Ranch†**/300 cap   I
• *2813 Cornell Rd., Agoura, 818-597-1036*

Pasadena Center/various spaces, 3,000 cap   N
• *300 Green St., Pasadena, 818-793-2122*

Pasadena Masonic Temple†/4 rms,   N
100-300 cap
• *200 S. Euclid Ave., Pasadena, 818-578-9776*

Petersen Museum†/4 rms, 170-550 cap   N
• *6060 Wilshire Blvd., LA, 213-964-6355*

Peter Strauss Ranch†**/300 cap   I
• *3000 Mulholland Hwy., Agoura, 818-991-9231*

Robert Mondavi Wine & Food   N
Center/3 rms, 14-175 cap
• *1570 Scenic Ave., Costa Mesa, 714-979-4510*

Saddlerock Ranch†**/various spaces,   VE
5,000 cap
• *31727 Mulholland Hwy., Malibu, 818-706-0888*

Santa Anita Race Track/various spaces,   N
25-2,000 cap
• *285 W. Huntington Dr. (Baldwin Ave.), 818-574-7223*

Santa Monica Museum of Art†/1 rm, 150 cap   E
• *2437 Main St., Santa Monica, 310-399-0433*

Southwest Museum†/2 rms, 40-125 cap   N
• *234 Museum Dr., Highland Park, 213-221-2164*

---

† BYO caterer.
**Outdoor facility only.

Party Sites

C

UCLA Fowler Museum of Cultural History†/150 cap N
• 405 Hilgard Ave., Westwood, 310-206-2310

Union Station†/2 rms, 100-500 cap E
• 800 N. Alameda, Downtown LA, 213-625-5865

Victorian at Heritage Sq., The/4 rms, E
25-160 cap
• 2640 Main St., Santa Monica, 310-392-4956

Will Rogers State Historic Park†*/200 cap I
• 14253 Sunset Blvd., Pacific Palisades, 310-454-8212

HOTELS

Argyle, The/4 rms, 50-180 cap VE
• 8358 Sunset Blvd., W. Hollywood, 213-654-7100

Bel Air Hotel/2 rms, 70-150 cap VE
• 701 Stone Canyon Rd., Bel Air, 310-472-1211

Beverly Hills Hotel/3 rms, 120-650 cap VE
• 9641 Sunset Blvd., Beverly Hills, 310-276-2251

Beverly Hilton/24 rms, 30-1,200 cap E
• 9876 Wilshire Blvd., Beverly Hills, 310-274-7777

Beverly Plaza/1 rm, 150 cap M
• 8384 W. Third St., LA, 213-658-6600

Beverly Prescott/2 rms, 65-150 cap M
• 1224 S. Beverwil Dr., LA, 310-277-2800

Biltmore/4 rms, 80-1,100 cap E
• 506 S. Grand Ave., Downtown LA, 213-624-1011

Burbank Airport Hilton & Convention Center/41 rms, 30-1,040 cap M
• 2500 Hollywood Way, Burbank, 818-843-6000

Century Plaza Hotel & Tower/30 rms, E
70-1,800 cap
• 2025 Ave. of the Stars, Century City, 310-277-2000

Chateau Marmont/2 rms, 50-200 cap E
• 8221 Sunset Blvd., Hollywood, 213-656-1010

Crowne Plaza Holiday Inn Redondo Beach/3 rms, 75-650 cap M
• 300 N. Harbor Dr., Redondo Beach, 310-318-8888

Doubletree Pasadena/18 rms, 20-450 cap M
• 191 N. Los Robles Ave., Pasadena, 818-792-2727

---

† BYO caterer.
**Outdoor facility only.

Party Sites   C

Four Seasons/3 rms, 60-250 cap   VE
● *300 S. Doheny Dr., LA, 310-273-2222*

Glendale Red Lion/5 rms, 25-700 cap   I
● *100 W. Glenoak Blvd., Glendale, 818-956-5466*

Hyatt Regency/15 rms, 80-2,000 cap   M
● *711 S. Hope St., Downtown LA, 213-683-1234*

Inter-Continental Hotel/3 rms, 150-700 cap   E
● *251 S. Olive St., Downtown LA, 213-617-3300*

JW Marriott Hotel at Century City/7 rms,   E
70-300 cap
● *2151 Ave. of the Stars, Century City, 310-277-7777*

LA Airport Hilton & Towers/6 rms, 70-900 cap   M
● *5711 W. Century Blvd., LA, 310-410-4000*

Loews Santa Monica Beach/4 rms, 100-500 cap   E
● *1700 Ocean Ave., Santa Monica, 310-458-6700*

Long Beach Hilton/23 rms, 20-1,400 cap   M
● *Two World Trade Ctr., Long Beach, 310-983-3400*

Miramar Sheraton/6 rms, 20-500 cap   E
● *101 Wilshire Blvd., Santa Monica, 310-576-7777*

Mondrian/3 rms, 25-80 cap   E
● *8440 Sunset Blvd., W. Hollywood, 310-650-8999*

New Otani and Garden/9 rms, 100-600 cap   M
● *120 S. Los Angeles St., Downtown LA, 213-629-1200*

Nikko at Beverly Hills, Hotel/2 rms, 60-360 cap E
● *465 S. La Cienega Blvd., Beverly Hills, 310-247-0400*

Omni Los Angeles/29 rms, 15-900 cap   E
● *930 Wilshire Blvd., Downtown LA, 213-629-4321*

Peninsula Beverly Hills/4 rms, 30-120 cap   VE
● *9882 Little Santa Monica Blvd., Beverly Hills,*
  310-551-2888

Portofino Hotel & Yacht Club/2 rms,   M
150-200 cap
● *260 Portofino Way, Redondo Beach, LA, 310-379-8481*

Radisson Bel Air Summit/5 rms, 30-300 cap   M
● *11461 Sunset Blvd., Brentwood, 310-476-6571*

Radisson Plaza Hotel/Golf Club/18 rms,   M
20-450 cap
● *1400 Parkview Ave., Manhattan Beach, 310-546-7511*

Regent Beverly Wilshire/4 rms, 40-810 cap   VE
● *9500 Wilshire Blvd., Beverly Hills, 310-275-5200*

---

† BYO caterer.
**Outdoor facility only.

Party Sites   C

Ritz-Carlton Huntington Hotel/8 rms,   E
30-770 cap
• *1401 S. Oak Knoll Ave., Pasadena, 818-568-3900*

Ritz-Carlton Marina del Rey/6 rms, 45-530 cap   VE
• *4375 Admiralty Way, Marina Del Rey, 310-823-1700*

Sheraton Grande/26 rms, 30-725 cap   E
• *333 S. Figueroa St., Downtown LA, 213-617-1133*

Sheraton Universal/14 rms, 60-1,000 cap   M
• *333 Universal Terr. Pkwy., Universal City, 818-980-1212*

Shutters on the Beach/6 rms, 40-220 cap   VE
• *1 Pico Blvd., Santa Monica, 310-458-0030*

Sofitel Ma Maison, Hotel/1 rm, 240 cap   E
• *8555 Beverly Blvd., LA, 310-278-5444*

Sportsmen's Lodge/5 rms, 25-130 cap   I
• *12825 Ventura Blvd., Studio City, 818-769-4700*

Universal City Hilton & Tower/21 rms,   M
20-1,300 cap
• *555 Universal Terr. Pkwy., Universal City, 818-506-2500*

Warner Center Marriott/10 rms, 40-770 cap   M
• *21850 Oxnard St., Woodland Hills, 818-887-4800*

Westin Bonaventure Hotel and Suites/   M
6rms, 80-2,000 cap
• *404 S. Figueroa St., Downtown LA, 213-624-1000*

Westlake Inn Hotel and Restaurant/4 rms,   I
90-225 cap
• *31943 Agoura Rd., Westlake Village, 818-889-1662*

Westwood Marquis and Garden/5 rms,   VE
50-150 cap
• *930 Hilgard Ave., Westwood, 310-208-8765*

Wyndham Bel Age/5 rms, 80-350 cap   E
• *1001 N. San Vicente Blvd., W. Hollywood, 310-854-1111*

Wyndham Checkers/2 rms, 45-70 cap   VE
• *535 S. Grand Ave., Downtown LA, 213-624-0000*

RESTAURANTS & CLUBS
(For additional listings, see the
Zagat Los Angeles Restaurant Survey)

Alto Palato/1 rm, 42 cap/Italian   M
• *755 N. La Cienega Blvd. (bet. Melrose Ave. & Santa
Monica Blvd.), W. Hollywood, 310-657-9271*

---

† BYO caterer.
**Outdoor facility only.

Party Sites

Beaurivage/4 rms, 16-100 cap/Mediterranean   **M**
- *26025 P.C.H. (north of Malibu Canyon Rd.), Malibu, 310-456-5733*

Belvedere, The/1 rm, 8-22 cap/Continental   **VE**
- *Peninsula Beverly Hills Hotel, 9882 Little Santa Monica Blvd., Beverly Hills, 310-273-4888*

Bistro 45/1 rm, 44 cap/Cal-French   **E**
- *45 S. Mentor Ave. (bet. Colorado Ave. & Green St.), Pasadena, 818-795-2478*

Bistro Garden/2 rms, 50-160 cap/Continental   **E**
- *176 N. Cañon Dr. (north of Wilshire Blvd.), Beverly Hills, 310-550-3900*

Bistro Garden/Coldwater/1 rm, 80 cap/   **E**
Continental
- *12950 Ventura Blvd. (west of Coldwater Canyon Ave.), Studio City, 818-501-0202*

Ca'Brea/2 rms, 30-60 cap/Italian   **M**
- *346 S. La Brea Ave. (3 blocks north of Wilshire Blvd.), LA, 213-938-2863*

Ca'del Sole/2 rms, 10-90 cap/Italian   **M**
- *4100 Cahuenga Blvd. (bet. Moorpark St. & Lankershim Blvd.), N. Hollywood, 818-985-4669*

Cafe Bellissimo/1 rm, 60 cap/Italian   **I**
- *22458 Ventura Blvd. (1 block west of Shoup Ave.), Woodland Hills, 818-225-0026*

Cafe '50s/1 rm, 50 cap/Diner-American   **I**
- *4609 Van Nuys Blvd. (bet. Ventura Blvd. & Ventura Frwy.), Sherman Oaks, 818-906-1955*
- *11623 Santa Monica Blvd. (2 blocks east of Barrington Ave.), West LA, 310-479-1955*

Cafe Santorini's Rococo/2 rms, 20-175 cap/   **M**
Mediterranean
- *70 W. Union St. (bet. Delancy & Fair Oaks Sts.), Pasadena, 818-564-4200*

Camelions/3 rms, 36-60 cap/Californian   **E**
- *246 26th St. (south of San Vicente Blvd.), Santa Monica, 310-395-0746*

Campanile/3 rms, 20-80 cap/   **VE**
California-Mediterranean
- *624 S. La Brea Ave. (north of Wilshire Blvd.), LA, 213-938-1447*

---

† BYO caterer.
**Outdoor facility only.

Party Sites

C

Cava/1 rm, 150 cap/Spanish-Latin M
• Beverly Plaza Hotel, 8384 Third St. (2 bl. east of La
Cienega Blvd.), LA, 213-658-8898

Chez Helene/1 rm, 40 cap/French bistro M
• 267 S. Beverly Dr. (2 blocks south of Wilshire Blvd.),
Beverly Hills, 310-276-1558

Chez Melange/5 rms, 45-250 cap/Int'l-Eclectic M
• Palos Verdes Inn, 1716 PCH (bet. Palos Verdes Blvd. &
Prospect Ave.), Redondo Beach, 310-540-1222

Chianti/Cucina Chianti/1 rm, 25 cap/Italian M
• 7383 Melrose Ave. (bet. La Brea & Fairfax Aves.), LA,
213-653-8333

Ciao Trattoria/1 rm, 120 cap/Italian M
• 815 W. Seventh St. (bet. Flower & Figueroa Sts.),
Downtown LA, 213-624-2244

Cicada/1 rm, 50 cap/Italian E
• 8478 Melrose Ave. (La Cienega Blvd.), West Hollywood,
213-655-5559

Citrus/1 rm, 150 cap/Californian VE

Bistro Bar/1 rm, 65 cap/French Bistro M
• 6703 Melrose Ave. (west of Highland Ave.), LA,
213-857-0034

Clearwater Cafe/1 rm, 40 cap/Seafood M
• 168 W. Colorado Blvd. (Pasadena Ave.), Pasadena,
818-356-0959

Dar Magreb/2 rms, 18-100 cap/Moroccan M
• 7651 Sunset Blvd. (6 blocks east of Fairfax Ave.),
Hollywood, 213-876-7651

DC3/2 rms, 10-170 cap/American M
• Santa Monica Airport, 2800 Donald Douglas Loop N. (off
28th St. & Ocean Park Blvd.), Santa Monica, 310-399-2323

Depot/1 rm, 70 cap/Cal-Pacific New Wave M
• 1250 Cabrillo Ave. (Torrance St.), Torrance, 310-787-7501

Derby, The/1 rm, 400 cap/Italian N
• 4500 Los Feliz Blvd. (Hillhurst Ave.), Los Feliz,
213-663-8979

Drago/1 rm, 26 cap/Italian E
• 2628 Wilshire Blvd. (26th St.), Santa Monica, 310-828-1585

Dynasty Room/1 rm, 20 cap/Continental VE
• Westwood Marquis Hotel, 930 Hilgard Ave., Westwood,
310-208-8765

† BYO caterer.
**Outdoor facility only.

Empress Pavilion/2 rms, 10-30 cap/Chinese   `I`
- *Bamboo Plaza, 988 N. Hill St. (Bernard St.), Chinatown,*
  213-617-9898

Engine Co./1 rm, 20 cap/American   `M`
- *644 S. Figueroa (bet. 7th St. & Wilshire Blvd.), Downtown*
  LA, 213-624-6996

Farfalla on La Brea/1 rm, 80 cap/Italian   `M`
- *143 N. La Brea Ave. (south of Beverly Blvd.), LA,*
  213-938-2504

Fenix/4 rms, 50-80 cap/Cal-French   `VE`
- *The Argyle, 8358 Sunset Blvd., W. Hollywood,*
  213-654-7100

Four Oaks/3 rms, 25-30 cap/Californian   `VE`
- *2181 N. Beverly Glen Blvd. (2 miles north of Sunset Blvd.),*
  Bel Air, 310-470-2265

Gardens/1 rm, 12-22 cap/Cal-French   `M`
- *Four Seasons Hotel, 300 S. Doheny Dr., LA, 310-273-2222*

Gate, The/3 rms, 75-150 cap/American   `N`
- *643 N. La Cienega Blvd. (Melrose Ave.), LA, 310-289-8808*

Gladstone's University City**/2 rms,   `M`
35-60 cap/Seafood
- *1000 Universal CityWalk (next to Universal Studios Tour),*
  Universal City, 818-622-3474

Gordon Biersch/1 rm, 35 cap/American   `I`
- *41 Hugus Alley (bet. Fair Oaks Ave. & Colorado Blvd.),*
  Pasadena, 818-449-0052

Granita/3 rms, 25-50 cap/Californian   `VE`
- *23725 W. Malibu Rd. (Webb Way & PCH), Malibu,*
  310-456-0488

Hal's/1 rm, 40 cap/Californian   `M`
- *1349 Abbot Kinney Blvd. (bet. Venice Blvd. & Main St.),*
  Venice, 310-396-3105

House of Blues/various spaces, 999 cap/   `N`
Cajun-Creole
- *8430 Sunset Blvd., W. Hollywood, 213-848-2516*

Il Cielo/2 rms, 30-40 cap/Italian   `M`
- *9018 Burton Way (east of Doheny Dr.), Beverly Hills,*
  310-276-9990

Il Moro/1 rm, 16 cap/Italian   `M`
- *11400 W. Olympic Blvd. (3 blocks west of #405 Frwy.),*
  West LA, 310-575-3530

---

† BYO caterer.
**Outdoor facility only.

Party Sites

C

Inn/Seventh Ray/2 rms, 45-55 cap/Health Food **M**
- *128 Old Topanga Rd. (4 miles north of PCH), Topanga, 310-455-1311*

Jimmy's/4 rms, 10-200 cap/Continental **VE**
- *201 Moreno Dr. (east of Century Park East), Beverly Hills, 310-552-2394*

Lawry's Prime Rib/2 rms, 40-80/Steakhouse **E**
- *100 N. La Cienega Blvd. (north of Wilshire Blvd.), Beverly Hills, 310-652-2827*

Le Chardonnay/1 rm, 34 cap/French bistro **E**
- *8284 Melrose Ave. (Sweetzer Ave.), LA, 213-655-8880*

Le Dome/3 rms, 20-80 cap/French bistro **E**
- *8720 Sunset Blvd. (La Cienega Blvd.), W. Hollywood, 310-659-6919*

Le Petit Greek/1 rm, 15 cap/Greek **M**
- *Beverly Connection, 100 N. La Cienega Blvd., 2nd fl. (bet. Beverly Blvd. & 3rd St.), LA, 310-657-5932*

L'Opera/2 rms, 50-120 cap/Italian **M**
- *101 Pine St. (1st St.), Long Beach, 310-491-0066*

L'Orangerie/1 rm, 40 cap/French **VE**
- *903 N. La Cienega Blvd. (bet. Melrose Ave. & Santa Monica Blvd.), West Hollywood, 310-652-9770*

Luna Park/3 rms, 50-100 cap/Californian **M**
- *665 N. Robertson Blvd. (bet. Melrose Ave. & Santa Monica Blvd.), W. Hollywood, 310-652-0611*

Lunaria/5 rms, 10-120 cap/French bistro **M**
- *10351 Santa Monica Blvd. (Beverly Glen Blvd.), Century City, 310-282-8870*

Maple Drive/1 rm, 18 cap/American **E**
- *345 N. Maple Dr. (Burton Way), Beverly Hills, 310-274-9800*

Matsuhisa/1 rm, 16 cap/Japanese **VE**
- *129 N. La Cienega Blvd. (north of Wilshire Blvd.), Beverly Hills, 310-659-9639*

Michael's/2 rms, 10-40 cap/Californian **VE**
- *1147 Third St. (North of Wilshire Blvd.), Santa Monica, 310-451-0843*

Ocean Avenue Seafood/1 rm, 40 cap/Seafood **M**
- *1401 Ocean Ave. (Santa Monica Blvd.), Santa Monica, 310-394-5669*

Ocean Seafood/2 rms, 120-400 cap/Chinese **I**
- *747 N. Broadway (bet. Alpine & Ord Sts.), Chinatown, 213-687-3088*

† BYO caterer.
**Outdoor facility only.

Ocean Star/6 rms, 10-70 cap/Chinese I
- *145 N. Atlantic Blvd. (Emerson Ave.), Monterey Park, 818-308-2128*
- *112 N. Chandler Ave. (east of Atlantic Blvd.), Monterey Park, 818-300-8446*

On Cañon/1 rm, 22 cap/Italian M
- *301 N. Cañon Dr., Beverly Hills, 310-247-2900*

Original Sonora Cafe/1 rm, 14 cap/Southwest M
- *180 S. La Brea (bet. 3rd St. & Beverly Blvd.), LA, 213-857-1800*

Pangaea/1 rm, 12 cap/Pacific New Wave E
- *Hotel Nikko, 465 S. La Cienega Blvd., Beverly Hills, 310-246-2100*

Papadakis Taverna/4 rms, 12-92 cap/Greek M
- *301 W. Sixth St. (Centre St.), San Pedro, 310-548-1186*

Parkway Grill/1 rm, 35 cap/California M
- *510 S. Arroyo Pkwy. (California Blvd.), Pasadena, 818-795-1001*

Patina/3 rms, 20-55 cap/Californian-French VE
- *5955 Melrose Ave. (west of Cahuenga Blvd.), LA, 213-467-1108*

Pinot Bistro/3 rms, 30-85 cap/French bistro E
- *12969 Ventura Blvd. (bet. Coldwater Canyon & Fulton Aves.), Studio City, 818-990-0500*

Pinot Hollywood/4 rms, 20-85 cap/Country French E
- *1448 N. Gower St., Hollywood, 213-461-8800*

Posto/2 rms, 26-30 cap/Italian M
- *14928 Ventura Blvd. (Kester Ave.), Sherman Oaks, 818-784-4400*

Prego/1 rm, 70 cap/Italian M
- *362 N. Camden Dr. (north of Wilshire Blvd.), Beverly Hills, 310-277-7346*

Primi/1 rm, 60 cap/Italian M
- *10543 W. Pico Blvd. (bet. Overland Ave. & Beverly Glen Blvd.), Rancho Park, 310-475-9235*

Ritz-Carlton Marina del Rey1 rm, 16 cap/ E
Mediterranean
- *3475 Admiralty Way, Marina del Rey, 310-823-1700*

Ritz-Carlton Pasadena/2 rms, 18-20 cap/ E
Californian-Continental
- *Ritz-Carlton Huntington Hotel, 1401 S. Oak Knoll Ave. (Huntington Dr.), Pasadena, 818-568-3900*

† BYO caterer.
**Outdoor facility only.

Remi/1 rm, 14 cap/Italian   M
• *1451 Third St. Promenade (B'way), Santa Monica, 310-393-6545*

Roxbury/4 rms, 30-140 cap/Californian-Italian   M
• *8225 Sunset Blvd. (Crescent Hts. Blvd.), LA, 213-656-1750*

Saddle Peak/3 rms, 14-27 cap/American   E
• *419 Cold Canyon Rd. (east of Malibu Canyon Rd., bet. Mulholland Hwy. & Puma Rd.), Calabasas, 818-222-3888*

Sanctuary/3 rms, 78-125 cap/Californian   E
• *180 N. Robertson Blvd. (Wilshire Blvd.), Beverly Hils, 310-358-0303*

72 Market Street/1 rm, 60 cap/American   E
• *72 Market St. (west of Pacific Ave.), Venice, 310-392-8720*

Spago/1 rm, 100 cap/Californian   E
• *8795 Sunset Blvd. (Horn Ave.), W. Hollywood, 310-652-4025*

St. Marks/1 rm, 85 cap/Californian   M
• *23 Windward Ave. (Venice Boardwalk), Venice, 310-452-2222*

Sylvie/1 rm, 30 cap/Mediterranean   E
• *Beverly Prescott Hotel, 1224 S. Beverwill Dr. (Pico Blvd.), LA, 310-772-2999*

Terrazza Toscana/1 rm, 65 cap/Italian   M
• *17401 Ventura Blvd. (bet. White Oak Ave. & Balboa Blvd.), Encino, 818-905-1641*

Thousand Cranes, A/4 rms, 8-30 cap/Japanese   M
• *New Otani Hotel, 120 S. Los Angeles St., Little Tokyo, 213-629-1200*

Valentino/4 rms, 25-80 cap/Italian   VE
• *3115 Pico Blvd. (2 blocks west of Bundy Dr.), Santa Monica, 310-829-4313*

Vida/1 rm, 25 cap/Pacific New Wave   M
• *1930 Hillhurst Ave. (Los Feliz Blvd.), Los Feliz, 213-660-4446*

West Beach Cafe/1 rm, 45 cap/Californian   M
• *60 N. Venice Blvd. (bet. Pacific Ave. & Venice Boardwalk), Venice, 310-823-5396*

World Cafe/2 rms, 20-200 cap/International   I
• *2820 Main St., Santa Monica, 310-392-1661*

Xiomara/1 rm, 45 cap/French bistro   E
• *69 N. Raymond Ave. (Walnut St.), Pasadena, 818-796-2520*

† BYO caterer.
**Outdoor facility only.

Yamashiro/2 rms, 90-110 cap/Japanese `M`
• *1999 N. Sycamore Ave. (bet. La Brea & Highland Aves.),
Hollywood, 213-466-5125*

PRIVATE CLUBS
(Members only or member sponsored)

Beverly Hills Country Club/3 rms, 20-180 cap `M`
• *3084 Motor Ave., Cheviot Hills, 310-836-4400*

City Club on Bunker Hill, The/8 rms, `E`
10-225 cap
• *Wells Fargo Ctr., 333 S. Grand Ave., Downtown LA,
213-620-9662*

Foundation Room at House of `VE`
Blues/5 rms, 8-36 cap
• *8430 Sunset Blvd., W. Hollywood, 213-848-2516*

Friars Club, The/various spaces, 300 cap `M`
• *9900 Santa Monica Blvd., Beverly Hills, 310-553-0850*

Hollywood Park Turf Club/1 rm, 350 cap `M`
• *1050 S. Prairie Ave., Inglewood, 310-419-1529*

Los Angeles Athletic Club/9 rms, 350 cap `N`
• *431 W. 7th St., Downtown LA, 213-625-2211*

Los Angeles Police Revolver & `N`
Athletic Club/2 rms, 200-500 cap
• *L.A. Police Academy, 1880 N. Academy Dr., LA, 213-222-9136*

La Cañada/Flintridge Golf & `M`
Tennis Club/3 rms, 75-250 cap
• *5500 Godbey Dr., La Cañada, 818-790-0611*

Malibu Lake Mountain Club†**/1 rm, 200 cap `VE`
• *29033 Lake Vista Dr., Agoura Hills, 818-889-1211*

Malibu Racquet Club/1 rm, 140 cap `N`
• *23847 Stuart Ranch Rd., Malibu, 310-457-9783*

Malibu Riding & Tennis Club/1 rm, 200 cap `N`
• *33905 PCH, Malibu, 310-457-9783*

Manhattan Country Club/5 rms, 15-300 cap `M`
• *1330 Park View Ave., Manhattan Beach, 310-546-5656*

Marina City Club/3 rms, 25-300 cap `N`
• *4333 Admiralty Way, Marina del Rey, 310-822-0611*

Mountaingate Country Club/1 rm, 220 cap `N`
• *12445 Mountaingate Dr., Brentwood, 310-476-6215*

Mulholland Tennis Club/3 rms, 150-200 cap `N`
• *2555 Crestview Dr., Hollywood, 213-654-0550*

† BYO caterer.
**Outdoor facility only.

Party Sites

C

Riviera Country Club/3 rms, 70-360 cap
M
• *1250 Capri Dr., Pacific Palisades, 310-454-6591*

Stadium Club/various spaces, 500 cap
N
• *Dodger Stadium, 1000 Elysian Park Ave., LA,
213-223-3341*

University Club of Pasadena/7 rms,
M
10-300 cap
• *175 N. Oakland Ave., Pasadena, 818-793-5157*

---

† BYO caterer.
**Outdoor facility only.

Prepared Foods

In the land of the cellular phone and beeper, time is always of the essence. Which is why prepared foods are a major part of the Southern Californian lifestyle. These days, take-out can be every bit as good as the stuff made in your own kitchen – and sometimes a lot better. And thanks to our area's ethnic stew, the variations on the chow-to-go theme are endless. You can cuddle up in front of the big screen with anything from an Italian to a French or Chinese feast with no difficulty at all. Besides the sources listed below, just about every ethnic restaurant and many others offer takeout.

Top Quality
28 Julienne
    Pascal Epicerie
27 Michel Richard
26 Bristol Farms
    Kitchen for Exploring

Top Variety
25 Bristol Farms
    Julienne
24 Gelson's Markets
23 Kitchen for Exploring
    Marmalade

Top Service
25 Pascal Epicerie
    Bristol Farms
24 Misto Caffe
    Gelson's Markets
    Divine Pasta

Best Buys
    Misto Caffe
    Divine Pasta
    California Chicken
    Trader Joe's
    Zankou Chicken

Q	V	S	C
24	22	22	M

Baducco's 🚲
- *Village Glen Plaza, 2839 Agoura Rd. (1 block south of Westlake Blvd.), Westlake Village, 818-991-4670*
  Every day 9am-7pm

☑ In a part of SoCal not famous for its ethnic enclaves, this popular "NY Italian" takeout is a "tasty surprise", offering "great bread", salami, fresh pasta and more along with a "neighborhood feel" in a suburb without neighborhoods; a few critics say "so-so", but for most this "well-run", "beautiful" store is a "favorite haunt."

23	18	21	M

Benny's BBQ 🚲▣
- *4077 Lincoln Blvd. (bet. Maxella Ave. & Washington Blvd.), Marina del Rey, 310-821-6939*
  M-F 11am-10pm/Sat noon-10pm/Sun 4pm-10pm

■ Probably the best place for BBQ on the Westside, this busy take-out window (with a table or two for eat-ins) pleases 'cue buffs with "bodacious ribs" and "finger-lickin'-good" hot links; fans call it "the best west of Oklahoma or south of Oakland" and say the "divine smell" alone is worth "driving up and down Lincoln" to inhale.

Beverly Glen Market Place ⚲✉ ⎡22⎤⎡21⎤⎡22⎤⎡E⎤
- *2964 Beverly Glen Circle (1 block south of Mulholland Dr.), Bel Air, 310-475-0829*
  Every day 7am-10pm

◪ An exclusive neighborhood market with prepared foods that admirers say are "really like home cooking", including "good roast turkey" and "generous meatball sandwiches"; detractors say it's "too expensive for ordinary fare", but it is "convenient", which is one reason why "everyone from Betsy Bloomingdale to drywall workers goes here."

BG to Go ⚲ ▽ ⎡26⎤⎡21⎤⎡19⎤⎡M⎤
- *12930 Ventura Blvd. (½ block west of Coldwater Canyon Ave.), Studio City, 818-366-3246*
  M-F 11am-9pm/Sat & Sun 7:30am-9pm

■ "A real find", this take-out place opened by Bistro Garden (hence the name) next to their Studio City location provides "definitive chocolate soufflés" as well as pastas, rotisserie items and other "quality" fare at a relatively "low price"; the offerings are "well made" and "different": "where else can you get crème brûlée to go?"

BRISTOL FARMS ⎡26⎤⎡25⎤⎡25⎤⎡E⎤
- *See listing in Supermarkets section.*

■ "You need a truck to haul all the good stuff" home from this beloved supermarket minichain with some of the most creative take-out fare anywhere; their "awesome displays" of "gourmet meals" include "great salads", comfort foods, desserts, even sushi from the "best on-site sushi makers"; as one addict says: "glad they're not near me – I'd be broke."

Broadway Deli ⚲ ⎡21⎤⎡20⎤⎡18⎤⎡E⎤
- *See listing in Baked Goods section.*

◪ "Hit-and-miss" quality may explain mixed reactions to this love-it-or-hate-it quasideli with a big take-out section; to supporters it offers "high-quality" food at "fair prices", to critics it's "edible but boring" with an "odd selection" of "costly" fare; desserts win praise, especially the "good bread pudding" and "delicious cookies."

California Chicken Cafe ⌑ ⎡24⎤⎡21⎤⎡21⎤⎡I⎤
- *2005 Westwood Blvd. (bet. Olympic & Santa Monica Blvds.), West LA, 310-446-1933*
- *2401 Wilshire Blvd. (24th St.), Santa Monica, 310-453-0477*
- *6805 Melrose Ave. (3 blocks east of La Brea Ave.), LA, 213-935-5877*
- *15601 Ventura Blvd. (½ mile west of Sepulveda Blvd.), Encino, 818-789-8056*
  M-F 11am-10pm/Sat noon-10pm

■ Poultry pundits say this rapidly expanding chain provides "good healthy fast food" – rotisserie chicken, "fantastic" salads, chicken wraps and so on – plus terrific "value" and speedy service; it's a "great concept" – "if you like chicken and only chicken."

Q	V	S	C

Chalet Gourmet 🚲

22	21	22	E

- *See listing in Cheese section.*

▤ "One of the trendsetters" in terms of high-rent takeout, this Hollywood landmark offers "unusual dishes" (some even "a little scary looking") that can be "wonderful" or "disappointing" but which can be "expensive"; "excellent pasta and rice salads" are hits, but "bring tons of dough."

Chin Chin 🚴

-	-	-	I

- *8618 Sunset Blvd. (bet. La Cienega & San Vicente Blvds.), W. Hollywood, 310-652-1818*
- *11740 San Vicente Blvd. (bet. Montana & Barrington Aves.), Brentwood, 310-826-2525*
- *12215 Ventura Blvd. (Laurel Canyon Blvd.), Studio City, 818-985-9090*
- *Marina Marketplace Ctr., 13455 Maxella Ave. (east of Lincoln Blvd.), Marina del Rey, 310-823-9999*
- *16101 Ventura Blvd. (Woodley Ave.), Encino, 818-783-1717 Sun-Th 11am-11pm/F & Sat 11am-midnight*

An always busy, very popular Chinese-as-you-want-it chain famed for Chinese chicken salad and 'dim sum and then sum', all offered to go from a separate take-out section at the Sunset Plaza flagship shop (and at the counter at other branches); there's also a choice of fat-free Chinese dishes.

Divine Pasta

26	23	24	M

- *1303 Montana Ave. (Euclid), Santa Monica, 310-394-7930 M-F 11am-7:30pm/Sat & Sun 11am-7pm*
- *443 N. Beverly Dr. (½ block south of Little Santa Monica Blvd.), Beverly Hills, 310-858-8786 M-Sat 10am-7pm*
- *615 N. La Brea (south of Melrose), LA, 213-939-1148 M-Sat 11am-8pm*
- *12616 Ventura Blvd. (bet. Whitsett & Coldwater Canyon Aves.), Studio City, 818-761-1874 M-Sat 11am-8pm*

■ "It's a marvel to shop" at this expanding Italian take-out chain and pasta bar; "fabulous lasagna", "wonderful lobster ravioli" and other "better-than-homemade" pasta dishes plus "terrific sauces" are "good to have on hand" and make for "great fast meals"; aficionados say "life would be much better with more Divine Pastas."

Dr. Hogly Wogly's Tyler Texas BBQ

24	20	21	M

- *8136 Sepulveda Blvd. (½ block south of Roscoe Blvd.), Van Nuys, 818-780-6701 Every day 11:30am-10pm*

■ SoCal's top-rated BBQ joint is also a top place for 'cue to go, served with the speed of summer lightning, especially if you phone ahead on your cellular; this "hog heaven" has what many consider to be the "best ribs anywhere", plus brisket, beans and more, so if you like meat that "falls off the bone", "pass the napkins...a stack of 'em."

Elite Cuisine   ▽ 24 | 20 | 21 | M
- *See listing in Caterers section.*
■ "Proof that kosher need not be boring", the take-out arm of this kosher caterer offers a "nice selection" of "very tasty", moderately priced fare for those who want to observe the strictures of kashruth without sacrificing flavor.

Feast From the East   23 | 17 | 19 | I
- *1949 Westwood Blvd. (bet. Olympic & Santa Monica Blvds.), Westwood, 310-475-0400*
  M-Sat 11:30am-7:30pm
■ This small Chinese storefront has a permanent line of hungry Westsiders waiting for take-out orders of the "best Chinese chicken salad ever" – it's "impossible to eat any other" version after trying this; with big crunchy noodles, lots of chicken and great sesame dressing, it's so popular many patrons don't know there's more on the menu.

Flora Kitchen ⚲   25 | 21 | 18 | M
- *460 S. La Brea Ave. (6th St.), LA, 213-931-9900*
  Every day 8am-11pm
☑ "Wonderful sandwiches and pastries" are offered by this terminally "trendy" take-out cafe next to a pretty flower shop; though critics claim "quality varies", most advise going for the "best grilled eggplant sandwich anywhere", "creative salads" and "great pasta combos", but not for what can seem like the "worst service in LA" – "rude, rude!"

Fresh to Go ⌖   ▽ 19 | 16 | 18 | M
- *259 Hampton Dr. (Main St.), Venice, 310-450-6013*
  M-F 8am-8pm/Sat & Sun 9am-5pm
☑ Known for cooking with no oil (as in no-oil tuna-pasta salad, no-oil turkey chili), this "hole-in-the-wall" take-out shop caters to the many body building gyms in Venice; admirers like its "healthy", low- and no-fat food, but detractors say they left out the taste along with the oil.

Gelson's Markets   24 | 24 | 24 | E
- *See listing in Supermarkets section.*
☑ "My second kitchen" is how many view the prepared foods section of LA's biggest upscale market chain; a "dizzying array" of "high-quality" fare makes it "easy to put together a picnic or dinner", and the staff "goes out of their way to help"; foes say "oily", "uneven" and "overpriced", but "there's always a crowd – it must be good."

Gianfranco Delizie Italiane   21 | 20 | 19 | M
- *11363 Santa Monica Blvd. (Purdue Ave.), West LA, 310-477-7777*
  M-Sat 10:30am-10:30pm/Sun 1pm-9:30pm
☑ "Reminiscent of Italy", this busy Westside deli has fans for its "good selection" of "tasty" Italian fare, including "exotic stuff", but it also has critics who claim it "fluctuates in quality"; it's a "good place to practice your Italian", if you don't mind sometimes "grumpy" staffers.

Gourmet Grub to Go – – – M
- *1627 Montana Ave. (17th St.), Santa Monica, 310-451-2021*
  M-F 9:30am-6pm/Sat 10am-5pm

Large bowls of freshly prepared, Pritiken-approved dishes
are attractively presented at this popular take-out Health
Foodery located in the back of the Ashford Marketplace
behind Il Fornaio; while not every item is as satisfying as
the "real thing", the shop does an admirable job for those
who must watch their fat, salt and caloric intake.

Jackson's Farm – – – M
- *439 N. Beverly Dr. (bet. Little Santa Monica Blvd. &*
  Brighton Way), Beverly Hills, 310-273-5578
  Every day 7am-10pm

This spin-off of Jackson's bistro, opened by Alan Jackson
(son of KABC's Michael Jackson, not that other one),
offers an impressive selection of light French-American
bistro dishes and platters to go, including one of the best
choices of cheeses around, baked goods with crust, lots
of tempting salads and as good a roast chicken as you'll
find in Beverly Hills.

Judy's Carry Out Cuisine 🚴 ▽ 24 22 21 M
- *129 N. La Brea Ave. (bet. Beverly Blvd. & 1st St.), LA,*
  213-934-7667
  Sun-Th 10am-10pm/F 7am-1 hour before sundown

■ Though the name doesn't give much of a clue, this is a
kosher takeout, and to admirers it's the "best by far in the
kosher category"; the fare can be "delicious and
innovative" (anything from lo mein salad to chicken
paprikash), but some find it a bit "expensive for what it is."

JULIENNE 28 25 23 E
- *2649 Mission St. (bet. El Molino & Los Robles), San Marino,*
  818-441-2299
  M-F 9am-6:30pm/Sat 9am-5pm

■ "The royalty of prepared foods", this cafe/caterer is
top-rated for the quality of its "inventive, colorful"
prepared foods with a Country French spin; "each flavor is
distinctive", whether it's a "great lamb sandwich",
rosemary raisin bread or peppermint ice cream; the tab's
"a bit costly", but even so fans urge "don't leave San
Marino without bringing something home."

Kitchen for Exploring 26 23 22 E
Foods, The 🚴
- *1434 W. Colorado Blvd. (Ave. 64), Pasadena, 818-793-7218*
  T-Sat noon-6pm

■ The name's a bit strange but the kitchen lives up to it,
turning out some "wonderful Eclectic food" that's
"innovative" and "delicious"; surveyors especially like the
"healthy" items and side dishes at this "really cute"
Pasadena shop (which also does full-service catering),
but you're advised to "bring a book for the line."

Koo Koo Roo ☙ $\quad$ 22 $\mid$ 20 $\mid$ 19 $\mid$ I

- 8393 Beverly Blvd. (3 blocks east of La Cienega Blvd.), LA, 213-655-9045
- 301 N. Larchmont Ave. (Beverly Blvd.), LA, 213-962-1500
- 11066 Santa Monica Blvd. (Sepulveda Blvd.), West LA, 310-473-5858
- Villa Marina Shopping Ctr., 4325 Glencoe Ave., Marina Del Rey, 310-305-8100
- 17136 Ventura Blvd. (bet. Balboa Blvd. & White Oak Ave.), Encino, 818-783-5576
- 11650 San Vicente Blvd. (Darlington Ave.), Brentwood, 310-207-3232
- 262 S. Beverly Dr. (bet. Wilshire & Olympic Blvds.), Beverly Hills, 310-274-3121
- 255 S. Grand Ave., Downtown LA, 213-620-1800
- Manhattan Village Shopping Ctr., 3294 Sepulveda Blvd., Manhattan Beach, 310-546-4500
- 2002 Wilshire Blvd. (20th St.), Santa Monica, 310-453-8767
- 2385 Lake Ave., Pasadena, 818-683-9600
  All locations: every day 11am-10pm

■ "Excellent", "simple", "dependable" – and the price is right, which is why this upscale chicken chain is hatching new branches; "lots of choices", all "fast" and "tasty", wins votes as "best takeout chicken", and yups and Xers like its "healthy" skinless choices; turkey, salads and side dishes have fans too; one gripe: "needs better service."

La Brea Bakery $\quad$ – $\mid$ – $\mid$ – $\mid$ E

- See listing in Baked Goods section.

Known as the place to go for "bread and breakfast" – customers can now pick up some of La Brea's (and its companion Campanile Restaurant's) high-quality salads, pastries, cheeses and the like to have at home with their loaves and rolls; N.B. quality like this does not come cheap.

Le Marmiton $\quad$ 26 $\mid$ 22 $\mid$ 22 $\mid$ E

- 1327 Montana Ave. (14th St.), Santa Monica, 310-393-7716 T-Sat 10am-7pm

■ Both "old favorites and new dishes" are "excellent" at this Westside French takeout and cafe that's arguably "LA's only authentic charcuterie and pâtisserie"; shoppers feel they're "in Paris" as they pick up anything from an "old-fashioned French stew or roast chicken" to "wonderful tarts and pâtés"; frozen items make easy "gourmet feasts."

Main Course, The $\quad$ 24 $\mid$ 18 $\mid$ 22 $\mid$ M

- 10509 W. Pico Blvd. (Patricia St.), Rancho Park, 310-475-7564 M-Sat 11am-9pm

■ "Just like grandma's" describes the "delicious", "healthy home cooking" at this "real treasure"; there's "not much selection" but what they make each day (and they really do make it: even the pie crusts are from scratch) is "good and economical"; surveyors especially "love the Hungarian goulash" and the "best turkey with gravy", a signature dish.

Maria's Italian Kitchen ⚲   21 | 21 | 20 | M |
- *11723 Barrington Ct. (½ block south of Sunset Blvd.),*
  Brentwood, 310-476-6112
  Every day 10am-10pm
- *10761 W. Pico Blvd. (bet. Overland Ave. & Westwood Blvd.),*
  West LA, 310-441-3663
  Sun-Th 11am-10pm/F & Sat 11am-11pm

■ Not to be confused with the Maria's pizza and pasta chain, this "good old standby" with "quick service" is a "decent neighborhood place" for take-out standards such as "great pizzas", pasta salads and "meatball sandwiches like in Hoboken"; a "true sleeper", it's "very handy" for "lazy" lovers of Italian food.

Marmalade   25 | 23 | 21 | E |
- *710 Montana (7th St.), Santa Monica, 310-395-9196* ⚲
  M-F 6:30am-8pm/Sat 7am-8pm/Sun 7am-7pm
- *3894 Cross Creek Rd. (PCH), Malibu, 310-317-4242*
  Sun-Th 7:30am-9:30pm/F & Sat 7:30am-11pm
- *14910 Ventura (Kester Ave.), Encino, 818-905-8872* ⚲
  Every day 7am-10pm

◪ Admirers say this take-out spot, which has grown into full-service restaurants in its Malibu and Encino locations, provides "creative" Californian cuisine that's a "feast for the eyes" and "tastes as good as it looks"; "great for Hollywood Bowl picnics", they offer "many choices, all good" including "excellent baked goods" and "wonderful salads"; critics say the food "costs too much" and comes with too much "attitude": "tell them they didn't invent pasta."

Michel Richard   27 | 22 | 22 | E |
- *See listing in Baked Goods section.*

■ Create "a bistro sensation at home" with some "great" Gallic takeout from what devotees dub the "Le Nôtre of LA"; though chef Michel Richard is now connected in name only, the staff carries on in his tradition, preparing "excellent pâtés", the "best croissants" and other "sinfully wonderful" (and "expensive") fare; you may risk "death by cholesterol", but what a way to go.

Misto Caffe & Bakery   26 | 22 | 24 | M |
- *Hillside Village Shopping Ctr., 24558 Hawthorne Blvd.*
  (½ mile south of PCH), Torrance, 310-375-3608
  M 11:30am-3pm/T-Th 11:30am-9:30pm/
  F 11:30am-10pm/Sat 10am-1opm/Sun 10am-9pm

■ Replacing the old Chez Allez take-out shop, this "very tasty" South Bay operation (part of the Chez Melange, Descanso and Depot restaurant family) is liked for its "to-die-for salads", sandwiches, cold dishes, "yummy desserts" and more; "everything they do is fabulous", but some lament there "aren't enough choices."

Q V S C

Mrs. Gooch's Whole Foods Market

24 22 23 E

• *See listing in Health/Natural Food section.*

☑ "Good, healthy and fresh" say those who like the "large variety" of take-out choices at this top-of-the-line natural foods chain; sandwiches, salads and more are made with mostly "guilt-free" ingredients and are "great for vegans", but critics say you must "choose carefully to find flavor" at this "healthy for the wealthy" place.

Panda Express &

_ _ _ I

• *145 S. Barrington Ave. (Sunset Blvd.), Brentwood, 310-440-1974*
• *Beverly Ctr., 121 N. La Cienega Blvd. (Beverly Blvd.), LA, 310-659-4568*
• *Century City Marketplace, 10250 Santa Monica Blvd. (Century Park West), Century City, 310-252-8438*
• *Seventh Market Pl., 735 S. Figueroa St. (bet. 7th & 8th Sts.), Downtown LA, 213-624-1131*
• *17870 Ventura Blvd. (Zelzah Ave.), Encino, 818-881-3968*
• *1216 Fair Oaks Ave. (Huntington Dr.), S. Pasadena, 818-799-8085*
• *4325 Glencoe Ave. (Lincoln Blvd.), Marina del Rey, 310-577-9818*
• *UCLA-Ackerman Union, Level 1, 308 Westwood Plaza, Westwood, 310-206-8447*
• *Westside Pavilion, 10800 W. Pico Blvd. (Overland Ave.), West LA, 310-470-7789*
• *14561 Ventura Blvd. (Vesper), Sherman Oaks, 818-906-8061*
• *326 Fox Hills Mall (Sepulveda Blvd.), Culver City, 310-390-7845*
• *3214 Glendale Galleria (bet. Orange & Central Aves.), Glendale, 818-507-7010*
• *1134 Glendale Galleria (bet. Colorado & Central Aves.), Glendale, 818-548-4648*
• *218 S. Lake Ave. (Del Mar Blvd.), Pasadena, 818-796-7710*
• *5945 E. Spring St. (Los Coyotes), Long Beach, 310-421-0283*
• *129 Los Cerritos Ctr. (bet. South St. & Gridley Ave.), Cerritos, 310-665-7938*
• *Media Ctr., 4100 W. Alameda (Riverside Dr.), Burbank, 818-567-9989*
• *18427 Nordhoff St. (Reseda Blvd.), Northridge, 818-700-2829*
• *15201 Sunset Blvd. (Monument St.), Pacific Palisades, 310-459-9801*
• *Sherman Oaks Fashion Sq. 14006 Riverside Dr. (Woodman Ave.), Sherman Oaks, 818-981-0713*
• *The Galleria at South Bay, 1815 Hawthorne Blvd. (Artesia Blvd.), Redondo Beach, 310-542-3466*
• *Topanga Plaza Shop Ctr., 6600 Topanga Canyon Blvd., Canoga Park, 818-887-6688*
• *The Plaza at W. Covina, 1200 W. Covina Pkwy. (Vincent Blvd.), W. Covina, 818-814-9027*

Panda Express (Cont.)
- *Baldwin Hills Crenshaw Plaza, 3850 Martin Luther King Jr. Blvd. (Crenshaw Blvd.), LA, 213-291-9200*
- *5718 E. Seventh St. (bet. PCH & Bellflower Blvd.), Long Beach, 310-986-9850*
- *Palm Court, 161 E. Orange Grove (San Fernando Rd.), Burbank, 818-972-9800*
- *California Plaza, 350 S. Grand Ave. (4th St.), Downtown LA, 213-626-6018*
- *Cal State LA, Eagle Landing Food Court, 5156 State University Dr., LA, 213-343-4932*
- *Cal State Long Beach, 6049 E. Seventh St. (University), Long Beach, 310-597-8198*
- *Valencia Town Ctr., 24201 Valencia Blvd. (McBean Pkwy.), Valencia, 805-254-0379*
- *44415 Valley Central Way (bet. Central St. & Ave. J), Lancaster, 805-940-6058*
- *Granary Sq., 25902 McBean Pkwy. (Arroyo Park Dr.), Santa Clarita, 805-288-1507*
  General hours: M-F 11am-9pm/Sat 11am-9:30pm/ Sun 11am-8:30pm
  Other locations in Vons and Pavilions Supermarkets and Fedco stores

A rapidly expanding chain of Chinese fast-food outlets, with a distinctive leaning toward the fine flavors of Mandarin-style cooking, along with a few hot Szechuan dishes tossed in for good measure; popping up in every mall, on every corner, and in a number of supermarkets as well, they make for some of the best Chinese takeout around.

Pascal Epicerie 🚲   28 | 22 | 25 | E |
- *1000 N. Bristol (1 block north of Jamboree Rd.), Newport Beach, 714-261-9041*
  M-Sat 7am-7pm

◼ "What you'd expect from a world-class chef", this take-out shop next to OC's top-rated Pascal Restaurant shows the perfectionist touch of Pascal Olhats; homemade pâté and sandwiches of marinated albacore or grilled lamb loin typify the choices that change daily but always feature "original" presentation and "marvelous" flavor; it's hard to top for "a French fix", but it may "bankrupt you if used for a large party."

Pasta, Etc. 🚲   ▽ 25 | 23 | 23 | M |
- *8650 Sunset Blvd. (2 blocks west of La Cienega Blvd.), W. Hollywood, 310-854-0094*
  Every day 9am-11pm

◼ One of several tempting upscale take-out cafes in the Sunset Plaza area, with a house specialty of polenta pie and a "wonderful selection" of "extremely fresh", "unusual" pasta salads; this reasonably priced "bit of Beverly Hills" also provides "great platters for meetings and parties."

Pasta Shoppe, The 🏠   ▽ 26 | 21 | 24 | M

- *1964 Hillhurst Ave. (Franklin Ave.), Los Feliz, 213-668-0458*
  M-F 10:30am-6:30pm/Sat 9:30am-5:30pm
- *3820 Ocean View Blvd. (bet. Honolulu & Florencita Aves.),*
  Montrose, 818-541-9091
  T-F 10:30am-7:30pm/Sat 9:30am-5:30pm

■ "Ravioli to die for", "very good pastas", lasagna, stuffed
peppers and "quality pastries" are just some of the
moderately priced "rich" offerings of these "little-known"
Italian take-out "gems" in Los Feliz and Montrose.

Pavilions   17 | 19 | 18 | M

- *See listing in Supermarkets section.*

◪ Trying hard to upscale its prepared foods section, this
chain still has a way to go; fans say it's "better than most"
supermarkets, citing "good salads, fried chicken" and other
"nicely presented" fare, while foes say it's "too expensive"
for "second-rate quality"; maybe "they need new recipes."

Reddi Chick BBQ 🏠   24 | 19 | 21 | I

- *225 26th St. (San Vicente Blvd.), Santa Monica, 310-393-5238*
  M-Sat 9am-7pm

■ "An old standby that never changes", this "yummy"
Brentwood Country Mart chicken shop provides what
may be the "best rotisserie chicken" ("you can smell it two
blocks away") and "immortal fries with seasoned salt";
"kids love it" and adults can't get enough; "if this place
closes, they might as well blow up the rest of the Mart."

Rosetree Cottage 🍽   23 | 16 | 20 | E

- *824 E. California Blvd. (Lake Ave.), Pasadena, 818-793-3337*
  T-F noon-6pm/Sat 10am-6pm/Sun noon-6pm

◪ "The place to go for a *Wind in the Willows* picnic", this
British tea shop and garden offers takeout you'd expect to
find in Stratford on Avon, e.g. pork pies, sausage rolls, "cute
box dinners" and "expensive scones"; fans call the selection
"small but choice", while foes say it's "better for tea."

Rosti   23 | 20 | 20 | M

- *908 S. Barrington Ave. (south of San Vicente Blvd.),*
  Brentwood, 310-447-8695 🚴
  M-Th 11am-10pm/F-Sun 11am-10:30pm
- *7475 Beverly Blvd. (Gardener St.), LA, 213-938-8335* 🚴
  M-Th noon-10pm/F noon-11pm
- *931 Montana Ave. (10th St.), Santa Monica, 310-393-3236*
  M-Th 11am-10pm/F-Sun 11am-10:30pm
- *Encino Marketplace, 16403 Ventura Blvd. (Hayvenhurst*
  Ave.), Encino, 818-995-7179
  Every day 11am-10pm

◪ What started as the to-go arm of Toscana Restaurant is
now a chain of Italian takeout/cafes; fans cite "always good
risotto", "delicious roast potatoes", "baked chicken" and
other "terrific Tuscan tastes" – it's "country Italian cooking
at home", but critics find the fare "oily" and "overrated."

Prepared Foods

Trader Joe's

• *See listing in Supermarkets section.*

◪ Judging from high surveyor response, more people pick up prepared foods at "dependable" Trader Joe's than at any other SoCal market; it offers "everything from A to Z", including "fresh salads", "tasty frozen meals" and "brown-bag lunch items", and if "not gourmet", most find it all of "high quality" and "a good buy"; critics shrug "so-so."

Wesley's Place 🚲

• *Penguin Plaza, 711 Foothill Blvd. (Oakwood), La Cañada, 818-790-4622*
   M-F 9am-8pm/Sat 9am-7pm/Sun 10:30am-4pm

This one-stop gourmet market, located in the foothills of the San Gabriel Valley, offers freshly made hot entrees, salads, breads and desserts to work-weary Eastsiders who would rather pick up (or have delivered) a roasted vegetable lasagna than cook themselves; the menu changes daily so call ahead.

Wild Oats Market 🚲

• *603 S. Lake Ave. (California), Pasadena, 818-792-1778*
• *1425 Montana Ave. (15th St.), Santa Monica, 310-576-4707*
   Every day 8am-10pm

■ Pasadena and Santa Monica's "richest hippies feast" on the "good variety" of "fresh, healthy" prepared foods offered by these "magical" natural markets with sizable take-out counters; the "interesting" choices include "nice tamales" and items from the "great salad bar", but it's "too expensive" for some; the new Santa Monica location has become the Westside place to see and be seen.

Wok Fast 🚲

• *3115 Washington Blvd. (Lincoln Blvd.), Marina del Rey, 310-574-1781*
   Every day 5am-10pm
• *703 Montana Ave. (7th St.), Santa Monica, 310-917-2793*
   Every day 11am-11pm
• *4203 W. Alameda Ave. (1 block west of Pass Ave.), Burbank, 818-558-1080*
   Every day 11am-10pm
• *46 W. Colorado Ave. (Delacy St.), Pasadena, 818-356-9651*
   Every day 11am-10pm

A home delivery staple, this ubiquitous Chinese take-out chain is known for slightly undercooking their dishes so they arrive at your door at the peak of doneness, which sometimes works, sometimes doesn't; but it's quickly turning into the Domino's of Chinese takeout – fast and satisfying, if not always good.

Prepared Foods   Q V S C

Wolfgang Puck Express   -|-|-|I
- *1315 Third St. Promenade (Arizona Ave.), Santa Monica,
  310-576-4770* 🚲
  M-Th 11am-10pm/F-Sun 11am-midnight
- *LAX Terminal 2, 201 World Way, LA, 310-215-5166
  Every day 5:30am-11:30pm*
- *LAX Terminal 7, 701 World Way, LA, 310-215-5169
  Every day 5:30am-11:30am*

Wolfgang Puck To-Go
- *Gelson's Market, 16450 Ventura Blvd. (Hayvenhurst Ave.),
  Encino, 818-379-8464*
- *Gelson's Market, 15424 Sunset Blvd. (Via de la Paz),
  Pacific Palisades, 310-573-9653
  Every day 8am-10pm*

A step below the Wolfgang Puck Cafes, these simplest of
Puck eateries have a counter where you place your order
to eat in at simple tables or to take out (Wolfgang Puck
To-Go); the Chinois chicken salad may be the single best
bargain in town: a heaping order of one of Puck's greatest
creations for not much more than the cost of a Big Mac.

Zabies ⌘   24 | 20 | 20 | M
- *3003 Ocean Park Ave. (30th St.), Santa Monica, 310-392-9036
  M-Sat 7:30am-4pm*

◪ After briefly closing, this take-out shop across from SM
Airport and the Museum of Flying is up and running again
under new ownership, offering California cuisine with
Mediterranean flourishes; "always a treat", "eclectic and
delicious" say fans, noting that "you meet all types of
people" in this friendly little place; foes deem it "way
overrated", but they're a minority.

Zankou Chicken ⌘   25 | 18 | 20 | I
- *5065 Sunset Blvd. (Normandie Ave.), Los Feliz, 213-665-7845
  Every day 10am-midnight*
- *5658 Sepulveda Blvd. (½ block north of Burbank Blvd.),
  Van Nuys, 818-781-0615
  Every day 10am-10pm*
- *1415 E. Colorado Blvd. (Verdugo Rd.), Glendale,
  818-244-2237
  Every day 10am-11pm*

■ "Almost perfect", "to die for", "best take-out chicken
ever" – the raves are for a trio of Armenian chicken
shacks where dozens of "wonderfully garlicky" birds spin
on the rotisserie, ready to go in moments but impossible
to get home in one piece because the smell will drive you
to distraction; "it's beyond great" and "cheap" to boot.

Produce*

It can be argued that Southern California has the best produce in the world – and looking at the impressive fruits and vegetables displayed at everything from supermarkets to small shops and outdoor markets, it's a hard point to dispute. From the best of the local seasonal harvest to out-of-season specialties shipped in from exotic climes, the produce sold here is often the crème de la crème. It has to be – many of us have been known to grow a tomato or two in our own backyards, so we have alternatives. The markets have to do well to compete.

Top Quality		Top Service	
29	Bristol Farms	26	Bristol Farms
28	Tanaka	25	Tanaka
	Gelson's Markets		Gelson's Markets
	Southland Farmers' Mkt.	23	Mrs. Gooch's
27	Tapia Brothers		Southland Farmers' Mkt.

Top Variety		Best Buys	
27	Bristol Farms		Southland Farmers' Mkt.
	Gelson's Markets		Bristol Farms
24	Southland Farmers' Mkt.		Gelson's Markets
	Mrs. Gooch's		Tapia Brothers
23	Vicente Foods		Mrs. Gooch's

	Q	V	S	C

Beverly Glen Market Place 🚲 | 22 | 19 | 22 | E |
- *2964 Beverly Glen Circle (Mulholland Dr.), Bel Air, 310-475-0829 Every day 7:30am-11pm/Sun 8am-11pm*

☑ Where the rich and famous go to buy carrots and zucchini, this market just below Mulholland usually has "great quality" but "not great variety"; it's "ok" "in a pinch", but prices "make Gelson's seem like a bargain basement."

BRISTOL FARMS | 29 | 27 | 26 | E |
- *See listing in Supermarkets section.*

■ Expect "farmer's market quality" at these highly rated supermarkets, where the "wonderful variety" of produce is especially welcome "out of season"; "you get hungry just looking" at the "beautiful, bountiful" displays that are "so seductive to the eye and nose, so reductive to the wallet."

Charlie Lopez 🚲 | 25 | 22 | 22 | M |
- *Farmer's Market, 633 W. Third St., Stall 130, LA, 213-937-2477 M-Sun 9am-6pm*

■ A longtime favorite at the Farmer's Market (where surprisingly little produce is actually sold), this stand has "gorgeous displays" of produce, especially "fresh, delicious corn and strawberries"; it's a "friendly" "mom-and-pop spot."

* Top ratings lists exclude sources in outlying areas.

Chino Ranch ⊟   30 | 27 | 22 | E

- *6123 Calzada del Bosque (Via de la Valle exit, 5 miles east off #I-5 Frwy.), Rancho Santa Fe, 619-756-3184 T-Sat 10am-4pm/Sun 10am-1pm*

■ Wolfgang Puck and Alice Waters order their fruits and vegetables from this remarkable roadside stand located just north of San Diego; it's the "quintessential country experience" (to upscale urbanites, perhaps) where "artisan farmers" sell "edible art", including dozens of varieties of tomatoes, melons, corn and so forth; "you'll have to mortgage your house to pay for it, but it's worth every cent."

Cicero Farms ⊟   25 | 19 | 19 | M

- *22600 Sherman Way (bet. Fallbrook & Shoup), Woodland Hills, 818-346-6338 Every day 9:30am-6:30pm (May-January)*

■ This "old-fashioned" farm stand in Woodland Hills is known for "good seasonal produce, especially delicious white corn" and "fabulous tomatoes"; they "do fun things for kids during the holidays" and there's a "great pumpkin patch at Halloween."

Co-Opportunity   23 | 21 | 20 | M

- *See listing in Health/Natural Food section.*

■ Those who worry about the purity of their broccoli find "peace of mind" at this "best bet for organic produce"; "excellent quality" and "reasonable prices" make it "*the* place to shop between farmer's markets."

Fedco   17 | 19 | 13 | I

- *See listing in Supermarkets section.*

◪ A membership store that draws a wide range of love it or hate it comments; some declare it's "surprisingly good and fresh" with a "decent selection" at "great prices"; naysayers howl "dreadful", "grade Z", "steer clear"; the bottom line – "be careful what you buy."

GELSON'S MARKETS   28 | 27 | 25 | E

- *See listing in Supermarkets section.*

■ Ranking just a jot below Bristol Farms, with a lot more branches, this "class all the way" chain has an "excellent selection" of "beautifully displayed" produce, including some "exotic" choices; "you can close your eyes and pick a perfect specimen", so while "you pay more, it's worth it."

Hughes Markets   21 | 22 | 18 | M

- *See listing in Supermarkets section.*

◪ "The best of the regular, moderate supermarkets" seems to be the consensus on this chain that offers usually "fresh", "well-priced and displayed" fruits and vegetables including "good ethnic varieties"; though some claim "quality varies" by branch, overall it's a "good place for everyday produce."

Lopez Ranch 🥕   24 20 17 M
• *12681 W. Jefferson Blvd. (Lincoln Blvd. & Centinela Ave.),*
  Culver City, 310-306-4288
  Every day 9:30am-7pm (May-December)
■ A "tradition" that's "better than a drive to the country",
this venerable produce stand across the street from the
Marina wetlands is popular for "pumpkins at Halloween"
and "super" sweet corn and strawberries; "consistently
fresh and well-priced" fruits and vegetables keep
generations returning year after year; open seasonally.

Marina Farms   24 23 18 M
• *5454 Centinela Ave. (½ block north of Jefferson Blvd.),*
  Culver City, 310-827-3049
  M-Sat 9am-7:30pm/Sun 9am-7pm
■ A "farm in the middle of a residential area", this "excellent
neighborhood greengrocer" carries a "gorgeous and varied"
selection of "in and out of season fresh veggies"; while a bit
out of the way, "everything you could possibly want is here."

Mrs. Gooch's Whole   27 24 23 E
Foods Market
• *See listing in Health/Natural Food section.*
☑ "Beautiful", "organic" fruits and vegetables appeal to
the Save-the-Bay crowd and others who insist on "fresh,
fresh, fresh" produce – too bad "the price will kill you" ("a
head of lettuce costs more than a car"); while most rate
the quality "wonderful", some find these "ultimate yuppie
healthy living markets" a bit "too precious."

Pavilions   22 23 18 M
• *See listing in Supermarkets section.*
☑ Admirers praise these upscale Vons as among the
"best for produce" of the large chain supermarkets, with
a "surprising selection of exotics", including a wall of
gourmet vegetables and bins of wild mushrooms; "terrific
variety" makes them "a cut above", but demanding types
shrug them off as "so-so."

Price/Costco 🚲   19 16 10 I
• *See listing in Supermarkets section.*
☑ For those who don't mind buying produce in quantities
that could feed whole villages, this membership store
offers "ok"-quality bulk fruits and veggies – if you need
"10,000 grapes", "eight pounds of mushrooms" or "500
oranges", head here; it's a "godsend if you hate paying
retail" but if there are "just two of you, better eat fast."

Ralphs Grocery Company   17 20 16 M
• *See listing in Supermarkets section.*
☑ "Good, not great" produce that's "better at some"
outposts "than at others" is sold by this midlevel chain;
most say you get "good value" and it's usually "fine in a
pinch", but pickier shoppers sniff "I don't think so."

Produce

Santa Monica Farms   21 21 18 M
- *2015 Main St. (bet. Pico Blvd. & Ocean Park Ave.),
  Santa Monica, 310-396-4069
  Every day 8am-8pm*
◪ Opinion is split over this small neighborhood fruit,
vegetable and juice place on the north end of trendy Main
Street; fans praise its "unusual variety" of "very fresh"
produce sold by "nice people", while critics say "nothing
special", "be careful", "hit and miss."

Southland Certified Farmers'   28 24 23 I
Markets ✌

Monday
- *John Sim Park, (bet. Oak & Clark Aves.), Bellflower,
  310-804-1424
  9am-1pm*
- *South Gate Park (Tweedy & Walnut), South Gate, 213-774-0159
  9am-1pm*
- *Plummer Park, 7377 Santa Monica Blvd., W. Hollywood,
  310-967-4202
  9am-2pm*

Tuesday
- *Alondra Blvd. (west of Pioneer, opposite Excelsior High
  School), Norwalk, 310-863-7365
  10am-2pm*
- *Charles H. Wilson Park, 22000 Crenshaw Blvd. (bet.
  Carson St. & Sepulveda Blvd.), Torrance, 310-618-2930
  8am-1pm, Sat 8am-noon*
- *12000 block of Bailey St. (bet. Greenleaf & Comstock),
  Whittier, 714-526-5814*
- *Culver Blvd. (bet. Main & Ince Sts.), Culver City, 310-839-3808
  4pm-8pm (April-October)*

Wednesday
- *St. Agnes Catholic Church (Adams Blvd. & Vermont Ave.),
  LA, 213-777-1755
  2pm-5pm (Sept.–mid-June), 1pm-6pm (mid-June–Aug.)*
- *Arizona Ave. (2nd St.), Santa Monica, 310-458-8712
  9:30am-3pm*
- *6200 W. 87th St. (in The Triangle), Westchester, 310-375-5900
  8:30am-1pm*

Thursday
- *100 N. Brand Blvd., Glendale, 818-449-0179
  9:30am-1:30pm*
- *Redondo Beach Pier (end of Torrance Blvd.), Redondo
  Beach, 310-540-0722
  9am-1pm*
- *Ports O' Call Village, Berth 77, San Pedro, 310-433-3881
  10am-2pm*
- *Oak Shopping Ctr. (Wilbur Rd. & Thousand Oaks Blvd.),
  Thousand Oaks, 805-529-6266
  4pm-7:30pm*

- *Weyburn Ave. (Westwood Blvd.), Westwood, 310-208-6115*
  3pm-7pm

Friday

- *"Hub City", Alameda at Compton, Compton, 310-537-5415*
  10am-5pm (March-Nov.), 11am-5pm (Nov.-March)
- *13th St. & Hermosa Ave., Hermosa Beach, 310-379-1488*
  noon-4pm
- *Promenade North (bet. 3rd St. & Broadway), Long Beach,*
  310-433-3881
  10am-4pm
- *Library Park (bet. Myrtle & Lime), Monrovia, 818-359-2529*
  5pm-9pm
- *Venice Blvd. (Venice Way), Venice, 310-399-6690*
  7am-11am
- *12000 Bailey St. (bet. Greenleaf & Comstock Aves.),*
  Whittier, 714-526-5814
  8:30am-1pm

Saturday

- *Third St. & Orange, Burbank, 818-308-0457*
  8am-1pm
- *Calabasas Rd. & El Cañon, Calabasas, 818-223-8696*
  8am-noon
- *Hollypark Methodist Church, 13000 S. Van Ness Ave.,*
  Gardena, 213-777-1755
  6:30am-noon
- *Dooley's parking lot, 51st St. (west of Long Beach Blvd.),*
  Long Beach, 310-433-3881
  7:30am-11:30am
- *Second St. (west of Garey), Pomona, 714-623-1031*
  7:30am-11:30am
- *Cloverfield & Pico Blvds., Santa Monica, 310-458-8712*
  8am-1pm
- *Charles H. Wilson Park, 2200 block of Crenshaw Blvd.*
  (Jefferson), Torrance, 310-618-2930
  8am-noon
- *W. Covina Plaza, Sunset & Plaza Way, W. Covina,*
  818-338-8496
  8am-noon
- *Arizona Ave. (2nd St.), Santa Monica, 310-458-8712*
  8:30am-noon
- *Van Nuys City Hall parking lot (Van Nuys Blvd. & Sylvan St.),*
  818-908-5066
  8am-noon

Sunday

- *The Victorian at Heritage Sq. parking lot, 2640 Main St.*
  (Ocean Park Blvd.), Santa Monica, 310-458-8712
  9am-noon
- *100 S. Monterey St. (Bay State St.), Alhambra, 818-308-0457*
  9am-1pm

- *200 block of NW Cañon Dr. (Wilshire Blvd. & Dayton Way),*
  Beverly Hills, 310-285-2103
  9am-1pm
- *Organization for The Needs of the Elderly, 17400 Victory*
  Blvd. (bet. Balboa Blvd. & White Oak Ave.), Encino,
  818-708-6611
  8am-noon
- *Ivar St. (bet. Hollywood & Sunset Blvds.), Hollywood,*
  213-963-4151
  8:30am-1pm
- *Peninsula Ctr. parking lot, Palos Verdes, 310-375-5900*
  9am-1pm
- *College of the Canyons, Rockwell & Valencia Blvds.,*
  Santa Clarita, 805-529-6266
  8:30am-noon
- *Van Nuys City Hall parking lot, Van Nuys Blvd. & Sylvan St.,*
  Van Nuys, 818-908-5066
  8am-noon

■ An organization of genuine farmer's markets (there's even one in Beverly Hills!) that has changed the way many shoppers buy produce; allowed to sell only what they grow, they offer "vastly superior freshness and quality" with a focus that helps put SoCal locals back in touch with the seasons; fans consider them "simply the best" and say they "put the fun back" into buying fruits and vegetables.

Stan's Produce ⊟   <u>-</u> <u>-</u> <u>-</u> <u>M</u>

- *9307 W. Pico Blvd. (bet. Beverly & Doheny Drs.), LA,*
  310-274-1865
  M-F 8am-6pm/Sun 8am-5pm

This no-frills shop in the Pico-Robertson area is a well-kept secret offering fine produce (including some organics and hard-to-find specialty items) for those who can't make it to Gelson's, and at a fraction of the price; N.B. Friday PMs can be very crowded since the store is closed on Saturdays.

Tanaka Quality Produce ☙   <u>28</u> <u>22</u> <u>25</u> <u>E</u>

- *1627 Montana Ave. (17th St.), Santa Monica, 310-394-2535*
  M-Sat 9am-6pm/Sun 9am-5pm

■ Trendy Montana Avenue's trendiest place to buy green beans and peaches, this "produce jewel" boasts "always excellent" quality, a "wonderful neighborhood feel" and a "very knowledgeable" owner; "it's all there" (including "beautiful gift baskets"), "you just have to pay for it."

Tapia Brothers ⊟   <u>27</u> <u>19</u> <u>22</u> <u>M</u>

- *5251 Hayvenhurst Ave. (Frwy. #134), Encino,*
  818-787-4358
  Every day 9am-6pm (March–mid-November)

■ For "great white corn, tomatoes and strawberries" and what some call the "world's best peaches" head for this freeway-adjacent produce stand in central San Fernando Valley; the "homegrown, delicious" produce tastes like "summertime incarnate", making it well "worth the drive."

Produce

Vicente Foods
26 | 23 | 23 | E
- *See listing in Supermarkets section.*

■ "You can find anything you want" at this well-respected neighborhood market offering "absolutely reliable", "year-round quality" produce sold by "helpful people"; "where else can you always get long-stemmed strawberries?" asks one regular; it's a pricey "place to indulge."

Wild Oats 🚴
25 | 22 | 23 | E
- *603 S. Lake Ave. (California), Pasadena, 818-792-1778*
- *1425 Montana Ave. (15th St.), Santa Monica,*
  310-576-4707
  All locations: every day 8am-10pm

◪ A Gooch equivalent that boosters say offers "consistently high-quality organic produce" including "great fruit" and a "good selection of beans and sprouts"; some find the general selection somewhat "limited", however, and nonbelievers complain that the "goods aren't always fresh."

Windward Farms
22 | 19 | 17 | M
- *105 Windward Ave. (Pacific Ave.), Venice, 310-392-3566*
  Every day 8:30am-7:30pm

◪ The "convenient" beach location is a big plus for this "quaint store" that offers an "ok" selection with some "interesting veggies and good value" in the land of the roller blader and skate boarder; foes say it has "deteriorated — now just an emergency stop for iceberg lettuce."

Restaurant Delivery Services

The perfect solution for those so fried after a long day they can't even deal with stopping for takeout: restaurant meals delivered hot to your door by any of the following services. Often, the feast comes complete with plates and utensils — all you have to do is open your mouth and chew. Since many upscale restaurants are involved (e.g. Ca'Brea, Le Dome, Locanda Veneta, The Mandarin), you're virtually assured of a great meal, with no more hassle involved than forking over your credit card.

Dining In

Q	V	S	C
▽ 23	21	21	E

- *1311 Ventura Blvd. #206 (Cold Water Canyon), Studio City, 818-986-3287*
  M-F 11am-1:30pm/F & Sat 5pm-10pm/Sun-Th 5pm-9:30pm

☑ Serving the Westside and Valley, with about 20 restaurant clients in each area, these runabouts will deliver meals and also do marketing, a definite plus; complainers say they "need more variety of restaurants and menu items" and are "overpriced", but they only charge $5 with a $15 food minimum.

Glendale Gourmet Delivery Service

–	–	–	M

- *815 S. Central Ave. (Garfield Ave.), Glendale, 818-243-4636*
  M-F 11am-1:30pm/M 5pm-9pm/T-Sat 5pm-9:30pm/ Sun 5pm-8:30pm

The name refers to the center point of this Eastsider's delivery area — they also service adjacent communities like Los Feliz and Burbank, with a $5 basic fee that rises as they get further from Glendale; meals from any of their 25 or so restaurants, including The Crocodile Cafe and Far Niente, are delivered by "very courteous drivers" who wear tuxedos and get to know their clients.

Gourmet Courier

–	–	–	M

- ***Beverly Hills/Pacific Palisades***
  8240 Beverly Blvd., LA, 213-655-8666, 310-788-9777
  Every day 5:30pm-10pm
- ***Encino/Studio City***
  12444 Ventura Blvd., Studio City, 818-766-7888
  M-F 11am-2pm/M-Th 5:30pm-10pm/F & Sat 5:30pm-10pm/ Sun 5pm-9:30pm
- ***Burbank/Glendale/Pasadena/Woodland Hills***
  12444 Ventura Blvd., Studio City, 818-766-7888

Gourmet Courier (Cont.)
*M-F 11am-2pm/M-Th 5:30 pm-9:30pm/F & Sat 5:30pm-10pm/
Sun 5pm-9:30pm*

The largest and, for some, the "best" delivery chain in town,
with branches all over LA (Beverly Hills, Pacific Palisades,
Encino, Studio City, Pasadena and more); this carrier deals
with some 150 restaurants, including upscale spots like The
Mandarin, Tribeca and Kate Mantilini, charging $3 to $6 –
a fair price to pay for "convenience" and "helpful" service.

LA to Go 23 | 23 | 23 | M
• *522 S. Sepulveda Blvd. (1½ blocks south of Montana Ave.),
Westwood, 310-440-4455
M-F 11am-2pm/M-Th 5pm-10:30pm/F 5pm-11pm/
Sat 4:30pm-11pm/Sun 4:30pm-10:30pm*

■ A "good idea for those who work late", this popular
Westside delivery service covers Santa Monica, Century
City, Brentwood, Westwood and West LA with a choice of
some 30 restaurants, including Cafe Montana, Bombay
Cafe, Mezzaluna and Babalu; service, much of it provided
by UCLA students and waiters, is "mostly very efficient
and runs about $4."

Takeout Taxi 22 | 22 | 21 | M
• *5301 Beethoven St. (Jefferson Blvd.), Marina del Rey,
310-301-7074
M-F 11am-2pm/M-F 5pm-9:30pm/Sat & Sun 5pm-10:30pm*

■ With "tons of restaurants to choose from", this "very
efficient", wide-ranging service that delivers from the South
Bay to Santa Monica is a "brilliant concept" that costs $4.50
and is run by "friendly folks"; perfect "on a lazy night."

Why Cook? ▽ 27 | 28 | 27 | E
• *8640 W. Third St. (bet. San Vicente & Robertson Blvds.),
LA, 310-278-3957
M-F 11:30am-2:30pm/Every day 5:30pm-9:30pm*

◪ With two service areas (one covering Hollywood Hills,
Beverly Hills and West LA, the other ranging west from
Brentwood to the Palisades), this firm offers meals from
some 30 restaurants including Locanda Veneta, Ca'Brea and
Le Dome with a $3-7 delivery charge; they claim to have
attractive actors and actresses delivering the food (didn't
Heidi Fleiss say something similar?), which may be one
reason why regulars use them "at least twice a week."

Supermarkets

We take them for granted because they're everywhere. But the fact is that we couldn't do without supermarkets: they've become the modern-day version of the general store, a social center and a nexus for all our needs. We're also lucky in that SoCal supermarkets are mostly pleasant, well-stocked places to shop, in contrast to some of the cramped, outmoded stores on the East Coast. The best of them, such as Bristol Farms and Gelson's, are virtual temples to the joys of consumerism — why else would there still be TV shows that involve people running up and down the aisles, madly filling their carts with food and any other goodies they can grab?

Top Quality
29 Bristol Farms
28 Gelson's Markets
   Owen's Market
27 Vicente Foods
25 Chalet Gourmet

Top Service
27 Owen's Market
26 Gelson's Markets
   Bristol Farms
24 Vicente Foods
22 Beverly Glen

Top Variety
27 Gelson's Markets
   Bristol Farms
23 Vicente Foods
   Pavilions
   Hughes Markets

Best Buys
Gelson's Markets
Trader Joe's
Bristol Farms
Vicente Foods
Hughes Markets

Q	V	S	C
17	19	16	M

Albertsons
- *3841 E. Sierra Madre (Michilinda), Pasadena, 818-351-0076*
- *12800 La Mirada Blvd., La Mirada, 310-943-3783*
- *19725 Vanowen St. (Corbin Ave.), Canoga Park, 818-348-9553*
- *11815 Artesia Blvd. (Pioneer), Artesia, 310-924-9429*
- *5595 Rosemead Blvd. (Las Tunas), Temple City, 818-287-0907*
- *9022 Balboa Blvd. (Nordhoff St.), Northridge, 818-894-6415*
- *331 N. Glendale Ave. (Lexington), Glendale, 818-247-2458*
- *7814 E. Firestone Blvd. (Rives), Downey, 310-923-0394*
- *5810 Downey Ave. (South St.), Long Beach, 310-634-8141*
- *1023 N. Grand Ave. (Covina), Covina, 818-332-1060*
- *6501 Spring St. (Palo Verde), Long Beach, 310-429-5611*
- *21035 Hawthorne Blvd. (Torrance Blvd.), Torrance, 310-540-6824*
- *298 E. Live Oak Ave. (Tyler), Arcadia, 818-446-1416*
- *11300 Firestone Blvd. (bet. Orr & Day Sts.), Norwalk, 310-929-1878*

Albertsons (Cont.)
- *17120 Colima Rd. (Azusa), Hacienda Hts., 818-964-7737*
- *123 N. Reino Rd. (Borchard), Newbury Park, 805-498-1719*
- *5135 Los Angeles St. (Stearns), Simi Valley, 805-520-9293*
- *2800 Cochran (Sycamore), Simi Valley, 805-522-9001*
- *1736 Ave. de los Arboles (#23 Frwy.), Thousand Oaks, 805-493-1551*
  All locations: every day 6am-midnight
  Other locations throughout Southern California.

☑ "Convenience", a "good" selection of ethnic foods and "friendly" staff are cited as virtues of this working-class chain, while "inconsistency" between branches, "tasteless bakery goods" and a "need to modernize" are turnoffs; it provides "reasonable value", but some are irked by "no double coupons anymore."

Beverly Glen Market Place 🚲   23 | 19 | 22 | E |
- *2964 Beverly Glen Circle (Mulholland Dr.), Bel Air, 310-475-0829*
  M-F 7:30am-10pm/Sat & Sun 7:30am-11pm

■ A "small but excellent" upscale specialty store in the hills above Bel Air that's considered "very convenient" "for limited use", but "expensive for regular shopping"; as is often true of tony neighborhood markets, it has a "friendly", "small-town feel", but cynics say the mood is broken at the register: "they should wear masks and point guns."

BRISTOL FARMS   29 | 27 | 26 | E |
- *606 Fair Oaks Ave. (Pasadena Frwy. #110), S. Pasadena, 818-441-5450*
  Every day 8am-9pm
- *1570 Rosecrans Ave. (bet. Aviation & Sepulveda Blvds.), Manhattan Beach, 310-643-5229*
  Every day 8am-9pm (10pm in summer)
- *837 Silver Spur Rd. (Hawthorne Blvd.), Rolling Hills Estates, 310-541-9157*
  M-Sat 8am-8pm/Sun 9am-7pm
- *6227 Topanga Canyon Blvd. (Erwin St.), Woodland Hills, 818-227-8400*

■ Top-rated for quality, this four-store chain that puts the "super" in supermarket was recently sold by its original owners, but assuming no major changes are made, fans expect it to remain "a shopper's dream" with "wide aisles", "helpful" staff, "beautiful presentations" and lots of "great samples" of its "terrific" goods; cost is a drawback, but this "carriage-trade winner" is "worth it."

Chalet Gourmet 🚲 ▭   25 | 20 | 22 | E |
- *7880 Sunset Blvd. (Fairfax Ave.), LA, 213-874-6301*
  Every day 9am-9pm

☑ On Sunset just below the affluent Hollywood Hills, this longtime boutique supermarket makes entertaining easy with its "interesting selection" of "high-quality" items, but those who feel it "needs more variety and lower prices" say it's "not for everyday use."

Supermarkets q | v | s | c

Fedco 18 | 16 | 13 | I
- *14920 Raymer St. (east of Sepulveda Blvd.), Van Nuys, 818-786-6863*
- *3535 S. La Cienega Blvd. (Rodeo), LA, 310-837-4481*
- *11525 South St. (Gridley), Cerritos, 310-860-7711*
- *3111 E. Colorado Blvd. (Rosemead), Pasadena, 818-449-8260*
- *3030 Harbor Blvd. (Baker), Costa Mesa, 714-979-2660*
- *2534 S. Archibald Ave. (#60 Frwy.), Ontario, 909-947-8300*
- *8450 La Palma Ave. (bet. Dale Ave. & Beach Blvd.), Buena Park, 714-236-1800*
  570 S. Mt. Vernon (Mill), San Bernardino, 909-888-4181
  All locations: M-F 10am-9pm/Sat & Sun 10am-6pm
  Other locations throughout Southern California.

■ A members-only chain where shoppers "stock up" on Bunyan-size quantities of household products at rock-bottom prices – a fair exchange for putting up with "long lines", "pushy crowds", "poor service" and spotty selection; fans say you can "save dollars" on liquor and find "good prices on Harris Ranch meats" at this "People's Republic of Shopping."

GELSON'S MARKETS 28 | 27 | 26 | E
- *Century City Marketplace, 10250 Santa Monica Blvd. (Century Park West), Century City, 310-277-4288 M-Sat 9am-10pm/Sun 9am-9pm*
- *15424 Sunset Blvd. (Via de La Paz), Pacific Palisades, 310-459-4483*
- *Marina Marketplace, 13455 Maxella Ave. (Lincoln Blvd.), Marina Del Rey, 310-306-2952*
- *16450 Ventura Blvd. (Hayvenhurst Ave.), Encino, 818-906-5780*
- *2734 Townsgate Rd. (Village Glen), Westlake Village, 805-496-0353*
- *4738 Laurel Canyon Blvd. (Riverside Dr.), N. Hollywood, 818-906-5743*
- *5500 Reseda Blvd. (Ventura Blvd.), Tarzana, 818-906-5752*
  All locations: every day 8am-10pm, unless noted otherwise

■ Ranking just a notch below Bristol Farms for quality, this midsized chain is SoCal's busiest group of upscale markets (only Trader Joe's receives more votes); "you can eat off the floor" at these carefully manicured stores where shopping is "a joy" thanks to "well-stocked" shelves, "top-notch" goods and "helpful" service; though not cheap, in many cases it's "only pennies more than the big chains."

Hughes Markets 22 | 23 | 20 | M
- *12842 Ventura Blvd. (Coldwater Canyon Ave.), Studio City, 818-761-6196*
- *14440 Burbank Blvd. (east of Van Nuys Blvd.), Sherman Oaks, 818-989-5640*
- *16940 Devonshire St. (Balboa Blvd.), Granada Hills, 818-363-3173*

Hughes Markets (Cont.)

- *15120 Sunset Blvd. (west of Chautauqua), Pacific Palisades, 310-454-3001*
- *2716 San Fernando Rd. (Fletcher Dr.), LA, 213-225-5127*
- *4520 Van Nuys Blvd. (Moorpark Ave.), Sherman Oaks, 818-788-3552*
- *11361 National Blvd. (Sawtelle Blvd.), West LA, 310-479-4351*
- *21431 Devonshire St. (Canoga Ave.), Chatsworth, 818-341-0950*
- *6657 Laurel Canyon Blvd. (Archwood), N. Hollywood, 818-765-2770*
- *1100 N. San Fernando Blvd. (Delaware), Burbank, 818-845-6424*
- *10400 N. Sepulveda Blvd. (Devonshire St.), Mission Hills, 818-365-3296*
- *26518 Bouquet Canyon (Soledad Canyon), Saugus, 805-296-8682*
- *30019 Hawthorne Blvd. (Crest), Palos Verdes, 310-377-6941*
- *22333 Sherman Way (Shoup Ave.), Canoga Park, 818-883-1230*
- *101 West LA Ave., Moorpark, 805-529-1604*
- *9040 W. Beverly Blvd. (Doheny Dr.), Beverly Hills, 310-278-1351*
- *1028 S. San Fernando Blvd. (Alameda Ave.), Burbank, 818-843-7553*
- *674 Las Posas (#101 Frwy.), Camarillo, 805-338-1781*
- *1101 W. Huntington Dr. (bet. Sunset Blvd. & Huntington Dr.), Arcadia, 818-447-3548*
- *320 W. Colorado Blvd. (east of Orange Ave.), Pasadena, 818-793-4179*
- *2909 Rolling Hills Rd. (Crenshaw Blvd.), Torrance, 310-325-0611*
- *3601 E. Foothills Blvd. (Rosemead), Pasadena, 818-351-8806*
- *23841 W. Malibu Rd. (PCH), Malibu, 310-456-2917*
- *2520 Glendale Blvd. (north of Silverlake Blvd.), LA, 213-666-5392*
- *1305 W. Whittier Blvd. (east of Harbor Blvd.), La Habra, 310-694-6397*
- *30805 Thousand Oaks Blvd. (Westlake Blvd.), Westlake Village, 818-706-9548*
- *330 N. Atlantic Blvd. (south of #10 Frwy.), Monterey Park, 818-289-0261*
- *19340 Soledad Canyon Rd. (White's Canyon), Canyon Country, 805-252-6226*
- *25930 McBean Pkwy. (Soledad Canyon), Valencia, 805-254-3440*

Hughes Markets (Cont.)
- *583 N. Ventura Park Rd. (Thousand Oaks Blvd.),*
  Newbury Park, 805-449-6743
  All locations: every day 24 hrs
  Other locations throughout Southern California.

◪ This popular chain offers "convenience" (there seems to be a branch in every neighborhood), "competitive prices" and variety ("look around, it's here"), which is why most call it a good all-around choice for "everyday needs"; a few foes claim it's "gone downhill" and note "service is not their strong suit", but "with coupons it's paradise."

Louis Foods   20 21 21 M
- *451 S. Sierra Madre Blvd. (San Pasqual Ave.),*
  Pasadena, 818-795-4281
- *South Hills Shopping Ctr., 1420 Azusa Ave. (2 miles*
  south of Frwy. #10), W. Covina, 818-916-2070
  All locations: every day 7am-11pm

■ "They try harder" say admirers of these San Gabriel Valley neighborhood gourmet markets that aim to please with a "great selection" of "offbeat items", including "hard-to-find specialties" and British goods; prices are "a bit higher" than some, but choices are "more interesting."

Lucky Stores   17 19 15 I
- *4211 Eagle Rock Blvd. (El Paso), LA, 213-255-9993*
- *28500 S. Western Ave. (Westmont), Rancho Palos Verdes,*
  310-832-4548
- *1516 S. PCH (Avenue H), Redondo Beach, 310-316-3551*
- *1120 S. Hacienda Blvd. (Gale), Hacienda Hts., 818-330-2444*
- *13051 Victory Blvd. (Coldwater Canyon), N. Hollywood,*
  818-760-3754
- *4848 W. 190th St. (Inglewood), Torrance, 310-371-2757*
- *3901 Crenshaw Blvd. (Martin Luther King), LA, 213-295-1919*
- *3105 Wilshire Blvd. (Franklin), Santa Monica, 310-829-2363*
- *615 N. PCH (Irina), Redondo Beach, 310-376-2170*
- *3828 N. Peck Rd. (Ramona), El Monte, 818-442-4020*
- *2515 Torrance Blvd. (Crenshaw), Torrance, 310-320-3258*
- *27631 W. Bouquet Canyon Rd. (Haskell Canyon), Saugus,*
  805-296-9655
- *6821 Lennox Ave. (Vanowen), Van Nuys, 818-781-1310*
- *18555 Devonshire St. (Reseda), Northridge, 818-368-3694*
- *7134 Sepulveda Blvd. (Sherman Way), Van Nuys,*
  818-782-2320
- *2400 Sepulveda Blvd. (Marine Dr.), Manhattan Beach,*
  310-546-2408
- *13925 Amar Rd. (Willow), La Puente, 818-962-3281*
- *543 N. Azusa Ave. (San Bernardino), Covina, 818-966-1604*
- *18730 E. Amar Rd. (Nogales), Walnut, 818-965-7377*
- *3830 W. Verdugo Ave. (Hollywood Way), 818-954-0817*
- *2510 PCH (Artesia), Hermosa Beach, 310-379-7437*
- *6801 Atlantic Blvd. (Florence), Bell, 213-560-0067*
- *2130 PCH (Narbonne), Lomita, 310-326-3351*

Lucky Stores (Cont.)
- *11029 Alondra Blvd. (Studentbaker), Norwalk, 310-863-9753*
- *933 E. Las Tunas Blvd. (San Gabriel), E. San Gabriel, 818-287-7581*
- *6255 E. Second St. (Marine Dr.), Long Beach, 310-430-4822*
- *5750 Mesmer Ave. (Jefferson), Culver City, 310-390-2373*
- *3456 S. Sepulveda Blvd. (Palms), West LA, 310-838-4123*
- *644 N. Redondo Blvd. (7th St.), Long Beach, 310-439-4004*
- *2120 Pacific Ave. (21st St.), Long Beach, 310-591-5808*
- *110 E. Carson St. (Main St.), Carson, 310-835-6402*
- *11660 E. Firestone Blvd. (Pioneer), Norwalk, 310-863-2217*
- *17220 S. Lakewood Blvd. (Artesia), Bellflower, 310-866-3724*
- *6000 Atlantic Ave. (60th St.), Long Beach, 310-423-2500*
- *1820 W. 182nd St. (Western), Torrance, 310-323-9303*
- *12122 Magnolia Blvd. (Laurel Canyon), N. Hollywood, 818-985-4780*
- *6235 E. Spring St. (Palo Verde), Long Beach, 310-425-8456*
- *2630 E. Workman Ave. (Citrus), W. Covina, 818-331-5532*
- *855 N. Wilcox (Via Campo), Montebello, 213-724-0462*
- *1636 W. 25th St. (Western), San Pedro, 310-831-1161*
- *8448 Lincoln Blvd. (Manchester), LA, 310-645-3518*
- *2627 Lincoln Blvd. (Ocean Park Blvd.), Santa Monica, 310-452-3811*
- *22840 Victory Blvd. (Fallbrook), Woodland Hills, 818-883-6565*
- *1855 W. Glenoaks Blvd. (Allen), Glendale, 818-244-8485*
- *1000 S. Central Ave. (Chevy Chase), Glendale, 818-244-8109*
- *3211 Firestone Blvd. (State St.), South Gate, 213-564-3713*
- *6240 Foothill Blvd. (Lowell), Tujunga, 818-248-6945*
- *14433 Ramona Blvd. (Maine Ave.), Baldwin Park, 818-337-0818*
- *432 W. Huntington Dr. (Mayflower), Monrovia, 818-357-4515*
- *11750 E. Whittier Blvd. (Hadley St.), Whittier, 310-696-3212*
- *14401 Inglewood Ave. (Rosecrans Ave.), Hawthorne, 310-644-7200*
- *15055 Mulberry Dr. (La Mirada Blvd.), Whittier, 310-944-8112*
- *1222 N. Avalon Blvd. (L St.), Wilmington, 310-835-1427*
- *1190 E. Carson St. (Orange Ave.), Long Beach, 310-426-2549*
- *8320 Firestone Blvd. (Downey Ave.), Downey, 310-862-7513*
- *7224 Mason Ave. (Sherman Way), Canoga Park, 818-346-8785*
- *2115 Artesia Blvd. (Rindge St.), Redondo Beach, 310-542-2122*
- *273 E. Gladstone Ave. (Azusa Ave.), Azusa, 818-334-7513*
- *19307 Saticoy St. (Tampa Ave.), Reseda, 818-772-0010*
- *4155 Tweedy Blvd. (Otis Ave.), South Gate, 213-569-1588*
- *9317 Whittier Blvd. (Durfee St.), Pico Rivera, 310-692-2151*
- *8725 Sepulveda Blvd. (Parthenia St.), 818-893-5767*
- *17202 S. Norwalk Blvd. (Artesia), Cerritos, 310-860-9211*
- *3963 Cochran St., Simi Valley, 805-526-1615*

Lucky Stores (Cont.)

- *8231 Woodman Ave. (Rosco Blvd.), Panorama City, 818-781-3544*
- *16201 San Fernando Mission Blvd. (Woodley Ave.), Granada Hills, 818-366-9555*
- *2035 Hillhurst Ave. (Sunset Blvd.), LA, 213-660-0687*
- *18571 Soledad Canyon (Sierra Hwy.), Canyon Country, 805-298-0219*
- *708 Yorktown Ave. (Golden West), Huntington Beach, 714-536-8816*
  All locations: every day 6am-midnight
  Other locations throughout Southern California.

■ If you're lucky you'll find "decent meat, produce" and other basics plus "shorter lines" at this big, not always beloved chain of blue-collar markets; "bargains are their specialty", but critics say they're "low in price, low in quality", with "surly" service and "not very clean" stores.

Mayfair Markets 21 | 19 | 19 | M

- *2725 Hyperion Ave. (Griffith Park Pl.), Silverlake, 213-660-0387*
- *1234 N. LaBrea Ave. (Fountain Ave.), W. Hollywood, 213-464-2171*
- *8330 W. Santa Monica Blvd. (Kings Rd.), W. Hollywood, 213-656-5580*
- *5877 Franklin Ave. (Bronson Ave.), Hollywood, 213-464-7316*
  All locations: every day 7am-midnight

■ Owned by Gelson's, this minichain strikes admirers as a handy "fallback" and "good for last-minute items" since it's "never crowded", but foes claim it approaches "Gelson's prices without the appearance" or service; still, "fresh produce" and meats win votes and optimists say it's "getting better" all-around.

Owen's Market 🚲�# 28 | 21 | 27 | E

- *9769 W. Pico Blvd. (Roxbury Dr.), LA, 310-553-8181*
  Every day 9am-6pm

■ Expect "service with a smile" at this "small boutique-style market" that's "great if they have what you need"; known for its "excellent butcher" and "fabulous" beef that's aged on the premises, it's among the "best of its kind", but be advised that "prices are to the moon"; they also deliver – a vanishing service in sprawling SoCal.

Pavilions 🚲 23 | 23 | 19 | M

- *130 W. Foothill Blvd. (Myrtle), Monrovia, 818-303-4547*
- *745 E. Naomi Ave. (Baldwin), Arcadia, 818-446-9483*
- *11030 Jefferson Blvd. (Sawtelle Ave.), Culver City, 310-398-1945*
- *11750 Wilshire Blvd. (Stoner Ave.), West LA, 310-479-5294*
- *1110 Alameda Ave. (bet. Main & Buena Vista), Burbank, 818-567-0257*
- *845 E. California St. (bet. Lake & Hudson), Pasadena, 818-449-3968*

Pavilions (Cont.)
- *6534 Platt Ave. (Victory Blvd.), West Hills, 818-999-5939*
- *14845 Ventura Blvd. (Kester Ave.), Sherman Oaks, 818-986-7213*
- *1213 Fair Oaks Ave. (Monterey), South Pasadena, 818-799-2261*
- *727 N. Vine St. (Melrose Ave.), LA, 213-461-4167*
- *8969 Santa Monica Blvd. (Robertson Blvd.), W. Hollywood, 310-273-0977*
- *820 Montana Ave. (Lincoln Blvd.), Santa Monica, 310-395-1682*
- *4705 Torrance Blvd. (Anza), Torrance, 310-370-1136*
- *7 Peninsula Ctr. (bet. Hawthorne Blvd. & Silver Spur), Rancho Palos Verdes, 310-377-1994*
- *9467 W. Olympic Blvd. (Beverly Dr.), Beverly Hills, 310-553-5734*
- *10800 W. Pico Blvd. (Overland Ave.), West LA, 310-470-2284*
- *5949 Spring St. (Woodruff), Long Beach, 310-496-2151*
- *5500 Woodruff, Lakewood, 310-866-3681*
- *1101 PCH (Seal Beach Blvd.), Seal Beach, 310-598-4251*
- *1135 Lindero Canyon Rd. (Kanan Rd.), Thousand Oaks, 818-597-1261*
  Hours vary according to location; please call to check.
◪ An upscale chain opened by Vons to compete with trendier supermarkets like Gelson's; with "good quality", "wide variety" and generally "courteous" service, it's fast becoming "a favorite for regular shopping" when "not feeling rich"; a few complainers say "some stores are better than others" and they're like "a zoo" when crowded; P.S. they'll even shop for you and deliver the groceries; call 800-756-6225 for home delivery.

Price/Costco   ♿   21 | 19 | 11 | I |
- *3560 W. Century Blvd. (Yukon Ave.), Inglewood, 310-672-1371*
- *8810 Tampa Ave. (bet. Nordhoff & Parthenia), Northridge, 818-755-1860*
- *21300 Roscoe Blvd. (Canoga Ave.), Canoga Park, 818-884-8968*
- *6100 Sepulveda Blvd. (Oxnard St.), Van Nuys, 818-989-3565*
- *1345 Montebello Blvd. (Paramount Blvd.), Montebello, 213-890-1901*
- *1220 W. Foothill Blvd. (Irwindale Ave. exit, #210 Frwy.), Azusa, 818-812-7911*
- *12324 Hoxie Ave. (Imperial Hwy., #60 Frwy.), Norwalk, 310-929-0826*
- *17301 E. Gale Ave. (Azusa Ave, #210 Frwy.), City of Industry, 818-964-6265*
- *10950 Sherman Way (Vineland Ave.), Burbank, 818-840-8115*
- *5175 W. Marine Ave. (Aviation Blvd.), Lawndale, 310-643-7332*
- *5175 W. Marino Ave. (Irwindale Ave., #210 Frwy.) Hawthorne, 310-643-7332*

Price/Costco (Cont.)

- *2207 W. Commonwealth Ave. (Freemont Ave.),*
  Alhambra, 818-281-8600
  M-F 11am-8:30pm/Sat 9:30am-6pm/Sun 10am-5pm
  Other locations throughout Southern California.

■ "A great secret if you know how to use them", these
members-only warehouse stores draw restaurateurs and
folks in search of "bargain" bulk buys; quality is surprisingly
good – fans tout it for anything from paper products and
chicken breasts to mushrooms and frozen fish; perfect if
"buying for a small army" or to see "how big cans can get."

Ralphs Grocery Company   ⎡20⎤ ⎡21⎤ ⎡17⎤ ⎡M⎤

- *2675 Foothill Blvd. (La Crescenta), La Crescenta,*
  818-249-5448
- *1010 S. Western Ave. (Olympic Blvd. & Western Ave.),*
  LA, 213-731-8525
- *1193 Huntington Dr. (Buena Vista), Duarte, 818-358-2338*
- *Every day 6am-1am*
- *17840 Ventura Blvd. (Zelzah Ave.), Encino, 818-345-6882*
- *23741 Calabasas Rd. (bet. Parkway Calabasas & Valley*
  Circle), 818-223-8646
- *Every day 6am-midnight*
- *8704 S. Sepulveda Blvd. (Manchester Ave.), Westchester,*
  310-670-2522
- *1745 Garfield (Huntington Dr.), S. Pasadena, 213-682-3149*
- *Every day 6am-11pm*
- *8340 Van Nuys Blvd. (Roscoe Blvd.), Panorama City,*
  818-892-7208
- *100 N. La Cienega Blvd. (Third St.), LA, 213-655-6226*
- *14049 Ventura Blvd. (Hazeltine Ave.), Sherman Oaks,*
  818-784-2674
- *3410 W. Third St. (Vermont Ave.), LA, 213-480-1421*
- *4949 Paramount Blvd. (Del Amo), Lakewood, 310-636-8470*
- *260 S. La Brea (Third St.), LA, 213-937-3263*
- *17020 Chatsworth St. (Balboa Blvd.), Granada Hills,*
  818-360-7323
- *5727 Kanan Dume Rd. (Thousand Oaks Blvd.), Agoura,*
  818-889-5428
- *7257 Sunset Blvd. (bet. La Brea & Fairfax Aves.), Hollywood,*
  213-874-6333
- *17840 Ventura Blvd. (Zelzah Ave.), Encino, 818-345-6882*
- *23741 Calabasas Rd. (Valley Circle Blvd.), Calabasas,*
  818-223-8646
- *1745 Garfield Ave. (Huntington Dr.), S. Pasadena,*
  818-799-5790
- *211 E. Foothill Blvd. (Second Ave.), Arcadia, 213-681-2262*
- *2500 W. Victory Blvd. (Buena Vista), Burbank, 213-849-5767*
- *3035 E. Huntington Dr. (San Gabriel), Pasadena, 213-681-1205*
- *12057 Wilshire Blvd. (Bundy Dr.), West LA, 310-272-5728*

Ralphs Grocery Company (Cont.)

- 20440 Devonshire St. (Mason), Chatsworth, 818-341-7151
- 7221 Woodman Ave. (Sherman Way), Van Nuys, 213-873-3321
- 521 W. Foothill Blvd. (Gould), La Cañada, 818-790-0584
- 10900 Magnolia Blvd. (Vineland St.), N. Hollywood, 818-760-4148
- 1416 E. Colorado Blvd. (Verdugo), Glendale, 213-245-7749
- 12921 Magnolia Blvd. (Coldwater Canyon Ave.), Van Nuys, 818-986-2292
- 20060 Ventura Blvd. (Winnetka Ave.), Woodland Hills, 818-883-7551
- 21909 Ventura Blvd. (Topanga Canyon Blvd.), Woodland Hills, 818-883-1907
- 3827 Culver Ctr. (bet. Washington Blvd. & Overland Ave.), Culver City, 310-558-4026
- 5035 PCH (Calle Mayer), Torrance, 310-378-0294
- 160 N. Lake Ave. (Walnut), Pasadena, 818-793-7420
- 1200 N. Central Ave. (Stocker), Glendale, 818-246-1751
- 3455 Sepulveda Blvd. (Hawthorne Blvd.), Torrance, 310-542-1639
- 1413 Hawthorne Blvd. (182nd St.), Redondo Beach, 310-370-9446
- 8201 Topanga Canyon Blvd. (Roscoe Blvd.), Canoga Park, 818-703-5959
- 851 W. Sepulveda Blvd. (Vermont Ave.), Torrance, 310-549-4870
- 5420 Sunset Blvd. (Western Ave.), Hollywood, 213-871-8011
- 4033 Laurel Canyon Blvd. (Ventura Blvd.), Studio City, 818-985-5401
- 22741 Victory Blvd. (Fallbrook Ave.), Canoga Park, 818-999-2320
- 10201 Reseda Blvd. (Devonshire St.), Northridge, 818-886-0460
- 10309 W. Olympic Blvd. (Fox Hills Dr.), Century City, 310-553-8117
- 2700 Sepulveda Blvd. (Marine), Manhattan Beach, 310-546-2471
- 6350 W. Third St. (Fairfax Ave.), LA, 213-930-1023
- 16 E. Live Oak (Santa Anita), Arcadia, 818-357-1942
- 1100 PCH (Aviation Blvd.), Hermosa Beach, 310-798-6800
- 3701 E. Foothill Blvd. (Rosemead Blvd.), Pasadena, 818-351-7731
- 11727 W. Olympic Blvd. (Barrington Ave.), West LA, 310-473-5238
- 16325 Ventura Blvd. (Haydenhurst Ave.), Encino, 818-386-0118

Supermarkets

Ralphs Grocery Company (Cont.)

- 3963 Thousand Oaks Blvd. (Westlake Blvd.), Thousand Oaks, 805-496-2468
  6am-midnight
  Every day 24 hrs unless otherwise noted
  Other locations throughout Southern California.

☑ One of the biggest, and most successful, chains in SoCal is called "good", "solid", "reliable" and "well stocked" by fans, but the less-impressed are more succinct: "average"; "fresh fish" and La Brea Bakery bread are pluses, and it's a "double-coupon heaven"; due to a recent merger, all Alpha Beta Boys and Viva Markets will become Ralphs.

Smart & Final

- 1755 Ximeno Ave. (PCH), Long Beach, 310-591-5693
- 210 N. Verdugo Rd. (Broadway), Glendale, 818-243-4239
- 1382 Locust St. (Hill), Pasadena, 818-793-2195
- 500 S. Pacific Ave. (5th St.), San Pedro, 310-832-4179
- 11460 E. Washington Blvd. (bet. Greenleaf & Washington), Whittier, 310-695-1093
- 1216 S. Compton Ave. (1 block south of Olympic Blvd.), 213-747-6697
- 401 W. Anaheim St. (bet. Avalon & Wilmington), Wilmington, 310-835-5251
- 5700 E. Olympic Blvd. (Poplar), Commerce, 213-888-2803
- 266 E. Huntington Dr. (California), Monrovia, 818-358-3261
- 12210 Santa Monica Blvd. (Bundy Dr.), West LA, 310-207-8688
- 5140 E. Florence Ave. (Central), Bell, 213-562-3421
- 708 W. Las Tunas Dr., San Gabriel, 818-281-2049
- 332 S. PCH (Torrance Blvd.), Redondo Beach, 310-540-7344
- 7720 Melrose Ave. (Fairfax Ave.), LA, 213-655-2211
- 10935 Firestone Blvd., Norwalk, 310-863-7057
- 1320 W. Magnolia Blvd. (Victory Blvd.), Burbank, 818-845-4544
- 10113 Venice Blvd. (Clarington), West LA, 310-559-1722
- 604 Lincoln Blvd. (Sunset), Venice, 310-392-4954
- 10910 Long Beach Blvd. (Imperial), Lynwood, 310-631-8639
- 2019 Pasadena Ave. (San Fernando Rd.), LA, 213-223-6252
- 8137 S. Vermont Ave. (81st St.), LA, 213-758-5734
- 1125 E. El Segundo Blvd. (Central), LA, 213-569-7148
- 2308 E. Fourth St. (Soto), LA, 213-268-9179
- 1433 W. Carson St. (Normandie), Torrance, 310-328-3023
- 7815 Van Nuys Blvd., Van Nuys, 818-780-7222
- 9535 Alondra Blvd. (Bellflower), Bellflower, 310-925-5065
- 19718 Sherman Way (Corbin Ave.), Winnetka, 818-996-1331
- 4865 W. Rosecrans (Inglewood), Hawthorne, 310-675-1146
- 939 N. Western Ave. (Romaine), Hollywood, 213-466-9289
- 2949 W. Pico Blvd. (bet. Western & Normandie), LA, 213-732-9101
- 3140 W. Imperial Hwy. (Crenshaw), Inglewood, 310-677-1107
- 541 N. Azusa Ave. (Roland), W. Covina, 818-915-6619
- 20410 Susana Rd., Carson, 310-762-2536

Smart & Final (Cont.)
- *10893 San Fernando Rd. (Van Nuys Blvd.), Pacoima, 818-896-6212*
- *11436 Garvey Ave. (Peck Rd.), El Monte, 818-443-1381*
- *11148 Chandler Blvd. (Lankershim Blvd.), N. Hollywood, 818-769-2292*
- *1050 S. La Brea (Century Blvd.), Inglewood, 310-673-8830*
- *6555 Foothill Blvd. (Tujunga), Azusa, 818-352-9399*
- *3607 S. Vermont Ave. (Jefferson), LA, 213-733-5875*
- *1575 Centinela Ave. (Beach), Inglewood, 310-673-4997*
- *25355 Crenshaw (PCH), Torrance, 310-539-3526*
- *2720 Beverly Blvd. (Lafayette St.), LA, 213-382-6434*
- *16210 Devonshire (Widley), Granada Hills, 818-892-3338*
- *3708 W. Burbank Blvd. (Hollywood Way), Burbank, 818-562-3234*
- *18204 E. Gale Ave. (Fullerton Rd.), City of Industry, 818-965-0483*
- *1041 Fuller Ave. (Santa Monica Blvd.), W. Hollywood, 213-876-0421*
- *16847 Ventura Blvd. (Balboa Blvd.), Encino, 818-789-0242*
- *Ward Plaza, 1835 S. La Cienega Blvd. (#10 Frwy.), LA, 310-558-0576*
- *6201 Alameda St. (bet. Gage & Randall Sts.), LA, 213-581-7973*
- *2400 W. Hillcrest Dr. (Rancho Conejo), Thousand Oaks, 805-375-1358*
- *1856 Erringer Rd. (Los Angeles St.), Simi Valley, 805-582-9232*
- *23640 Lyons Ave. (Peachland), Santa Clarita, 805-255-9822*
  Store hours are M-Sat 7am-7pm/Sun 9am-7pm; call to check for specific location

■ Membership isn't necessary to shop this bulk-product chain, a "grab bag of odd deals" in the form of "institutional", "economy"-size staples such as cleaning materials, candy, condiments and sauces; "prices are great if you think big" or have to "take care of large groups", but don't expect much service or variety.

Trader Joe's 24 | 22 | 21 | I
- *Topanga Plaza Shopping Ctr., 6600 Topanga Canyon Blvd. (Vanowen St.), Canoga Park, 818-883-4134*
- *11114 Balboa Blvd. (San Fernando Mission Rd.), Granada Hills, 818-368-6461*
- *17640 Burbank Blvd. (White Oak Ave.), Encino, 818-990-7751*
- *14119 Riverside Dr. (Hazeltine Ave.), Sherman Oaks, 818-789-2771*
- *3433 Foothill Blvd. (2 blocks west of Pennsylvania), La Crescenta, 818-249-3693*
- *6378 E. PCH (½ block north of Second St.), Long Beach, 310-598-3740*
- *10850 National Blvd. (Westwood Blvd.), West LA, 310-470-1917*
- *220 Citrus St. (1 block south of #10 Frwy.), W. Covina, 818-858-0408*

Trader Joe's (Cont.)

- *2738 Hyperion Ave. (bet. Griffith Park Blvd. & Rowena), Silver Lake, 213-665-6774*
- *613 Mission St. (1 mile west of Fremont), S. Pasadena, 818-441-6263*
- *7260 N. Rosemead Blvd. (Huntington Dr.), San Gabriel, 818-285-5862*
- *8645 Sepulveda Blvd. (bet. Manchester Ave. & La Tijera), Westchester, 310-338-9238*
- *1821 Manhattan Beach Blvd. (Aviation Blvd.), Manhattan Beach, 310-372-1274*
- *10011 Washington Blvd. (bet. Robertson Blvd. & Motor Ave.), Culver City, 310-202-1108*
- *Riviera Village Shopping Ctr., 1761 S. Elena Ave., Redondo Beach, 310-316-1745*
- *7304 Santa Monica Blvd. (Poinsettia), W. Hollywood, 213-851-9772*
- *15025 E. Whittier Blvd. (Colima Rd.), Whittier, 310-698-1642*
- *610 S. Arroyo Pkwy. (California Blvd.), Pasadena, 818-568-9254*
- *1566 Colorado Blvd. (Figueroa), Eagle Rock, 213-257-6422*
- *28901 S. Western Ave. (1½ miles south of PCH), Palos Verdes, 310-832-1241*
- *3835 E. Thousand Oaks Blvd. (Westlake Blvd.), Westlake Village, 805-494-5040*
  All locations: every day 9am-9pm
  Other locations throughout Southern California.

■ Not so much a supermarket as a way of life, this burgeoning "yuppie-paradise" chain (which is starting to go national) received more votes than any competitor; while it may not have the variety of some markets, it's a "bonanza" of discount "specialty" goods including cheeses, wines, beers, dried fruits and "surprises" galore; in some ways, it's the LA version of NYC's Dean & DeLuca, but far cheaper.

Vicente Foods   27 23 24 E

- *12027 San Vicente Blvd. (Bundy Dr.), Brentwood, 310-472-5215*
  M-Sat 9am-9pm/Sun 9am-8pm

■ Where Brentwoodians head when they don't feel like dealing with the big chains, this "neighborhood" "Gelson's wanna-be" offers "superb" quality and "helpful" service; there are "no bargains", but "you get what you pay for" – "everything is excellent" and it's a "treat" to shop here.

Vons Market   19 20 16 M

- *1311 Wilshire Blvd. (14th St.), Santa Monica, 310-394-1414*
- *1011 N. San Fernando Rd. (Burbank Blvd.), Burbank, 818-845-1447*
- *1260 W. Redondo Beach Blvd. (Normandie Ave.), Gardena, 310-324-4226*
- *1820 W. Verdugo Blvd. (Olive St.), Burbank, 818-848-3559*
- *311 W. Los Feliz Blvd. (Central), Glendale, 213-245-8479*

Vons Market (Cont.)

- *2355 E. Colorado Ave. (Sierra Madre), Pasadena, 818-449-4338*
- *18439 Ventura Blvd. (Reseda Blvd.), Tarzana, 818-705-9749*
- *16930 San Fernando Mission Blvd. (Balboa Blvd.), Granada Hills, 818-368-5929*
- *16130 Nordhoff St. (Woodley Ave.), North Hills, 818-894-4300*
- *23381 Mulholland Dr. (San Luis), Woodland Hills, 818-223-3221*
- *435 N. Altadena (Villa), Pasadena, 818-796-5381*
- *133 E. Foothill Blvd. (bet. 1st & 2nd Sts.), Arcadia, 818-357-3647*
- *1110 Alameda Ave. (Main), Burbank, 818-567-0257*
- *845 E. California St. (Lake), Pasadena, 818-449-3968*
- *6534 Platt Ave. (Victory Blvd.), W. Hills, 818-999-5939*
- *4705 Torrance Blvd. (Anza), Torrance, 310-370-1136*
- *7 Peninsula Ctr. (Silver Spur), Rancho Palos Verdes, 310-377-1994*
- *1820 W. Verdugo Ave. (Olive), Burbank, 818-980-0475*
- *311 W. Los Feliz Blvd. (Central), Glendale, 213-245-8479*
- *2355 E. Colorado Blvd. (Sierra Madre), Pasadena, 818-449-4338*
- *18439 Ventura Blvd. (Reseda), Tarzana, 818-881-5527*
- *16930 San Fernando Mission Blvd. (Balboa), Granada Hills, 818-368-5929*
- *1129 Fair Oaks Ave. (Monterey), S. Pasadena, 818-441-3898*
- *3118 S. Sepulveda Blvd. (National Blvd.), West LA, 310-477-8717*
- *9119 Reseda Blvd. (Nordhoff), Northridge, 818-349-2494*
- *9860 National Blvd. (Manning), Cheviot Hills, 310-836-4161*
- *4365 Glencoe Ave. (Lincoln), Marina Del Rey, 310-821-7208*
- *21821 Ventura Blvd. (Topanga Canyon), Woodland Hills, 818-347-7880*
- *17380 Sunset Blvd. (PCH), Pacific Palisades, 310-454-2502*
- *11674 Santa Monica Blvd. (Barrington), West LA, 310-820-1012*
- *4030 Centinela Ave. (Washington), LA, 310-391-1503*
- *245 Palos Verdes Blvd. (Catalina), Redondo Beach, 310-378-7434*
- *3930 Rosecrans Ave. (Prairie), Hawthorne, 310-793-7179*
- *410 Manhattan Beach Blvd. (Valley), Manhattan Beach, 310-379-3051*
- *1512 E. Amar Rd. (Azusa Ave.), W. Covina, 818-964-7112*
- *10001 Paramount Blvd. (Florence St.), Downey, 310-928-1619*
- *4550 Atlantic Blvd. (45th St.), Long Beach, 310-984-1421*
- *6921 La Tijera Blvd. (Centinela Ave.), LA, 310-641-5857*
- *18135 Sherman Way (bet. Lindley & Etiwanda Sts.), Reseda, 818-342-9202*
- *20151 Roscoe Blvd. (Winnetka Ave.), Winnetka, 818-341-4055*
- *6140 Lankershim Blvd. (Erwin St.), N. Hollywood, 818-980-0475*

Vons Market (Cont.)

- *1831 W. Third St. (Bonnie Brae), LA, 213-483-1053*
- *820 N. Western Ave. (Crestwood St.), San Pedro, 310-832-5654*
- *2122 S. Hacienda Blvd. (Newton), Hacienda Hts., 818-330-4216*
- *1212 Beryl St. (Prospect Ave.), Redondo Beach, 310-374-7987*
- *715 Pier Ave. (PCH), Hermosa Beach, 310-374-4484*
- *24160 Lyons Ave. (Wiley Canyon), Santa Clarita, 805-259-9214*
- *1390 N. Allen Ave. (bet. Washington & Alice Sts.), Pasadena, 818-798-7603*
- *635 W. Foothill Blvd. (Oakwood St.), La Canada, 818-790-7563*
- *155 W. California Blvd. (Pasadena Ave.), Pasadena, 818-577-7149*
- *10321 Sepulveda Blvd. (Devonshire St.), Mission Hills, 818-891-1325*
- *3461 W. Third St. (Vermont Ave.), LA, 213-384-6552*
- *4520 Sunset Blvd. (Virgil St.), Hollywood, 213-662-8107*
  Store hours vary according to location; call to check.
  Other locations throughout Southern California.

■ One of the oldest supermarket chains in SoCal, with branches everywhere, these "better-than-average" stores have spawned the Pavilions chain as a wedge into the upscale market, while maintaining their working-class roots; many describe it as "good" – "good selection", "good value", "good quality"; the "plain Jane" of supermarkets.

Westward Ho Markets   19 | 17 | 18 | M

- *11737 San Vicente Blvd. (west of Barrington Ave.), Brentwood, 310-826-4666*
  Every day 7am-midnight
- *1515 Westwood Blvd. (Ohio Ave.), Westwood, 310-479-6702*
  Every day 7am-midnight
- *29211 Heathcliff Rd. (PCH), Malibu, 310-457-9128*
  Every day 8am-10pm

Gibson & Cooke

- *508 N. Doheny Dr. (Santa Monica Blvd.), W. Hollywood, 213-272-7400*
  Every day 7am-10pm

Trancas Market

- *30745 PCH (Broadbeach), Malibu, 310-457-9776*
  Every day 8am-10pm

☑ An "average" supermarket chain that some appreciate for "easy shopping" with "no lines", but which others criticize for "limited selection" and "unappealing ambiance"; P.S. Trancas Market is one of their branches, and Gibson & Cooke (fka Carl's) is their new flagship store and word is that their remaining stores will eventually be upscaled.

Wines & Liquors*

To the far north, there's Napa and Sonoma. Closer by, there's the Central Coast and Santa Ynez Valley. Down south, there's Temecula. Los Angeles is surrounded by wine-growing regions, and that fortunate proximity is reflected in our many fine wine shops, where Europe is a side line and California is the name of the game, discounts abound and knowledge is a prized possession among the staff. Visiting the best of these shops is also something of a learning experience, since they always seem to have discovered a winery you've never heard of, whose product just has to be sampled.

Top Quality
- **29** Wally's
- **28** Wine Merchant
- **27** Wine House
  - Northridge Hills
  - Duke of Bourbon

Top Service
- **28** Northridge Hills
- **26** Wally's
  - Du Vin
- **25** Duke of Bourbon
  - Top Line

Top Variety
- **27** Wine House
  - Wally's
- **26** Northridge Hills
- **25** Red Carpet
  - Duke of Bourbon

Best Buys
- Top Line
- Wine House
- Wine Co.
- Northridge Hills
- Wally's

Q	V	S	C
–	–	–	M

Bel-Air Wine Merchant
- *10421 Santa Monica Blvd. (Beverly Glen), West LA, 310-474-9518*

Though not exactly in tony Bel Air, this well-respected wine and spirits outlet prides itself in its fine selection of French and California vintages, offered at some of the best prices around; for even bigger discounts, try shopping at Bel-Air's discount outlet, the 20/20 Wine Co.

Beverage Warehouse 🚲 🖃

24	22	20	I

- *4935 McConnell Ave. (north of Culver Blvd.), LA, 310-306-2822*
  M-Sat 9am-6pm/Sun 10am-4pm
- *Mail Order: 800-304-9463*

■ It's "ugly, but who cares?" say fans of this stripped-down outlet store that's awash with "discounts"; it's worth hunting through the "mess" to find the "great buys" and "occasional surprises" among its "good selection" of wines, spirits and microbrews; suds aficionados claim it's "actually best for beer", especially kegs.

---

* Top ratings lists exclude sources in outlying areas.

Wines & Liquors

Bristol Farms
27 | 24 | 24 | E
• *See listing in Supermarkets section.*
■ Top-rated among supermarket wine sources, this highbrow chain actually has a better choice of premium California vineyards than most wine shops, including "hard-to-find labels"; "knowledgeable people" can guide you, but a persistent gripe is that it's "too expensive" with "no deals."

Broadway Deli 🚲
23 | 17 | 18 | E
• *1457 Third St. Promenade (Broadway), Santa Monica, 310-451-0616*
  M-Th 7am-midnight/F 7am-1am/Sat & Sun 8am-1am
◪ Part of a gourmet Santa Monica deli, this glassed-in wine shop near the deli entrance is easy to overlook, especially if you're focusing on the smoked salmon and wheels of Parmesan; though "expensive" it's worth a look, offering a "boutique" (some say "unfocused") wine selection plus "lots of grappas" and "many novel items for a small store."

Cañon Liquor 🚲✉
24 | 22 | 18 | M
• *338 N. Cañon Dr. (Dayton Way), Beverly Hills, 310-246-9463*
  M-Sat 9am-9pm
■ "Better than local supermarkets", this neighborhood wine shop with a small deli counter allows you to grab a sandwich with your Cabernet; "unusually good values" for a "high-priced locale", including "many hidden bargains", make it a popular Beverly Hills destination.

DUKE OF BOURBON 🚲✉
27 | 25 | 25 | E
• *20908 Roscoe Blvd. (DeSoto Ave.), Canoga Park, 818-341-1234*
  M-Th 9am-7pm/F & Sat 9am-8pm
• *Mail Order: 800-434-6394*
■ Aside from its cute name, this family-owned-and-operated West Valley institution is known for its "very knowledgeable and helpful staff", "great selection" (including "amazing old Chardonnays") and, alas, "high prices"; wine-tasting seminars and trips are another reason why this "old-school survivor" has been around since 1967 and is still "tops."

Du Vin Wine & Spirits 🚲✉
26 | 22 | 26 | M
• *540 N. San Vicente Blvd. (south of Melrose Ave.), W. Hollywood, 310-855-1161*
  M-Sat 10am-7pm
■ This West Hollywood "find" is "jam-packed with fabulous wines"; fans say it's "best for French regional" vintages but it also features Italian wines, cognacs, single malts and more; with good quality, "classy" environs and a "helpful" owner, it's a "fun" place to shop.

| Q | V | S | C |

Epicurus &🖥
| – | – | – | M |

- *625 Montana Ave. (west of 7th St.), Santa Monica,*
  310-395-1352
  M-Sat 10am-9pm/Sun 10am-7pm

A welcome addition to the spirits scene, this well-named
wine shop has an interesting setting with changing
contemporary art shows; serving the affluent Santa
Monica–Brentwood crowd, it offers good-value wines,
wine tastings, a newsletter and the Chardonnays and
Cabs that are the essence of life on the Westside.

Fireside Cellars &
| 25 | 22 | 23 | E |

- *1421 Montana Ave. (bet. 14th & 15th Sts.), Santa Monica,*
  310-393-2888
  Every day 8am-10pm

■ This venerable "neighborhood" resource has an
"interesting", "boutique selection" with "great surprises
for a store of this size", including "lots of rare old" bottlings
and "good Scotch"; but it's "not cheap" and some say watch
out for "over-the-hill vintages."

Flask Liquor Store, The &🖥
| 25 | 22 | 24 | E |

- *12194 Ventura Blvd. (1½ blocks west of Laurel Canyon*
  Blvd.), Studio City, 818-761-5373
  M-Sat 10am-7pm/Sun 11am-4pm

■ A Valley institution with a fine collection of hard liquors
in exotic bottles, this "A-1 operation" has a loyal following
of actors, writers and directors who live in the Studio City
hills; "individual attention" from the staff and "unusual
finds" on the shelves help justify the cost; the pewter
flasks make nice gifts.

Gelson's Markets
| 24 | 21 | 22 | E |

- *See listing in Supermarkets section.*

■ For many, this "Rolls Royce of wine shops" has the "best"
supermarket selection, offering "respectable" vintages and
"wines that aren't carried" elsewhere; supporters say it's
"convenient" for "last-minute" needs and find "some good
buys" amidst the "high prices", but a few dissenters call it
"lackluster" with "not much variety."

Greenblatt's Deli
& Fine Wines &🖥
| 26 | 25 | 22 | E |

- *8017 W. Sunset Blvd. (Crescent Hts. Blvd.), Hollywood,*
  213-656-0606
  Every day 9am-2am

■ Arguably more wine shop than deli, attracting locals from
Laurel Canyon and Mulholland with "good-deal" specials
that are often advertised on a ticker-tape billboard out front;
"outstanding bargains" and "very rare finds" mix easily
here, and besides, where else can you drink Viognier while
eating chopped chicken liver on rye?

Q V S C

Hi Time Wine Cellars 🚲 ▣
-- -- -- E
- *250 Ogle St. (Orange Ave.), Costa Mesa, 714-650-8463*
  M-Th 9am-9pm/F & Sat 8am-9pm/Sun 9am-7pm
- *Mail Order: 800-331-3005*

Boasting the largest climate-controlled wine cellar on the
West Coast, this 18,000-square-foot facility in a marketplace
setting has a wine-tasting bar, cigar shop with walk-in
humidor, a large import beer room stocking over 400 brews,
a cafe, flower shop, candy store and coffee bar.

Los Angeles Wine Co. ▣
26 23 23 I
- *4935 McConnell Ave. (west of Culver Blvd.), LA, 310-306-9463*
  M-Sat 10am-6pm/Sun noon-5pm
- *72-608 El Paseo, Palm Desert, 619-346-1763*
  T-Sat 10am-6pm
- *Mail Order: 800-854-8466*

◼ In the same location as the Beverage Warehouse, this
wine and spirit shop has what many call "the best buys in
the city"; "you have to choose what they find deals on,
but when you do, you gotta winner" as there's "not a bad
bottle" in stock; "killer French and German choices" and
"trustworthy service" help make it the "No. 1 discounter."

NORTHRIDGE HILLS
LIQUORS 🚲 ▣
27 26 27 M
- *11249 Tampa Ave. (1 block north of Frwy. #118),*
  Northridge, 818-368-7330
  M-Th 9am-8pm/F & Sat 9am-9pm/Sun 11am-6pm
- *Mail order: 800-678-9463*

◼ Paul Smith is a "great" wine merchant and "makes you
feel comfortable" at his off-the-beaten-path North Valley
"oasis"; it's well "worth a visit" for its "hidden bargains" and
"deep" California selection with "oldies and goodies."

Pavilions
-- -- -- M
- *See listing in Supermarkets section.*

Currently redoing the wine sections in many of its stores,
this huge chain is trying to become *the* place for fine
wines in SoCal; an ongoing series of wine-tasting dinners
is being held at finer restaurants around town to highlight
the various vineyards carried in its stores.

Price/Costco
22 18 11 I
- *See listing in Supermarkets section.*

☑ You can find some "good wines" at "great prices" at
this out-of-the-box, members-only warehouse chain, but it
takes some luck and "know-how", since there's "not much
variety" and nothing in the way of informed staff; "hit it
right" and it's a "gold mine", but hit it wrong and it's "not
worth the trip" to locations that tend to be near airports
and industrial areas.

204

Q	V	S	C

Red Carpet &♿️🖼️
27	25	24	M

- *400 E. Glenoaks Blvd. (Jackson St.), Glendale, 818-247-5544*
  M-Th 9am-10pm/F & Sat 9am-11pm/Sun 10am-9pm
- *Mail order: 800-339-0609*

■ Expect red-carpet treatment at this "excellent, all-around wine shop" that keeps Glendale-ites buzzing with its wine bar, tasting events, monthly newsletter and hundreds of premium handmade cigars kept in the walk-in humidor; it has a "good selection" and "will match prices" with anyone.

Topline Wine & Spirits &♿️🖼️
25	23	25	I

- *4718 San Fernando Rd. (1 mile south of Frwy. #134),*
  Glendale, 818-500-9670
  M-Sat 10am-6pm/Sun noon-5pm

■ Surveyors say this popular "no-frills" Valley discounter is the "best place for vin ordinaire" and the "only place to buy champagne for large parties"; the stock is "somewhat limited" but it offers some "great values" and the "reliable advice" is free; N.B. first-timers are advised to call for directions, as this spot is hard to find.

Trader Joe's
21	22	20	I

- *See listing in Supermarkets section.*

☑ The selection's "erratic", but some of the "best deals in town" are found in this specialty chain's wine section; with more votes than any other wine shop, it's a "favorite" of many, yet critics say "it's not for serious oenophiles" and is a "shadow of its former self" since the sale by founding father Joe Coulombe; still, there's "always something new" to try, though be warned that "you may not find it again."

20/20 Wine Co. &♿️
26	23	22	M

- *2020 Cotner Ave. (bet. Santa Monica & Olympic Blvds.),*
  West LA, 310-447-2020
  M-Sat 10:30am-6pm

■ A bustling West LA "discount cousin" of the Bel Air Wine Merchant, with a back room "reminiscent of a speakeasy" where you'll find "gems dating back to the '40s"; it's a "great place for obscure wines" and the "prices are cheaper than in Europe."

Victor's Liquor & Spirits &♿️
–	–	–	M

- *1915 N. Bronson Ave. (Franklin Ave.), Hollywood,*
  213-464-0275
  M-Th 7am-11pm/F & Sat 7am-midnight/Sun 7am-10pm

This Hollywood Hills wine store/deli offers a sizable assortment of prepared foods, soups and sandwiches that are nicely complemented by a collection of fine wines collected over the years, and many years at that – Victor's has been around since the 1920s.

WALLY'S 🚲📧   29 27 26 E

- *2107 Westwood Blvd. (Olympic Blvd.), West LA, 310-475-0606*
  M-Sat 9am-8pm/Sun 10am-6pm
- *Mail order: 800-8-WALLYS*

■ "You can't beat Wally's" is how many oenophiles feel about this highly touted shop run by the avuncular Steve Wallace; it has an "excellent selection" and a setting that's "great for browsing and tasting"; if you need help, just ask the "reliable", well-educated staff or refer to the shelves of wine books; if Bacchus owned a wine shop, this would be it.

Wine Cask, The 🚲📧   29 26 28 E

- *813 Anacapa St. (Cañon Perdido), Santa Barbara,*
  805-966-9463
  M-Th 11:30am-9pm/F 11:30am-10pm/Sat 10am-10pm/
  Sun 10am-9pm
- *Mail order: 800-436-9463*

■ This tony Santa Barbara shop, next to the fine restaurant of the same name, makes for "a rare treat – you can enjoy a good meal after procuring the perfect vin" here; the stock emphasizes Santa Ynez Valley plus "the best" Central Coast and SB wineries; in sum, it's "highest quality in every way."

Wine Club 🚲📧   28 28 24 I

- *2110 E. McFadden #E (#55 Frwy.), Santa Ana, 714-835-6485*
  M-Sat 9am-7pm/Sun 11am-6pm
- *Mail order: 800-966-5432*

◨ A "great-value" wine outlet offering some of the "best prices and variety" in Orange County along with well-informed service; a "wine bar that permits tasting before buying" as well as a fine "variety of reds" help make it "a godsend" for grape lovers and "worth the trip south."

Wine Exchange 📧   – – – I

- *2368 N. Mall of Orange (Tustin Ave., 2 blocks south of*
  Lincoln Ave.), Orange, 714-974-1454
  M-F 9am-8pm/Sat 9am-7pm/Sun 10am-6pm
- *Mail order: 800-769-4639*

This discount warehouse is said to carry the most extensive selection of fine wines in Orange County, with unusually large selections of German, Italian, French and California bottlings, including one of the best arrays of zinfandels.

Wine Expo 🚲📧   ▽ 24 22 22 M

- *2933 Santa Monica Blvd. (3 blocks east of 26th St.),*
  Santa Monica, 310-828-4428
  M-Sat 10am-10pm/Sun 11am-8pm
- *Mail order: 800-946-3397*

■ Besides offering a "careful selection" of wines including some "good Italian" choices, this wine and specialty shop also has a nice array of caviars and smoked fish and does a sizable mail-order business, accessible through AOL and CompuServe; "if you like food and wine", you can "trust" the owner for some "helpful" advice.

WINE HOUSE, THE 🚴🖥   27 | 27 | 24 | M
- *2311 Cotner Ave. (bet. Olympic & Pico Blvds.), West LA,*
  310-479-3731
  M-Sat 10am-7pm/Sun 11am-6pm
- *Mail order: 800-626-9463*

■ The "helpful salespeople" "know their stuff" at what is
probably the best-known wine and beer warehouse in SoCal;
with an encyclopedic collection, "moderate prices" and
regular tastings and classes, it's a "fun place to go" to
explore "a broad spectrum" of choices: if they don't have
it, it may not exist.

WINE MERCHANT OF   28 | 25 | 24 | E
BEVERLY HILLS 🚴🖥
- *9701 Little Santa Monica Blvd. (Roxbury Dr.), Beverly Hills,*
  310-278-7322
  M-F 9:30am-6pm/Sat 10am-6pm

◪ The name says it all at this paradigm of "elegance" and
"sophistication", a major destination for Hollywood bigwigs
and others who "don't mind overpaying" for a "deluxe
selection" of "premium" wines; critics say expect a "snobby
attitude unless you're known" at this "chic" store where
you can "rub elbows with the rich and famous."

Wine Vintage Chart
1982-1994

This chart is designed to help you select wine. It is based on the same 0 to 30 scale used throughout this guide. The ratings (prepared by our friend Howard Stravitz, a law professor at the University of South Carolina) reflect both the quality of the vintage and the wine's readiness for *present* consumption. If you are buying wines to store for *future* consumption, you should focus on the recent vintages of red bordeaux and burgundies, sauternes, California cabernets and a few grand cru white burgundies. To help you select wines for cellaring, we've put recommended great vintages in bold type on the chart.

WHITES	'82	'83	'85	'86	'88	'89	'90	'91	'92	'93	'94
French:											
Burgundy	22	21	29	28	22	29	23	18	28	20	24
Loire Valley	–	–	–	–	–	24	23	15	19	22	19
Champagne	26	22	28	25	–	26	25	–	–	–	–
Sauternes	–	**25**	22	**28**	**29**	25	**24**	–	–	–	19
California:											
Chardonnay	–	–	–	–	–	17	25	24	27	26	19

REDS	'82	'83	'85	'86	'88	'89	'90	'91	'92	'93	'94
French:											
Bordeaux	**29**	25	27	**26**	**25**	**28**	**26**	17	19	**23**	**24**
Burgundy	18	23	26	13	**26**	**27**	**29**	20	22	**25**	21
Rhône	–	25	26	20	**26**	**28**	27	–	–	–	22
Beaujolais	–	–	–	–	–	–	–	23	16	21	22
California:											
Cab./Merlot	22	19	**28**	25	15	21	26	25	24	24	22
Zinfandel	–	17	–	17	19	–	17	18	18	17	17
Italian:											
Tuscany	15	–	27	15	**25**	–	25	–	–	–	19
Piedmont	**25**	–	26	–	20	26	26	–	–	19	19

Bargain sippers take note – some wines are reliable year in, year out, and are reasonably priced as well. These wines are best bought in the most recent vintages. They include: Alsatian Pinot Blancs, Côtes du Rhône, Muscadet, Bardolino, Valpolicella and inexpensive Spanish Rioja and California Zinfandel. (We do not include 1984 and 1987 because, with the exception of '87 cabernets, those vintages are not recommended.)

Indexes

Special Features
and Appeals

TYPES OF CUISINE*

Afghan
Hawthorne Mkt.

American
Babalu
Baskin Robbins
Ben & Jerry's
Benny's BBQ
Beverly Glen Mkt.
BG to Go
Bigg Chill
Breadworks
Bristol Farms
Caffe Latte
Cake & Art
Cakeplace, The
Cakeworks
Calif. Chicken Cafe
C.C. Brown's
Chalet Gourmet
Cheesecake Factory
Chino Ranch
Cicero Bros.
Cultured Class
Double Rainbow
Dr. Hogly Wogly's
Eiger Ice Cream
Emack & Bolio's
Fantasy Frosting
Farmer's Mkt. Poultry
Fosselman's Ice Cream
Gelson's Markets
Golden West Meats
Gourmet Grub to Go
Grand Choc. Pizza
Great Harvest
Häagen-Dazs
Hansen Cakes
Heidi's/Swenson's/Steve's
Heminger's Fudge
HoneyBaked Ham
Jackson's Farm
Kitchen for Exploring
Koo Koo Roo
La Brea Bakery
LA Desserts
La Mousse
Lopez Ranch
Main Course
Marina Farms
Marmalade
McConnell's
Misto Caffe
Mrs. Beasley's
Mrs. Field's
Noonan's Ribs
Old Town Bakery
Owen's Mkt.
Penguin's Place
Pier Ave. Bakery
Pioneer Boulangerie
Reddi Chick BBQ
Renaissance Cafe
Robin Rose
Rosebud Cakes
Rose Cafe

Santa Monica Farms
See's Candy
Slender Sweet Shoppe
Southern Bakery
Southland Farmer's
Sweet Lady Jane
Tanaka Quality Produce
Tapia Bros.
Trader Joe's
Wesley's Place
Wild Oats Mkt.
Windward Farms
Wolfgang Puck Cafe
Zabies

Argentinean
Catalina's Mkt.
Continental Gourmet
El Camaguay
Empanada's Place
Food Bag
Valley Food

Asian
Ai Hoa/Shun Fat
Asian Ranch
Bangluck Supermkt.
Dong Loi
Hong Kong Mkt.
Little Saigon
99 Ranch/Price
Seafood City
T & T Supermarket
Van's Bakery
Vin Hoa

Bar-B-Q
Benny's BBQ
Dr. Hogly Wogly's

Cambodian
Vin Hoa

Central American
Catalina's Mkt.
El Camaguay
Food Bag
La Adelita
La Plaza Mkt.
Liborio Mkt.
Valley Food

Chinese
Chin Chin
Dong Loi
Family Pastry
Feast from the East
Hong Kong Mkt.
Kowloon Mkt.
Kuo's Bakery
LA Man Wah
99 Ranch/Price
Panda Express
Seafood City
T & T Supermarket
United Foods
Van's Bakery
Vin Hoa
Yie Mei Pastry

---

* These indexes are not exhaustive, but rather represent a selective listing of some of the best from each category.

Continental
Atelier de Chocolat
Atlas Sausage
B & L Gourmet
Chez Nous
Europane
European Sausage
J&T European
Konditori
La Conversation
Odeon
Pasadena Baking
Patticakes
Röckenwagner
Zov's Bakery

Cuban
El Camaguay
Food Bag
Liborio Mkt.
Porto's

Dutch
Ann's Dutch Imports
Artesia Bakery
Holland American

English
Friar Tuck
Rosetree Cottage
Tudor House
Ye Olde Kings

Filipino
Asian Ranch
Goldilocks Bakery
Red Ribbon
Seafood City

French
Aristoff Caviar
Belwood Bakery
Chez Nous
Julienne
La Creme de la Creme
Le Marmiton
Michel Richard
Mousse Fantasy
Odeon
Paris Pastry
Pascal Epicerie
Pierre's Pastry
Q Bakery
Zov's Bakery

German/Austrian
Alpine Village
Atlas Sausage
B & L Gourmet
Ernie's European
Eschbach's
Old Vienna Strudel
Röckenwagner
Schreiner's
Van Nuys Deli

Greek
Bay Cities
C&K

Hawaiian
Aloha
Pacific Mkt.

Hungarian
Otto & Sons

Indian
Bharat Bazaar
Bombay Spiceland
Hawthorne Mkt.
India Sweets
Mirch Marsala

Indonesian
Ann's Dutch Imports
Holland American
Little Saigon
T & T Supermarket

International
Aristoff Caviar
Bay Cities
Broadway Deli
Cheese Store/BH
Flora Kitchen
Jody Maroni's
Julienne
Main Course
Marmalade
Ron's Market
Say Cheese
Surfas Inc.
Trader Joe's
Wesley's Place
Zabies

Italian
Al Dente
Al Gelato
A-1 Groceries
Baducco's
Bay Cities
Buona Forchetta
Ciao Livio
Claro's Ital. Mkt.
Divine Pasta
Domingo's
Gelato Desserts
Gianfranco Delizie
Il Fornaio
Maria's Kitchen
Monte Carlo
Nicolosi Pastries
Pasta, Etc.
Pasta Shoppe
Rosti
Sorrento Italian Mkt.

Japanese
Aloha
Ebisu
Enbun
Frances Bakery
Granada Mkt.
Mousse Fantasy
Nijiya Mkt.
Pacific Mkt.
Safe & Save
Yaohan

Jewish
(Bagel shops, delis
and the following)
Barney Greengrass
Bea's Bakery
Beverlywood Bakery
Brown's Victory
Diamond Bakery*
Doheny Kosher*
Elat Market

Elite Cuisine*
Fred's Bakery
G&K Kosher Meats*
Homarus Lox*
J & T Bread Bin
Judy's Carry Out*
Miller's Mkt.
Ventura Kosher*
Weby's Bakery
(*Kosher)

Korean
Koreatown Plaza
Market World

Latin
Catalina's Mkt.
Continental Gourmet
El Camaguay
Food Bag
Grand Central Mkt.
La Adelita
La Plaza Mkt.
Liborio Mkt.
Valley Food

Mexican
Carrillo's
El Gallo Bakery
El Gallo Giro
El Mercado
Gallegos Mexican
Grand Central Mkt.
Juanito's Tamales
La Adelita
La Azteca
La Plaza Mkt.
Los Cinco Puntos
Seafood City
Top Valu
Valley Food

Middle/Near Eastern
Bay Cities
Bezjian's
C&K

Elat Market
Good Food
Hawthorne Mkt.
Miller's Mkt.
Panos Pastry
Ron's Market
Tarzana Armenian
Zankou Chicken

Russian
Gastronom
Royal Gourmet
Tatiana
Tbilisy & Yerevan

Scandinavian
Olson's Deli

South American
El Camaguay
Food Bag
La Plaza Mkt.
Liborio Mkt.
Rincon Chileno
Valley Food

Spanish
La Española

Swiss
Emil's Pastry
Teuscher

Thai
Bangkok Supermkt.
Bangluck Supermkt.
Silom Thailand

Vietnamese
Ai Hoa
Buu-dien
Dong Loi
Little Saigon
99 Price Market
Song Long
T & T Supermarket
Van's Bakery

NEIGHBORHOOD LOCATIONS*

AIRPORT

LAX
Wolfgang Puck Express

Marina Del Rey
Benny's BBQ
Beverage Warehouse
Cheesecake Factory
Chin Chin
Del Rey Nut Co.
Gelato Desserts
Gelson's Markets
I & Joy

Jerry's Famous Deli
Koo Koo Roo
LA Wine Co.
Marina Coffee
Penguin's Place
Prebica Coffee
Rainbow Acres
Tasting Spoon
Wok Fast

Westchester
Special Foods

LA CENTRAL

Beverly/Fairfax
Bagel Broker
Breadworks
Caffe Latte
Canter's
Charlie Lopez
Diamond Bakery
Erewhon Food Mkt.
Farmer's Mkt. Poultry
Huntington Meats
I & Joy
J & T Bread Bin
J&T European
Littlejohns
Magee's Nuts
Manhattan Fruitier
Mani's Bakery
Nowhere Foods Mkt.
Rosti
Tusquella's Seafood
Ultimate Nut & Candy

Beverly/La Cienega
B & L Gourmet
Bed Bath & Beyond
Chado
Cook's Library
Floral & Hardy
Godiva
Humphrey Yogart
Jerry's Famous Deli
Koo Koo Roo
LA Desserts
Williams-Sonoma

Beverlywood/
Pico-Robertson
Al Gelato
Bagel Factory
Beverlywood Bakery
Doheny Kosher Meats
Elat Market
Factor's Deli
Fred's Bakery
G&K Kosher Meats
Gordon's Fish Mkt.
Homarus Lox
Michel Richard
Owen's Mkt.
Pico Kosher Deli
Stan's Produce

Superior Meat Co.
Viktor Benes/Mamolo's

Chinatown
Ai Hoa/Shun Fat
Buu-dien
Family Pastry
Kowloon Mkt.
LA Man Wah
99 Ranch/Price
Ten Ren Tea
United Foods

Downtown
Avery Kit. Supply
Chef's Store
Citi Deli
El Gallo Giro
Euro Coffee
Godiva
Grand Central Mkt.
I & Joy
Il Fornaio
Koo Koo Roo
La Adelita
Langer's
LA Nut House
LA Trade Tech.
LA Wholesale Flower
Pasqua Coffee
Rocky Mtn. Chocolate
Stanley Kirsten
Union Bagel

Echo Park
Brooklyn Bagel Co.

Hancock Park
Breadworks Cafe
Koo Koo Roo
Sam's Bagels
White Gate Flowers

Hollywood
Bangkok Supermkt.
Bangluck Supermkt.
Ben & Jerry's
Bezjian's
Catalina's Mkt.
C.C. Brown's
Greenblatt's
I & Joy
La Adelita

---

* Excluding caterers, restaurant delivery services and major chains
with multiple locations.

Mayfair Mkts.
Quinn's
Red Ribbon
Rincon Chileno
Ron's Market
Silom Thailand
Victor's

Koreatown
C&K
Koreatown Plaza
Liborio Mkt.
Market World

La Brea
B&B Bagels
Cakeworks
Divine Pasta
Elite Cuisine
Flora Kitchen
Judy's Carry Out
La Brea Bakery
Rita Flora
Wok Fast

Little Tokyo
Enbun
Frances Bakery
Yaohan

Artesia
Artesia Bakery
Goldilocks Bakery
India Sweets
Kuo's Bakery

Bellflower
Holland American

Cerritos
Fedco
Red Ribbon

Culver City
Bharat Bazaar
Empanada's Place
India Sweets
Lopez Ranch
Marc Fredericks
Marina Farms
Old Vienna Strudel
Sorrento Italian Mkt.
Surfas Inc.
Top Valu

Gardena
Eschbach's
99 Ranch/Price
Pacific Mkt.

Harbor City
La Española

Hawthorne
Continental Gourmet
Price/Costco

Hermosa Beach
Lappert's
Penguin's Place
Pier Ave. Bakery

Inglewood/Lennox
Ernie's European
Price/Costco
Southern Bakery

Los Feliz/Silverlake
La Conversation
Mayfair Mkts.
Nature Mart
Panos Pastry
Pasta Shoppe
Piacere Espresso
Say Cheese
Zankou Chicken

Melrose
Calif. Chicken Cafe
Campo dei Fiori
Double Rainbow
Epicurean School
Euro Coffee
Humphrey Yogart
Laurel's Florist
Urth Cafe

Mid-Wilshire
Goldilocks Bakery
Pasqua Coffee

Pico/Fairfax-Mid-City
Fedco
Hansen Cakes
Olson's Deli

LA SOUTH
Top Valu

Lawndale
Price/Costco

Long Beach
Ben & Jerry's
Bronx Bagels
Friedman Ovens
Home Economics
Papa John's
Penguin's Place
Top Valu
Vin Hoa

Los Alamitos
Al Dente
Penguin's Place

Manhattan Beach
Bristol Farms
Cuisine Sur La Mer
Growing Wild
Koo Koo Roo
La Creme de la Creme
Thee Cutlery

Redondo Beach
Ben & Jerry's
Capt. Kidd's
Cheesecake Factory
Mrs. Gooch's
Penguin's Place
Quality Seafood
Western Bagel

Rolling Hills/Rolling Hills Estates
Bristol Farms
Penguin's Place
Williams-Sonoma

San Pedro
A-1 Groceries

Torrance

Alpine Village
Bagel Factory
Ben & Jerry's
Cookin' Stuff
Hawthorne Mkt.
Kafeneo Coffee
Market World
Misto Caffe
Nijiya Mkt.
Penguin's Place
Red Ribbon
Yaohan

LA SOUTH CENTRAL

Bell Gardens/Downey

Penguin's Place

Compton

Top Valu

Huntington Park

El Gallo Giro

South Gate

Claro's Ital. Mkt.

LA WEST

Bel Air

Bel-Air Meats
Beverly Glen Mkt.
Solarium Florist

Beverly Hills

Arrosto Coffee
Barney Greengrass
Cañon Liquor
Caviarteria West
Cheesecake Factory
Cheese Store/BH
Divine Pasta
Edelweiss
European Sausage
Flower Fashions
Graffeo Coffee
Grand Choc. Pizza
Hansen Cakes
I & Joy
Il Fornaio
Jackson's Farm
Koo Koo Roo
LA Premiere Flower
Lee Gelfond
Miss Grace
Mrs. Beasley's
Mrs. Gooch's
Nate 'n Al's
Rosebud Cakes
Secret Garden
Standard Cutlery
St. Urbain
Teuscher
Williams-Sonoma
Wine Merchant/Bev. Hills

Brentwood

Arrosto Coffee
Belwood Bakery
Ben & Jerry's
Cheesecake Factory
Chin Chin
Coffee Baron
Comparte's
Eiger Ice Cream
Great Harvest
Humphrey Yogart
Koo Koo Roo
Maria's Kitchen
NY Bagel Co.
Noah's Bagels
Phil's Fish
Rosti
Vicente Foods
Westward Ho Mkts.

Woods, The

Century City

Bel-Air Wine
Ben & Jerry's
Crate & Barrel
Emil's Pastry
Gelson's Markets
Godiva
Pasqua Coffee
Stage Deli
Ultimate Nut & Candy

Malibu

Atelier de Chocolat
Ben & Jerry's
Marmalade
Pacific Coast Greens
Westward Ho Mkts.

Mar Vista

Empanada's Place
Fleurish
Gloria's
Yaohan

Pacific Palisades

Gelson's Markets
Il Sogno
Pierre's Pastry
Q Bakery
Wolfgang Puck To-Go

Rancho Park

Main Course

Santa Monica

Arrosto Coffee
Babalu
Bagel Nosh
Bay Cities
Ben & Jerry's
Breadworks Cafe
Broadway Deli
Calif. Chicken Cafe
Co-Opportunity
Divine Pasta
Emack & Bolio's
Epicurus
Fireside Cellars
Fromin's Deli
Gallegos Mexican
Golden West Meats
Gourmet Grub to Go
Humphrey Yogart
I & Joy
Il Fornaio
J&T European

Jean Brady School
Jody Maroni's
Koo Koo Roo
Larry's Shaver Shop
Le Marmiton
Mani's Bakery
Marmalade
Noah's Bagels
Odeon
One Life Foods
Pioneer Boulangerie
Reddi Chick BBQ
Röckenroll
Röckenwagner
Rosti
Sam's Bagels
Santa Monica Farms
Santa Monica Seafood
Seasonal Table
St. Urbain
Tanaka Quality Produce
Tudor House
Wild Oats Mkt.
Williams-Sonoma
Wine Expo
Wok Fast
Wolfgang Puck Express
Ye Olde Kings
Zabies

Venice
El Camaguay
Fresh to Go
Jody Maroni's
Pioneer Boulangerie
Robin Rose
Rose Cafe
Venice/Ocean Pk. Co-op
Windward Farms

West Hollywood
Aristoff Caviar
Arrow Market
Cake & Art
Campo dei Fiori
Chalet Gourmet
Chin Chin
City Roasters
Cultured Class
David Jones
Du Vin
Empty Vase
Euro Coffee
Flower Shop
Gastronom

Greenblatt's
La Conversation
Mayfair Mkts.
Pasta, Etc.
Quinn's
Royal Gourmet
St. Urbain
Sweet Lady Jane
Tatiana
Tbilisy & Yerevan
Urth Cafe

West LA
Aloha
Arrosto Coffee
Bagel Factory
Bed Bath & Beyond
Bel-Air Wine
Bigg Chill
Buona Forchetta
Cakeplace, The
Calif. Chicken Cafe
Danish Pastry
Dutch Flower House
Emil's Pastry
Fox Deli/LA Fresh
Gianfranco Delizie
Granada Mkt.
I & Joy
Junior's Deli
Koo Koo Roo
La Mousse
Maria's Kitchen
Mousse Fantasy
Mrs. Gooch's
Nijiya Mkt.
Penguin's Place
Rainbow Acres
Safe & Save
Wally's
Western Bagel
Wine House
Zen Bakery

Westwood
City Bean Coffee
Double Rainbow
Feast from the East
I & Joy
Jordan Market
Paris Pastry
UCLA Extension
Westward Ho Mkts.
Wok Fast

PASADENA & ENVIRONS

Altadena
Patticakes

Arcadia
Claro's Ital. Mkt.
Goldstein's
Kuo's Bakery
99 Ranch Market
Penguin's Place
Williams-Sonoma

La Cañada
Penguin's Place
Slender Sweet Shoppe
Wesley's Place

Montrose
Jane's Cakes
Pasta Shoppe

Pasadena
Bob Smith's Rest. Equip.
Bristol Farms
Bristol Kitchens
Cleo & Cucci
Cobbler Factory
Crate & Barrel
Europane
Fedco
Goldstein's
Good Food
Granny's Pantry

Heminger's Fudge
I & Joy
Il Fornaio
Jacob Maarse
Kitchen for Exploring
Konditori
Louis Foods
Old Town Bakery
Pasadena Baking
Peggy Rahn Cooks
Rosetree Cottage
Sam's Bagels
Silver Birches
Wild Oats Mkt.

Williams-Sonoma
Wok Fast

San Marino
Julienne
San Marino Hardware

Sierra Madre
Tommy Farmer's

South Pasadena
Bristol Farms
Bristol Kitchens
Euro Coffee
Penguin's Place
So. Calif. School

SAN FERNANDO VALLEY (EAST OF #405 FRWY.)

Burbank
Ben & Jerry's
LA Culinary Institute
Monte Carlo
Otto & Sons
Price/Costco
Ultimate Nut & Candy
Wok Fast

Glendale
Ben & Jerry's
Billy's Rest./Bakery
Cleo & Cucci
Fish King
Mrs. Gooch's
Panos Pastry
Piacere Espresso
Porto's
Red Carpet
Schreiner's
Topline
Zankou Chicken

North Hollywood
Atlas Sausage
Bangluck Supermkt.
Brown's Victory
Food Bag
Gelson's Markets
Herb Products
Seafood City

Northridge/North Hills
Bombay Spiceland
Brent's Deli
Davy's Fish
Humphrey Yogart
La Plaza Mkt.
Mirch Marsala
Mrs. Gooch's
Northridge Hills
Price/Costco
Van Nuys Deli

Panorama City
Valley Food

San Fernando
Carrillo's

Sherman Oaks
Ben & Jerry's
Ciao Livio
Cleo & Cucci
Coffee Roaster
I & Joy
Mark's Garden
Mrs. Gooch's
Williams-Sonoma

Studio City
Ann's Dutch Imports
Art's Deli
Bed Bath & Beyond
BG to Go
Bigg Chill
Chin Chin
Flask, The
I & Joy
Jerry's Famous Deli
Mani's Bakery
Weby's Bakery
Western Bagel

Toluca Lake
Chez Nous

Universal City
Jody Maroni's

Van Nuys
Dr. Hogly Wogly's
Fedco
Friar Tuck
Humphrey Yogart
I & Joy
99 Ranch Market
Price/Costco
Solley's Deli
Star Rest. Supply
Village, The
Western Bagel
Zankou Chicken

SAN FERNANDO VALLEY (WEST OF #405 FRWY.)

Canoga Park
Carrillo's
Cheesecake Factory
Crate & Barrel
Duke of Bourbon
Follow Your Heart
I & Joy
India Sweets

Kake Kreations
Price/Costco

Chatsworth
Penguin's Place

Encino
Bagel Nosh
Calif. Chicken Cafe
Chin Chin

Domingo's
Floral & Hardy
Friedman Ovens
Fromin's Deli
Gelson's Markets
I & Joy
Jerry's Famous Deli
Koo Koo Roo
Marmalade
Miss Grace
Nancy's
Nicolosi Pastries
Panos Pastry
Rosti
Tapia Bros.
Wolfgang Puck To-Go

Granada Hills
Penguin's Place

Northridge/North Hills
Bombay Spiceland
Brent's Deli
Davy's Fish
Humphrey Yogart
La Plaza Mkt.
Mirch Marsala
Mrs. Gooch's
Northridge Hills

Price/Costco
Van Nuys Deli

Reseda
Bangluck Supermkt.
Miller's Mkt.

Tarzana
Bea's Bakery
Bed Bath & Beyond
Cheesecake Factory
Cicero Bros.
Fish King
Gelson's Markets
Hansen Cakes
Mrs. Beasley's
Tarzana Armenian
Ventura Kosher

Woodland Hills
Bed Bath & Beyond
Cheesecake Factory
Cicero Bros.
I & Joy
Solley's Deli
Tarzana Armenian
Western Bagel
Williams-Sonoma

SAN GABRIEL VALLEY & EAST (EAST OF #605 FRWY.)

Azusa
Penguin's Place
Price/Costco

City of Industry
Price/Costco

Duarte
India Sweets

Glendora
Claro's Ital. Mkt.
Goldilocks Bakery
Louis Foods
Village Kitchen

Hacienda Heights
Kuo's Bakery

La Habra
Claro's Ital. Mkt.

La Mirada
LA Nut House

La Puente
Nijiya Mkt.
Van's Bakery

Norwalk
Price/Costco

Pomona
Bangluck Supermkt.

Rowland Heights
Hong Kong Mkt.
99 Ranch Market
T & T Supermarket

West Covina
Claro's Ital. Mkt.
Goldilocks Bakery
Louis Foods
Red Ribbon
Seafood City

Whittier
Fantasy Frosting

SAN GABRIEL VALLEY & EAST (WEST OF #605 FRWY.)

Alhambra
Fosselman's Ice Cream
Kuo's Bakery
Price/Costco
Top Valu

Boyle Heights
Top Valu

City of Commerce
Garvey Nut & Candy

City Terrace
Juanito's Tamales

Downey
Penguin's Place

East LA
El Gallo Bakery

El Gallo Giro
El Mercado
La Azteca
Los Cinco Puntos
Top Valu

El Monte
El Gallo Giro

Montebello
Price/Costco

Monterey Park
Kuo's Bakery
T & T Supermarket

Rosemead
Kuo's Bakery
T & T Supermarket

218

San Gabriel
Claro's Ital. Mkt.
Hong Kong Mkt.
Kuo's Bakery

99 Ranch Market
Ten Ren Tea
Van's Bakery
Yaohan

OUTLYING AREAS

Agoura/Westlake/Thousand Oaks
Baducco's
Ben & Jerry's
Let's Get Cookin'
Mrs. Gooch's
Western Bagel
Williams-Sonoma

Orange County
Bed Bath & Beyond
Cheesecake Factory
Claro's Ital. Mkt.
Crate & Barrel
Diedrich Coffee
Dong Loi
Ebisu
El Gallo Giro
Fedco
Graffeo Coffee
Hi Time
Humphrey Yogart
Il Fornaio
India Sweets
Kuo's Bakery
Little Saigon
Mother's Mkt.
Mrs. Gooch's
99 Ranch/Price
Panos Pastry
Pascal Epicerie
Prebica Coffee
Renaissance Cafe
Robert Mondavi
Santa Monica Seafood
Song Long

Store For Cooks
Top Valu
Vanco Foods
Van's Bakery
Western Bagel
Wine Club
Wine Exchange
Yaohan
Zov's Bakery
Zov's Bistro

Oxhard
India Sweets

Palm Desert
Hadley's Fruit
Upper Crust School

Rancho Santa Fe
Chino Ranch

Santa Barbara
Follow Your Heart
Jordano's Marketplace
McConnell's
Wine Cask

Simi Valley
Carrillo's

Thousand Oaks
Penguin's Place

Valencia
Penguin's Place
Western Bagel

Ventura
Atelier de Chocolat

SPECIAL FEATURES AND APPEALS*

Adventure
Alpine Village
Bangkok Supermkt.
Bangluck Supermkt.
Chino Ranch
Elat Market
El Gallo Giro
Grand Central Mkt.
Hong Kong Mkt.
Koreatown Plaza
La Adelita
Little Saigon
Los Cinco Puntos
99 Ranch/Price
Quality Seafood
Ron's Market
Royal Gourmet
Yaohan

Always Crowded
Art's Deli
Barney Greengrass
Bea's Bakery
Breadworks Cafe
Brent's Deli
Bristol Farms
Broadway Deli
Caffe Latte
Cheesecake Factory
Cheese Store/BH
Claro's Ital. Mkt.
Coffee Bean & Tea
Co-Opportunity
Crate & Barrel
Diedrich Coffee
Elat Market
El Gallo Giro
Feast from the East
HoneyBaked Ham
Humphrey Yogart
Il Fornaio
Jerry's Famous Deli
Koo Koo Roo
La Brea Bakery
Mani's Bakery
Marmalade
Michel Richard
Mrs. Gooch's
Nate 'n Al's
Noah's Bagels
NY Bagel Co.
Old Town Bakery
Pasadena Baking
Porto's
Price/Costco
Reddi Chick BBQ
Rose Cafe
Santa Monica Seafood
Stan's Produce
Starbucks
Sweet Lady Jane
Tatiana
Tbilisy & Yerevan
Trader Joe's
Wally's
Williams-Sonoma

Bargain Spots
Avery Kit. Supply
Bed Bath & Beyond
Coffee Baron
Crate & Barrel
Danish Amer. Farms
Del Rey Nut Co.
Dong Loi
Elat Market
Erewhon Food Mkt.
Feast from the East
Fedco
Garvey Nut & Candy
Golden West Meats
HoneyBaked Ham
Koo Koo Roo
LA Nut House
LA Trade Tech.
LA Wine Co.
Lucky Stores
Miller's Mkt.
99 Ranch/Price
Price/Costco
Stan's Produce
Topline
Trader Joe's
Wine Club
Wine House

Best of the Best
Al Dente
Al Gelato
Aristoff Caviar
Bangluck Supermkt.
Bel-Air Meats
Ben & Jerry's
Bharat Bazaar
Brent's Deli
Bristol Farms
C&K
Cheese Store/BH
Chino Ranch
Claro's Ital. Mkt.
Cook's Library
Co-Opportunity
Divine Pasta
Doheny Kosher Meats
Domingo's
Edelweiss
Eiger Ice Cream
European Sausage
Fish King
Food Bag
Frances Bakery
Gelson's Markets
Goldstein's
Graffeo Coffee
Jacob Maarse
Jean Brady School
Jordano's Marketplace
Julienne
Kitchen for Exploring
Koreatown Plaza
La Brea Bakery
Mark's Garden
Michel Richard

---

* These indexes are not exhaustive, but rather represent a selective listing of some of the best from each category.

Mrs. Gooch's
Nate 'n Al's
99 Ranch/Price
Noah's Bagels
Northridge Hills
Panos Pastry
Pascal Epicerie
Pasta, Etc.
Pasta Shoppe
Q Bakery
Rosebud Cakes
Santa Monica Seafood
Secret Garden
Southland Farmer's
Superior Meat Co.
Sweet Lady Jane
Tanaka Quality Produce
Tarzana Armenian
Ten Ren Tea
Teuscher
Valley Food
Van Nuys Deli
Wally's
Williams-Sonoma
Wine Cask
Yaohan
Zov's Bakery

Breakfast or Brunch

(In addition to delis and most
bagel and coffee places)
Babalu
BG to Go
Chez Nous
El Gallo Bakery
El Gallo Giro
Family Pastry
Flora Kitchen
Follow Your Heart
Julienne
La Brea Bakery
La Conversation
Mani's Bakery
Marmalade
Michel Richard
Misto Caffe
Mother's Mkt.
Nancy's
Odeon
Old Town Bakery
Pascal Epicerie
Pier Ave. Bakery
Porto's
Röckenwagner
Rose Cafe
Rosti
Say Cheese
Song Long
Sweet Lady Jane
Victor's
Yie Mei Pastry
Zen Bakery
Zov's Bakery

Buy in Bulk

Bharat Bazaar
Co-Opportunity
Del Rey Nut Co.
Erewhon Food Mkt.
Follow Your Heart
Garvey Nut & Candy
Granny's Pantry

Herb Products
LA Nut House
Mother's Mkt.
Nature Mart
One Life Foods
Price/Costco
Rainbow Acres
Smart & Final
Superior Meat Co.
Surfas Inc.
Venice/Ocean Pk. Co-op
Wild Oats Mkt.

Cafe on Premises

(In addition to delis)
Al Gelato
Babalu
Bagel Broker
Bagel Factory
Bagel Nosh
B&B Bagels
B & L Gourmet
Bangluck Supermkt.
Barney Greengrass
BG to Go
Breadworks Cafe
Bristol Farms
Bronx Bagels
Caffe Latte
C&K
Cañon Liquor
Capt. Kidd's
Carrillo's
Cheesecake Factory
Davy's Fish
Divine Pasta
El Gallo Giro
Elite Cuisine
Empanada's Place
Ernie's European
Fish King
Flora Kitchen
Gallegos Mexican
Gelson's Markets
Gianfranco Delizie
Gourmet Grub to Go
Grand Central Mkt.
Il Fornaio
Il Sogno
India Sweets
Jody Maroni's
Julienne
Koo Koo Roo
Kuo's Bakery
La Adelita
La Brea Bakery
Le Marmiton
Main Course
Maria's Kitchen
Marina Coffee
Marmalade
Michel Richard
Mirch Marsala
Misto Caffe
Nancy's
Odeon
Old Town Bakery
Pier Ave. Bakery
Porto's
Prebica Coffee
Reddi Chick BBQ

Röckenroll
Röckenwagner
Rose Cafe
Rosetree Cottage
Rosti
Say Cheese
Southern Bakery
Sweet Lady Jane
Tarzana Armenian
Victor's
Wesley's Place
Western Bagel
Wild Oats Mkt.
Yaohan
Yie Mei Pastry
Zen Bakery
Zov's Bakery

Foodies' Favorites

Al Dente
Al Gelato
Aristoff Caviar
Art's Deli
Atlas Sausage
Baducco's
Barney Greengrass
Bay Cities
Ben & Jerry's
Bharat Bazaar
Brent's Deli
Bristol Farms
Bristol Kitchens
Buona Forchetta
C&K
Cheese Store/BH
Chino Ranch
City Bean Coffee
Claro's Ital. Mkt.
Cook's Library
Co-Opportunity
Crate & Barrel
Diedrich Coffee
Divine Pasta
Domingo's
Duke of Bourbon
Edelweiss
Eiger Ice Cream
Emack & Bolio's
European Sausage
Fish King
Gelson's Markets
Golden West Meats
Graffeo Coffee
Häagen-Dazs
Homarus Lox
HoneyBaked Ham
Humphrey Yogart
I & Joy
Jackson's Farm
Jacob Maarse
Jean Brady School
Jody Maroni's
Jordano's Marketplace
Julienne
Kitchen for Exploring
La Brea Bakery
LA Desserts
Langer's
Lee Gelfond
Let's Get Cookin'
Mark's Garden
Marmalade

Michel Richard
Mrs. Gooch's
Nate 'n Al's
99 Ranch/Price
Noah's Bagels
Northridge Hills
NY Bagel Co.
Panos Pastry
Pascal Epicerie
Phil's Fish
Price/Costco
Reddi Chick BBQ
Röckenwagner
Rosebud Cakes
Santa Monica Seafood
Say Cheese
Seasonal Table
Secret Garden
Southland Farmer's
Standard Cutlery
Starbucks
Superior Meat Co.
Sweet Lady Jane
Tanaka Quality Produce
Tarzana Armenian
Ten Ren Tea
Teuscher
Van Nuys Deli
Vicente Foods
Wally's
Western Bagel
Williams-Sonoma
Wine Club
Wine House
Woods, The
Yaohan
Zankou Chicken

Game

Arrow Market
Bel-Air Meats
Bristol Farms
Chalet Gourmet
Farmer's Mkt. Poultry
Farms, The
Gelson's Markets
Huntington Meats
Louis Foods
Mrs. Gooch's
Phil's Fish
United Foods
Vicente Foods

Gift Ideas

Aristoff Caviar
Barney Greengrass
Bristol Farms
Bristol Kitchens
Bullock's
Caviarteria West
Cheese Store/BH
Comparte's
Cook's Library
Crate & Barrel
Edelweiss
Gelson's Markets
Godiva
Grand Choc. Pizza
Heminger's Fudge
Jacob Maarse
Jean Brady School
Jordano's Marketplace

Lee Gelfond
Let's Get Cookin'
Magee's Nuts
Manhattan Fruitier
Mani's Bakery
Miss Grace
Mrs. Beasley's
Mrs. Gooch's
Robinsons-May
Rose Cafe
Seasonal Table
Teuscher
Ultimate Nut & Candy
Upper Crust School
Village Kitchen
Wally's
Williams-Sonoma

Hard-To-Find Ingredients
Al Dente
Baducco's
Bay Cities
Bharat Bazaar
Bristol Farms
C&K
Cheese Store/BH
Chino Ranch
Claro's Ital. Mkt.
Gelson's Markets
Gloria's
Herb Products
Jane's Cakes
Koreatown Plaza
La Española
Let's Get Cookin'
Market World
Mrs. Gooch's
99 Ranch/Price
Ron's Market
Southland Farmer's
Store For Cooks
Surfas Inc.
Tanaka Quality Produce
Valley Food
Van Nuys Deli
Vicente Foods
Village Kitchen
Vin Hoa
Wally's
Williams-Sonoma
Yaohan

Historic Interest
1906 C.C. Brown's
1917 Magee's Nuts
1923 LA Nut House
1923 LA Wholesale Flower
1926 Greenblatt's
1928 Standard Cutlery
1929 Victor's
1931 Lucky Stores
1932 Hadley's Fruit
1933 Superior Meat Co.
1934 Littlejohns
1934 Santa Monica Seafood
1935 Graffeo Coffee
1935 LA Trade Tech.
1937 Hansen Cakes
1937 Surfas Inc.
1938 Tanaka Quality Produce
1940 Ernie's European
1940 Fosselman's Ice Cream
1940 Noonan's Ribs
1941 Phil's Fish
1942 A-1 Groceries
1942 Edelweiss
1945 Atlas Sausage

"In" Places
Art's Deli
Barney Greengrass
Bay Cities
Bed Bath & Beyond
Belwood Bakery
Ben & Jerry's
Breadworks Cafe
Bristol Farms
Caffe Latte
Cheese Store/BH
Chino Ranch
City Bean Coffee
City Roasters
Coffee Bean & Tea
Cook's Library
Co-Opportunity
Crate & Barrel
Diedrich Coffee
Divine Pasta
Eiger Ice Cream
Gelson's Markets
Great Harvest
Häagen-Dazs
Humphrey Yogart
I & Joy
Il Fornaio
Jackson's Farm
Jacob Maarse
Jean Brady School
Jerry's Famous Deli
Jody Maroni's
La Brea Bakery
Let's Get Cookin'
Mani's Bakery
Marmalade
Michel Richard
Nancy's
Noah's Bagels
NY Bagel Co.
Old Town Bakery
Pasadena Baking
Pascal Epicerie
Porto's
Reddi Chick BBQ
Röckenwagner
Rosebud Cakes
Santa Monica Seafood
Southland Farmer's
Starbucks
Sweet Lady Jane
Wally's
Wild Oats Mkt.
Williams-Sonoma
Wine Club
Wine House
Woods, The
Yaohan

Mail Order
(See Mail Order section
for additional sources)
Aristoff Caviar
Arrosto Coffee
Atelier de Chocolat
Barney Greengrass

Beverage Warehouse
Broadway Deli
Caffe Latte
Cakeplace, The
Cañon Liquor
Caviarteria
Chado
Cheese Store/BH
Cheesecake Factory
City Bean Coffee
Coffee Bean & Tea
Comparte's
Crate & Barrel
Danish Amer. Farms
Del Rey Nut Co.
Diedrich Coffee
Duke of Bourbon
Du Vin
Edelweiss
Enbun
Epicurus
Ernie's European
Flask, The
Flower Fashions
Garvey Nut & Candy
Godiva
Graffeo Coffee
Grand Choc. Pizza
Greenblatt's
Hadley's Fruit
Heminger's Fudge
Herb Products
HoneyBaked Ham
Jane's Cakes
Jody Maroni's
Jordano's Marketplace
Kuo's Bakery
La Española
LA Nut House
LA Premiere Flower
LA Wine Co.
Lee Gelfond
Littlejohns
Mani's Bakery
Miss Grace
Mother's Mkt.
Mrs. Beasley's
Mrs. Field's
Nancy's
Northridge Hills
Panos Pastry
Red Carpet
Renaissance Cafe
Robinsons-May
Rocky Mtn. Chocolate
Rosetree Cottage
See's Candy
Starbucks
Ten Ren Tea
Teuscher
Topline
Tudor House
Ultimate Nut & Candy
Urth Cafe
Wally's
Williams-Sonoma
Wine Cask
Wine Expo
Wine House
Wine Merchant/Bev. Hills
Yaohan

Noteworthy Newcomers
Belwood Bakery
BG to Go
Bronx Bagels
Buona Forchetta
Emack & Bolio's
Europane
Home Economics
Jackson's Farm
Nancy's
Noah's Bagels
Pascal Epicerie
Pier Ave. Bakery
Royal Gourmet
Sam's Bagels
Seasonal Table
So. Calif. School
St. Urbain
Union Bagel
Urth Cafe
Wild Oats Mkt.

Office Meals
(In addition to delis)
Bonaventure Hotel*
Calif. Chicken Cafe
California Crisp*
Cal. Pizza Kitchen*
Drago Catering*
Feast from the East
Flora Kitchen
410 Boyd*
Hubba Hubba*
Il Pastaio*
Julienne
Kitchen for Exploring
Koo Koo Roo
Panecaldo*
Patinette*
Powell's*
Yang Chow*
(* Not in *Survey*)

Open Late
(After 8pm Mon-Fri;
*open 24 hrs;
check locations)

Bagels & Bialys
Bagel Factory
Bronx Bagels*
Brooklyn Bagel Co.
Goldstein's
I & Joy (Van Nuys)*
Union Bagel
Western Bagel (Van Nuys)*

Baked Goods
Babalu
Bea's Bakery
Bristol Farms
Broadway Deli
Cheesecake Factory
Chez Nous
Hughes Markets*
Il Fornaio
J & T Bread Bin
Mani's Bakery
Michel Richard
Misto Caffe
Mrs. Field's

Mrs. Gooch's
Nancy's Kitchen
Odeon
Old Town Bakery
Pasadena Baking
Pavilions
Pier Ave. Bakery
Price/Costco
Ralphs Markets*
Röckenroll
Röckenwagner
Rose Cafe
Sweet Lady Jane
Trader Joe's
Viktor Benes/Mamolo's
Wild Oats Mkt.

Candy & Nuts
Godiva
Hadley's Fruit
Heminger's Fudge
Robin Rose
See's Candy
Trader Joe's
Ultimate Nut & Candy

Caviar & Smoked Fish
Bristol Farms
Gelson's Markets
Ron's Market
Wally's

Cheese
Bristol Farms
Gelson's Markets
Pavilions
Trader Joe's
Wally's

Coffee & Tea
Arrosto Coffee
Bristol Farms
Caffe Latte
Cleo & Cucci
Coffee Bean & Tea
Diedrich Coffee
Euro Coffee
Il Fornaio
Kafeneo Coffee
Marina Coffee
Piacere Espresso
Prebica Coffee
Renaissance Cafe
Starbucks
Ten Ren Tea
Trader Joe's
Urth Cafe

Cookware & Supplies
Bed Bath & Beyond
Bristol Kitchens
Broadway
Cookin' Stuff
Crate & Barrel
Jordano's Marketplace
Let's Get Cookin'
Robinsons-May
Store For Cooks
Thee Cutlery
Village Kitchen
Williams-Sonoma

Delis
Broadway Deli
Canter's*
Factor's Deli
Fox Deli/LA Fresh
Fromin's Deli
Gallegos Mexican
Jerry's Famous Deli*
Junior's Deli
Pico Kosher Deli
Solley's Deli
Stage Deli

Ethnic Food Sources
Ai Hoa/Shun Fat
A-1 Groceries
Bangkok Supermkt.
Bangluck Supermkt.
Buu-dien
Dong Loi
Elat Market
El Gallo Bakery
El Gallo Giro*
Gallegos Mexican
Gastronom
Good Food
Hawthorne Mkt.
Hong Kong Mkt.
India Sweets
Jordan Market
Koreatown Plaza
Kuo's Bakery
La Adelita
Liborio Mkt.
Little Saigon
Market World
Mirch Marsala
Nijiya Mkt.
99 Price Market
99 Ranch Market
Rincon Chileno
Ron's Market
Royal Gourmet
Seafood City
Silom Thailand
Tarzana Armenian
Tatiana
Tbilisy & Yerevan
Top Valu
United Foods
Valley Food
Vin Hoa
Yie Mei Pastry

Fish
Bristol Farms
Capt. Kidd's
Chalet Gourmet
Davy's Fish
Gelson's Markets
Hughes Markets*
99 Ranch Market

Flowers
Empty Vase
Flower Shop
LA Premiere Flower
Rita Flora

Health/Natural Food
Erewhon Food Mkt.
Follow Your Heart

Mother's Mkt.
Mrs. Gooch's
Nature Mart
Nowhere Foods Mkt.
One Life Foods
Pacific Coast Greens
Papa John's
Quinn's
Rainbow Acres
Venice/Ocean Pk. Co-op
Wild Oats Mkt.

Herbs & Spices
Co-Opportunity
Erewhon Food Mkt.
Wild Oats Mkt.

Ice Cream & Frozen Yogurt
Al Gelato
Ben & Jerry's
Bigg Chill
C.C. Brown's
Ciao Livio
Cultured Class
Double Rainbow
Eiger Ice Cream
Emack & Bolio's
Fosselman's Ice Cream
Häagen-Dazs
Heidi's/Swenson's/Steve's
Humphrey Yogart
Penguin's Place
Robin Rose
TCBY

Meat & Poultry
Arrow Market
Bel-Air Meats
Bristol Farms
Chalet Gourmet
Danish Amer. Farms
Gelson's Markets
Hughes Markets*
Jody Maroni's
Louis Foods
Noonan's Ribs
Pavilions
Price/Costco
Vicente Foods

Prepared Foods
Benny's BBQ
Beverly Glen Mkt.
BG to Go
Bristol Farms
Broadway Deli
Calif. Chicken Cafe
Chalet Gourmet
Chin Chin
Dr. Hogly Wogly's
Elite Cuisine
Flora Kitchen
Gallegos Mexican
Gelson's Markets
Gianfranco Delizie
Jackson's Farm
Judy's Carry Out
Koo Koo Roo
Main Course
Maria's Kitchen
Marmalade
Michel Richard

Misto Caffe
Mrs. Gooch's
Pasta, Etc.
Pavilions
Rosti
Trader Joe's
Wild Oats Mkt.
Wok Fast
Wolfgang Puck Express
Zabies
Zankou Chicken

Produce
A 1 Groceries
Beverly Glen Mkt.
Bristol Farms
Co-Opportunity
Gelson's Markets
Hughes Markets*
Mrs. Gooch's
Pavilions
Price/Costco
Santa Monica Farms
Tanaka Quality Produce
Wild Oats Mkt.

Supermarkets
Albertson's
Beverly Glen Mkt.
Bristol Farms
Chalet Gourmet
Gelson's Markets
Hughes Markets*
Louis Foods
Lucky Stores
Mayfair Mkts.
Pavilions
Price/Costco
Trader Joe's
Vicente Foods
Von's Market*
Westward Ho Mkts.

Wines & Liquors
Bristol Farms
Broadway Deli
Cañon Liquor
Epicurus
Fireside Cellars
Gelson's Markets
Pavilions
Price/Costco
Red Carpet
Trader Joe's
Victor's
Wally's
Wine Expo
(* open 24 hrs.)

Open Sunday
(With the exception of most liquor stores, butchers and fish markets, most places are open on Sunday; here are some sources in those hard-to-find categories.)
Arrow Market
Bel-Air Meats
Beverage Warehouse
Bristol Farms
Broadway Deli
Cañon Liquor

Capt. Kidd's
Chalet Gourmet
Danish Amer. Farms
Davy's Fish
Epicurus
Farmer's Mkt. Poultry
Fireside Cellars
Flask, The
Hi Time
Huntington Meats
J&T European
Louis Foods
Mrs. Gooch's
Noonan's Ribs
Northridge Hills
Owen's Mkt.
Price/Costco
Quality Seafood
Red Carpet
Topline
Trader Joe's
Tusquella's Seafood
Vicente Foods
Wally's
Wine Expo

Pasta
Al Dente
A-1 Groceries
Baducco's
Bay Cities
Bristol Farms
Claro's Ital. Mkt.
Divine Pasta
Domingo's
Gianfranco Delizie
Monte Carlo
Pasta, Etc.
Pasta Shoppe
Sorrento Italian Mkt.

Picnics
(May only be available
seasonally and/or require
advance notice)
BG to Go
Bristol Farms
Broadway Deli
Elat Market
Flora Kitchen
Fresh to Go
Gastronom
Gelson's Markets
Gourmet Grub to Go
Jackson's Farm
Julienne
Kitchen for Exploring
La Brea Bakery
Le Marmiton
Marmalade
Michel Richard
Misto Caffe
Mrs. Gooch's
Nancy's
Old Town Bakery
Pascal Epicerie
Pasta, Etc.
Röckenroll
Röckenwagner
Rose Cafe
Rosti
Royal Gourmet

Say Cheese
Tarzana Armenian
Tatiana
Wally's
Wesley's Place
Wild Oats Mkt.
Zabies

Well-Kept Secrets
Al Gelato
Atelier de Chocolat
Atlas Sausage
Bel-Air Meats
Belwood Bakery
Ciao Livio
Citi Deli
Dutch Flower House
El Gallo Bakery
Fantasy Frosting
Fleurish
Flower Shop
Frances Bakery
Friar Tuck
Gelato Desserts
Goldilocks Bakery
Grand Choc. Pizza
Growing Wild
Herb Products
Huntington Meats
J&T European
La Creme de la Creme
La Española
Laurel's Florist
Manhattan Fruitier
Miller's Mkt.
Northridge Hills
Pasta, Etc.
Pasta Shoppe
Pier Ave. Bakery
Q Bakery
Quality Seafood
Red Ribbon
Rincon Chileno
Special Foods
Stan's Produce
Superior Meat Co.
Tbilisy & Yerevan
Ten Ren Tea
Topline
United Foods
Urth Cafe
Van Nuys Deli
Wonderful Parties

Worth A Trip
Al Dente (Los Alamitos)
Alpine Village (Torrance)
Baducco's (Westlake Village)
Chino Ranch (Rancho Santa Fe)
Ebisu (Fountain Valley)
El Gallo Giro (Huntington Bch.)
Jordano's Marketplace
  (Santa Barbara)
Little Saigon (Westminster)
Mother's Mkt. (Costa Mesa)
99 Ranch Market (San Gabriel)
Pascal Epicerie (Costa Mesa)
Porto's (Glendale)
Village Kitchen (Glendora)
Wine Cask (Santa Barbara)
Zov's Bakery (Tustin)

ALPHABETICAL INDEX

234